IMPLEMENTING THE NEW COMMUNITY CARE

Jane Lewis and Howard Glennerster

Open University Press
Buckingham • Philadelphia

Open University Press
Celtic Court
22 Ballmoor
Buckingham
MK18 1XW

and
1900 Frost Road, Suite 101
Bristol, PA 19007, USA

First Published 1996

A catalogue record of this book is available from the British Library

ISBN   0 335 19609 8 (pb)   0 335 19610 1 (hb)

Library of Congress Cataloging-in-Publication Data
Lewis, Jane (Jane E.)
    Implementing the new community care / Jane Lewis and Howard
Glennerster.
        p.   cm.
    Includes bibliographical references and index.
    ISBN 0-335-19610-1 (hb). — ISBN 0-335-19609-8 (pb)
    1. Community health services—Great Britain—Finance. 2. Human
services—Great Britain—Finance. 3. Aged—Services for—Great Britain—
Finance. 4. Handicapped—Services for—Great Britain—Finance. I.
Glennerster, Howard. II. Title.
RA485.L49   1996
362.1'2'0941—dc20   96-4760
                                                                                         CIP

Typeset by Type Study, Scarborough
Printed in Great Britain by Biddles Ltd, Guildford and King's Lynn

Contents

List of figures and tables

Figures

Tables

Acknowledgements

The study on which this book is based was financed by a grant from the Economic and Social Research Council (ESRC) Grant No. R 000 23 3936. We should like to record our thanks to the ESRC for their support and encouragement.

Above all we would like to thank the staff in the five local authorities who proved so hospitable to our researchers, who attended feedback meetings, and who have read drafts of our work.

The research officers on the project, Penny Bernstock, Virginia Bovell and Fiona Wookey, were extremely committed to the project. Their field work was exemplary and without their help we would not have been able to interpret the mass of material they gathered.

We are also indebted to many people who have discussed ideas with us, in particular: our colleague at the LSE, Sally Sainsbury, who attended many of the research meetings, and Barbara Meredith of the National Consumers' Council.

We should also like to thank the Suntory and Toyota International Centres for Economics and Related Disciplines (STICERD) for providing such a fruitful and congenial research environment for the project.

The purpose of the reforms

What was Mrs Thatcher's government trying to achieve when it introduced its community care reforms in the legislation it passed in 1990? Governments of all hues have been attempting to introduce something called 'community care' ever since at least 1948, and arguably earlier. So, what was the government up to? To understand the origins of the 1990 National Health Service and Community Care Act, or at least the community care part of it, it is important to try to review the rather confused tangle of events that preceded it and indeed to clarify the confusing term itself.

Community care

At first sight the term has been used to convey a bewildering range of policy goals through time. In 1948 the new National Health Service (NHS) and local authorities inherited 500 old workhouses that catered for, or 'warehoused', a mixture of elderly people, some of whom were incapable of looking after themselves, some of whom needed medical or nursing care, and some of whom simply had nowhere else to go. Understandably the NHS wanted to rid itself of these embarrassing institutions, which contained hundreds of people confined to large wards with no privacy and receiving no significant medical treatment (Townsend 1962). The Nuffield Foundation issued a report from a committee chaired by Seebohm Rowntree in 1947 on the circumstances of old people living in these homes, in smaller residential accommodation and at home. It recommended the development of small units, of no more than 35 people, sited in the community. Central government issued guidance to local authorities encouraging them to develop such smaller residential homes, though its own expenditure restrictions made this difficult to achieve until the 1960s when closure of the remaining workhouses became a major policy goal and local authorities began to build up services that supported elderly people in their own homes, such as home helps and meals on wheels. In NHS terminology these alternatives to long-stay care in the old hospitals and workhouses came to be called community care.

The same approach can be seen in the next group to be considered ripe for care in the community – the mentally ill. The Royal Commission on the Law Relating to Mental Illness and Mental Deficiency in 1957 saw a decline in the number of people needing long-term compulsory detention in hospital. Many were there and their civil liberties denied merely because no alternatives were available. Just what these alternatives ought to be was never fully agreed between the professions concerned, but there was agreement that long-term hospitalisation could become less necessary. The Commission advocated an expansion of local authority provision in a chapter entitled 'The Development of Community Care'.

The preparation for the closure of large long-stay hospitals for the mentally ill began in the early 1960s but it progressed very slowly at first. It was the scandals that hit the long-stay institutions for the mentally handicapped in the late 1960s and early 1970s that began a large programme of hospital closure for that group, too (Martin 1984; Korman and Glennerster 1990). Once more the term community care came to be applied to those facilities that were developed to replace long-stay hospital care. The expectation, though not the reality in the end, was that local authorities would take on the role of providing such alternative care.

In the 1980s the emphasis changed again. In their very early statement of policy priorities for the elderly, *Growing Older*, the new Conservative government emphasised the importance not of care *in* the community but of care '*by* the community' (Department of Health and Social Security 1981: 3, italics added). This essentially meant care by the family and support by neighbours and local voluntary groups – not the local authority.

A common pattern, therefore, begins to emerge in the use of the term community care by statutory agencies or government. Briefly put it can be summarised as 'not *our* problem guv'. This is not to say that people wish to be incarcerated in large institutions or do not wish to live on their own with help where possible, but the policy thread that binds all these official attempts to promote community care has been a concern to shift the responsibility for care from one agency to another – from the NHS to local authorities, from local authorities to families. The 1990 reforms were no exception to that rule.

The immediate origins of the 1990 Act

Runaway vouchers

Searching for the origins of the 1990 reforms takes us down an unlikely route. We have to go back to complaints made by the poverty lobby about the way supplementary benefits were being administered in the 1970s. Claimants' organisations argued that individual officers and local offices had too much discretion in interpreting claims. They called for more clearly defined legal entitlements. Paradoxically perhaps, government also saw a case for tighter legal controls, but from the opposite motive. Discretionary payments were rising fast and there was a view that by reducing the scope for discretion by individual officers this creeping growth could be checked. After an enquiry by the Supplementary Benefits Commission, it was concluded that the scheme should move to a more closely defined system of rules and entitlements.

What has all this to do with community care? One of the very small elements in the discretionary payments officers could make was to assist old people and others who were resident in a private residential or nursing home who found themselves in financial difficulties. This was a little known and rarely used power. In 1979 the total sum of money allocated in this way to individuals in distress was £10 million – out of a total supplementary benefit budget of about £2000 million.

From November 1980 the rules under which people could claim board and lodging expenses were regulated by statute under Parliamentary statutory instruments. These allowed someone who was a boarder to claim the full board and lodging charge plus an amount to cover personal expenses. A 'lodger' included not only those lodging with a landlady, say, in the normal sense of the word, but also those living in hostels and residential homes for the elderly and disabled and in nursing homes. A maximum sum for fee reimbursement was set, which had to be a reasonable charge for a facility 'of no more than a suitable standard' for the purpose in hand. It was fixed in relation to the normal levels of residential home fees in operation in a supplementary benefit office's area and became known as the 'local limit'.

There is still some dispute about how far politicians and officials were aware of what they were doing when they drew up these regulations, but their effects became all too clear before long. If you were a resident in such a home and you had no more savings or capacity to pay, the social security system would meet your fees. If you did have savings and hoped to hand them on to your children why not do so at once, become officially poor and let the social security system pay the fees? If this had not occurred to you, a thoughtful owner of the old people's home was likely to put you in the picture. One of the authors remembers just this happening to him when he finally arranged for his father to enter a home. Faced with advice that 'the social security can handle all this' he pointed out that his father had always had a dread of becoming dependent on the 'assistance' and would not wish to do so as long as his small pension and savings would suffice. The owner accepted the position with a rather quizzical look and a remark that few other people seemed to take that view.

Owners also soon caught on to the fact that the fees that were met were the average or normal local fee in the office's area. If all the fees in the area rose, so would the local limits and hence the sums payable to the owners by the local social security office.

Local-authority treasurers and politicians began to ask why they should go on providing old people's homes if individuals could seek a home for themselves in the private sector and get the social security system to pay. Indeed, why not transfer the local authorities' homes into the private sector and get social security to pay the costs? Certainly there seemed no point in opening new local authority homes. Local authorities were, at this point, coming under great pressure to cut their spending, and central government grants were being reduced or stabilised while increasing numbers of people over 80 years old were needing care. Here was a way of getting another part of central government to pay, and serve them right.

The NHS was also under great budgetary pressure, trying to cope with the growing demands on its geriatric facilities. Geriatric medicine at its best in the UK has been very good. Hospitals sought to rehabilitate those old people who may have come in with a stroke or a cracked hip after a fall. Yet all their good work was useless if they could not discharge the elderly person because there was no domiciliary care or residential care to take them. If a hospital had an official arrangement with a nursing home or a hospice to take its patients, the patient could not claim any fees from the social security system. If, however, the patient went to a private home independently, the social security system would pay and resources would be freed for more NHS care in the hospital. It is not surprising that more and more patients began to be encouraged to make private arrangements funded by social security. As one geriatric consultant said to one of us, 'the social security route made an otherwise intolerable situation possible'. Many hospitals concerned with the mentally ill and the handicapped began to follow suit.

In short, the social security budget had inadvertently come to the rescue of families, local authorities and the NHS, all of them under tight budgetary limits and increasing demand. What the government had done was to create an effective voucher system for old people and their families (Jackson and Haskins 1992). Families chose the private facility and the government paid. This maximised individual choice of residential care but it was causing an explosion of public expenditure. The whole story exposed one of the central problems with a voucher-type solution in this situation – who was to decide how big the voucher should be and who should get it? How was expenditure to be rationed? The answer the government had stumbled into was: the family should make the decision and the government will pay. That answer was not viable in the long term.

Rein in the runaway

At precisely this point the Treasury was undertaking a long-range review of public spending and the social security budget was its prime target. Here in the middle of this budget was the fastest-rising element in public spending and it seemed to have no ceiling. By the mid-1980s, the sum spent had risen from £10 million to £500 million.

The government began to try to recover from its mistake. In 1983 the amounts being paid for homes in some areas amounted to little over £50 but as much as £215 at the upper limit. New private homes were coming into being at a great rate and existing ones were expanding. It was not only officially registered homes that were covered. Homes with fewer than four residents also came within the scope of the regulations designed to cover board and lodgings. Social security officers were issued with simple instructions to decide whether such facilities were suitable for old people or not. They had no link with the local authority social workers who were doing the same with homes taking more than four people.

The government's first step was to introduce a freeze on the 'local limits' in December 1984. Then, in April 1985, the government introduced national limits on what could be paid for each resident, depending on the type of incapacity and type of facility. The regulations were generally tightened further in December 1985. None of this stemmed the rising tide of spending on the social security budget, which continued to accelerate.

External criticism

It was at this point that the recently created and independent agency responsible for overseeing local authority spending – the Audit Commission – stepped in. Its report was called *Making a Reality of Community Care* (Audit Commission 1986). It was a cogent and highly critical document. It discussed the fragmented nature of the so-called spectrum of care that was supposed to be available, from hospital to domiciliary care. It pointed out that many agencies were involved and that many people were either getting the wrong kind of care or not getting care at all. It criticised funding arrangements that gave more central government support to hospital care than to local authorities, which were providing an alternative.

None of this was new. The same points had been made by the Guillebaud Committee nearly three decades earlier (Cmd. 9663, 1956). The Labour government had gone some way to tackle the issues in its joint planning and joint finance arrangements in the mid-1970s. Academics had certainly been critical in a similar vein (Wistow 1983; Webb and Wistow 1983, 1986; Glennerster 1983). What was new was the exposure of what was happening to the social security funding of residential care. Under the heading 'Perverse effects of social security policies', the Audit Commission documented the rise in spending and argued that the government was being wholly inconsistent. It was telling local authorities that it wanted old people to stay at home for as long as possible because that was the most cost-effective and desirable thing to do, but at the same time it was pushing large sums of public money into expensive residential and nursing home care. The government was going to elaborate trouble to set its local government grant levels, in line with demography, between one local authority and another, but it was happily handing out far more to some areas than others through its social security budget. As a result, the Commission claimed: 'there are now nearly ten times as many places per 1,000 people aged 75 or over in private or voluntary homes for elderly people in Devon and East Sussex than there are in Cleveland, for example' (Audit Commission 1986: 3). These perverse incentives, the Commission concluded, must be removed. It reviewed a range of possible ways forward and recommended that a high-level review be undertaken: 'The one option that is not tenable is to do nothing' (p. 4).

Nothing

Yet, that is what the government did for the next four years. During that time social security expenditure rose from the original £10 million to over £2000 million in 1991. There was one major stumbling block in the way of reform – and its name was Mrs Thatcher.

Simply to cut off the flow of social security money to new applicants would lead to the bankruptcy of many small private homes. Not only had they become an influential pressure group but they were exactly the kind of small family businesses of which Mrs Thatcher approved. It was also clear to nearly all of those involved in discussing the policy options that if government money was to be devoted to care in the community, however defined, there would have to be one budget holder, one gatekeeper, accountable for the decisions taken in respect of those old or disabled people who needed care. It was difficult to see any agency at that point that could perform the task except the local authority social services departments – and that was anathema to Mrs Thatcher. One of the authors remembers being drawn into discussions at this time with senior Conservative politicians to see if there were any other way out. At the end of a long discussion the conclusion was reached that there was no other way. Sighing, the chair looked up at a painting of the lady in question, who looked down on the assembled group, and said: 'But she will not have it.'

More advice

Sir Roy Griffiths, Mrs Thatcher's trusted advisor on the NHS, had already reported to her on the management of the NHS. He was called into service again. His terms of reference were: 'To review the way in which public funds are used to support community care policy and to advise me [the Secretary of State] on options which would improve the use of these funds' (Department of Health and Social Security 1988). His essential job was to sort the money problem.

His eventual report, *Community Care: An Agenda for Action* (Department of Health and Social Security 1988) was also clear:

> I recommend that public finance for people who require either residential home care or non-acute nursing home care, whether that is provided by the public sector or by private or voluntary organisations, should be provided in the same way. Public finance should only be provided following separate assessments of the financial means of the applicant and of the need for care. The assessments should be managed through social services authorities.
>
> (para. 6.39)

The social security payments to individuals for *care* should cease and the sums spent be transferred to local authorities to meet the needs of those who were in the vulnerable groups affected. It should be transferred as 'targeted specific grants', to ensure that the money was not spent on projects that had nothing to do with community care.

Then, in a section of the report on the duties of the state, Griffiths made it clear that the social services departments might be getting more funds under his scheme but that did not mean that their own budgets and facilities should expand. On the contrary, 'The primary function of the public services is to design and arrange the provision of care and support in line with people's needs', and such support could and should come from a variety of sources. A 'mixed economy' would encourage choice, flexibility and innovation in a climate of competition (para. 3.4). Two of the most influential advisors to Griffiths, Ken Judge, Director of the King's Fund Institute, and Herbert Laming, then Director of Social Services in Hertfordshire, had been advocating such an approach for several years. Moreover, there was nothing new about the idea as far as Conservative policy was concerned. Ever since 1980 local authorities had been statutorily obliged to contract out a growing proportion of their activities to private firms. Norman Fowler, Secretary of State for Social Services, had urged social service departments to follow suit and become 'enabling authorities' in his Buxton speech in 1984. (For an extended discussion of the antecedents see Wistow *et al.* 1994b.)

Yet little had actually happened in the personal social services in most areas. Now the idea was being pushed to centre stage. Why? Certainly it reflected the temper of the times and the Conservative Party's third election victory in a row. The NHS, housing departments and indeed the rest of local government were being pushed in the same direction. The NHS was to become a 'quasi-market' too. But it is fairly clear that the main purpose was to get Mrs Thatcher to accept the Griffiths package. If the money being transferred to social services departments was *not* going to end up by further enlarging bloated local councils' social work staffs and *would* end up with private providers, her objections might be removed. So it proved. Griffiths' main proposals were accepted and a White Paper, *Caring for People*

(Cm. 849 1989), embodied most of the ideas strengthening, if anything, the explicitness of the mixed-economy enabling model.

Lessons

This history is crucial to understanding the reforms and the way they were implemented. They were not primarily driven by a desire to improve the relations between the various statutory authorities, or to improve services for elderly people, or to help those emerging from mental hospital. They were driven by the need to stop the haemorrhage in the social security budget and to do so in a way that would minimise political outcry and not give additional resources to the local authorities themselves. Most of the rest of the policy was, as the Americans would say, for the birds. Like the Health Service reforms that were part of the same legislation, these were hurried ideas (Glennerster *et al.* 1994) pushed through to meet a crisis.

If capping spending was the prime motive, the other elements were not insignificant. They were designed to appeal to other involved interests, not least those representing users, carers and those in the social services departments who would have to carry the policy through.

The White Paper – a policy at last

The White Paper set out six 'key objectives':

- to promote the development of domiciliary, day and respite care to enable people to live in their own homes;
- to provide support for carers;
- to make proper assessment of need and good case management 'the corner-stone of high quality care';
- to promote a flourishing independent sector;
- to clarify the responsibilities of agencies, notably between the NHS and local authorities;
- to secure better value for taxpayers' money.

The last point was merely Whitehall-speak for stopping the social security budget fiasco. The others were introduced to mollify particular interests. The one important new policy objective, which picked up a theme in the Griffiths report, was the central role given to assessment and the role of the 'case' manager. This term was in itself a change from the designation 'care manager', which Griffiths had used.

All those whose needs went 'beyond' health care should be assessed by the local authority. 'Assessments should apply both to people seeking domiciliary and day care services, and to people seeking admission to residential or nursing home care' (para. 3.2.2). The White Paper then slides into combining the discussion of assessment with what it called 'case-coordinators'. These workers would need to manage the links between all the various public, voluntary, private formal agencies or family members involved in the care of an individual. As we shall see later, this confusion about the precise meaning of care or case management was to prove bothersome for authorities trying to implement the government's intentions.

Nevertheless, the right to an assessment was written into the eventual statute and went a long way to reassure those who felt the new arrangements would deny them or their parents access to a home and it reassured social workers, who were made to feel that the changes were a positive move, creating needs-based services, with clients having a right to an assessment. How this was to be consistent with a policy primarily driven by the need to curtail public expenditure was not a question many people asked at the time.

The social services departments were to be obliged to produce community care plans reviewing the needs of their areas, setting objectives and priorities, and they were to discuss these with local people and voluntary organisations. This was the first time social planning had been made a statutory requirement!

The one major departure from Griffiths' recommendations was to reject his proposal for specific community care grants to local authorities. The Treasury's 70-year-old implacable opposition to such funding defeated the idea, at least temporarily. Additional funding was to be subsumed into local authorities' general grant. This issue provoked the one real focus of opposition to the reforms from the advocacy groups and professions concerned. The government later gave way, partially, and arranged for the funds that were being transferred from the social security budget to be earmarked for community care purposes for a temporary period. The Secretary of State used powers available to her in the 1988 Local Government Act to give a specific grant to local authorities for a designated purpose. The result was the 'community care special grant', which could be spent only on community care as defined by the 1990 NHS and Community Care Act. Within that grant there was a 'social security transfer element', 85 per cent of which had to be spent within the 'independent sector'. This was interpreted to include voluntary organisations and trust hospitals. The rest of the grant covered additional administrative costs and a replacement for the Independent Living Fund, which helped those with severe disabilities. (An amended circular had to be rushed out to do this.) The grant was to last for three years – 1993/4 to 1995/6, hence the title always used in official material 'the special *transitional* grant'! (We discuss this in detail in Chapter 3.)

Clouds of guidance

The other part of the NHS and Community Care Act, the changes to the NHS, coming on top of the poll tax fiasco, were causing such political embarrassment that ministers decided that one battle front at a time was quite enough. The community-care reforms were therefore delayed – 'staged' – with the main element, the ending of the social security payments, to wait until April 1993. This left local authorities with time to plan and the Department of Health with the opportunity to give guidance. This they did in good measure. There was more guidance given to local authorities in interpreting the purposes of this legislation than for any other recent statute. It took the form not just of Departmental circulars but glossy manuals written by management consultants and guidance for practitioners written by the Social Work Inspectorate. There should, at least, have been no doubt what the government wanted to achieve.

A volume of *Policy Guidance* was issued by the Department of Health (1990a) in 1990 after a draft had been circulated for comments. It covered the main areas of work that local authorities and health authorities, but mainly the former, would have to undertake in the next two to three years:

- They should gear themselves up to produce annual rolling plans for community services in their area and discuss them with the other statutory and voluntary agencies in their area.
- Systems for assessment should be in place by 1993, and 'local authorities should progressively introduce care management systems with supporting budgetary frameworks'.
- The pros and cons of different kinds of 'purchasing' and contracting were set out. Above all, authorities must secure a variety in the agencies providing services.
- Advice was given on setting up 'arm's length' inspection units charged with inspecting local authority as well as private and voluntary provision.
- There was advice, too, on setting up complaints procedures, care programmes for the mentally ill and the way the specific grants for mental health and drug abuse services would work.

It must be said that this advice took authorities little further in hard, practical terms. The advice was couched in generalities but it had given a timetable for action. The detail, it was expected, would follow.

To help draw up such advice and to ensure that the Health Service and the local authorities were both progressing the reforms together *and* that the independent sector was included, a 'Community Care Support Force' was created. It was headed by the Director of Social Services for Hampshire – Terry Butler – and Andrew Foster, Deputy Chief Executive of the NHS Management Executive. On it were representatives of different parts of the NHS, a carer, the voluntary and the private sectors of care provision, as well as local authorities. The Social Services Inspectorate was given a major role in monitoring and advising local social services departments. In terms of the classic top-down model of implementation, the machinery cannot be easily faulted. The model itself and its appropriateness is discussed in the next chapter.

The process began well. In March 1992 Andrew Foster and Herbert Laming, the Chief Inspector, sent out a joint circular that set out the 'key tasks' that had to be completed by April 1993, when the transfer of social security money and the main parts of the legislation were to be enacted (EL (92)13 1992):

- agreeing the basis for assessment systems;
- agreeing arrangements for continuing the care of those in care;
- ensuring mutually acceptable discharge procedures from hospital into the community for those in need of long-term care;
- clarifying the roles of general practitioners;
- ensuring adequate purchasing arrangements were in place;
- ensuring financial and management systems were in place and that staff were trained for new responsibilities;
- informing the public.

By the autumn, warning bells were beginning to ring. The results of the early monitoring suggested that authorities were falling behind in what was the most politically sensitive area – assessing the needs of and placing those who were being discharged from hospital, and using the new money in ways that would buy places in private homes and not face many residential homes with bankruptcy.

A new circular was issued in September (EL (92)65). It stressed these as top priorities. In doing so it *increased* the government's estimates of the number of people who would be in need of some kind of care who would previously have been paid for out of the social security budget. In March 1992 authorities had been told to plan for another 100,000 people a year. In this circular the number was increased to 120,000. Local authorities were reminded that they would have to spend 85 per cent of the money transferred to them on the private sector. Then, in November 1992, came a thick document from the Support Force, produced by Price Waterhouse, the management consultants, translating the key tasks into detailed steps, with timing and sequence for each (Department of Health and Price Waterhouse 1992). Advice for managers was followed by detailed advice on the implications for social work practice produced by the Social Services Inspectorate. The Social Services Inspectorate regularly visited authorities to monitor their progress towards the government's policy goals. Their function was explicitly not merely to inspect standards of residential accommodation or of social work practice. They were given a *policy* monitoring role. Despite protestations to the contrary, local authorities were being treated as if they were local branches of the Sainsbury's chain.

Explicit policy goals

As always when examining the impact of a policy, it is necessary to distinguish between what a government or politicians say they are trying to do and what really lies behind their actions. There is more of this in the next chapter, but already we can deduce from the history we have told that the government's prime concern was to hold public spending and if possible reduce it. That did not feature as such in the guidance, but the need to make the most of the infusion of new money into local authorities' budgets did.

Effective use of the extra money

About £1.5 billion extra was to be pumped into local authorities' budgets every year by the end of the transition period. This would increase their personal social service spending by nearly a third. Was the extra to be spent on community care and would it be spent effectively enough not to embarrass the government with stories of neglected old people? The flow of detailed rules and returns concerning the transitional grant attest to this concern. Authorities were required to make community care plans, specifying how the authorities were to use the money, and to submit them to the Department of Health. The Audit Commission and the Social Work Inspectorate combined forces to monitor results. This was the first time such a substantial combined operation had been undertaken.

Reorganising social services departments

A strong and long-standing political goal was to see social services departments become much more like the new health authorities created in the same legislation. Hospitals were rapidly being floated off to become independent agencies run by self-governing trusts, leaving the district health authorities as planning agencies. The same was happening to schools, which were eagerly assuming control of their own budgets even if they were not opting out of local authority ownership. The government wanted the same thing to happen to social services activities. Yet the organisational reality was very different. Hospitals already were distinct organisational entities, with their own formal and informal structures and identities. Their histories had been as independent entities long before the NHS ever existed. Schools, too, have a social organism that goes on as local education departments come and go. Social services departments had been created only 20 years earlier. They had been created as hierarchical entities precisely to give their varied and low-status activities some identity. They had gone through several reorganis-ations since. How did you separate the purchaser and the provider functions? Who were the purchasers? Were they care managers or were they the providers? Where was child care to go? The last was probably even more politically sensitive and also subject to new legislation – the Children Act 1989. Here the government trod very carefully. It would be going too far to dictate to local authorities what internal structures they should adopt. They did produce some detailed specifications for the 'arm's length' inspection agencies that social services departments were to set up to inspect not only private but their own facilities. How to separate purchasing and providing functions was left largely unanswered, although a range of models were suggested.

Creating enabling authorities

This was a closely related issue – how much of an authority's functions should be privatised? Here the problem was not only organic but political. Labour authorities might be expected to fight any requirement to privatise their services although rarely did it turn out that simple in practice. The government was trying to avoid getting drawn into a dogfight over community care of the kind it was involved in over the NHS. Local councils were party-political entities and in the three years during which the reforms were being implemented the Conservatives suffered massive local election defeats. By 1995 they had lost control of nearly all the local authorities in the country. The new Labour and Liberal Democrat councils and the large number with no overall majorities were not about to embark on a massive programme of privatisation. Nor did the Social Services Inspectorate want to sully its reputation by entering such territory. It is no wonder that the guidance was Delphic.

Assessment and care management

An early and more legitimate concern was to help authorities develop a system of care management and assessment. This was to be a needs-based service, and local authorities were given the clear responsibility to assess need. Considerable weight had been placed on the fact that all those in need would have a right to be assessed and that the individuals and their families would continue to be able to exercise the same kind of choice that they had under the old 'quasi-voucher' system. In a speech to the Social Services Conference on 2 October 1992, Mrs Bottomley, Secretary of State for Health, had said,

> At present [people] exercise these choices by spending their income
> support in homes of their preference, provided that the costs can be

covered. It is essential that this freedom of individual choice should be carried forward into the new policy.

(Department of Health press release, 2 October 1992)

Yet the new policy was precisely designed to ration that choice in order to save public money. The right to be assessed and sensitive care management that would take account of everyone's preferences, including carers', seemed a way of squaring the circle. The difficulty was that circles have the rather irritating property of not being squares.

Who was to be assessed – everyone who turned up at the social services departments' door, all those referred by their general practitioner, all those leaving hospital? Should everyone judged to be in need by a specialist assessment team be given the services the team judged necessary? That would solve the political problem but it would cause an explosion in public spending that would dwarf the rise that the reforms were designed to quench. What was 'need' anyway, and who was to determine it?

The Social Services Inspectorate and the Scottish Office Social Work Services Group (Department of Health *et al.* 1991b) had a go at defining the concept of need. Need was a 'complex' concept. It was a 'dynamic' concept. It was a 'relative' concept. It was a 'multi faceted' concept. It was 'defined by the particular care agency or authority' but it was also a 'personal concept'. A social policy student would be in great danger of getting a gamma minus for such stuff. The manual was, however, very clear that assessment had to be developed as a separate function within each agency, free from the constraints to thinking that come from being associated with a service-providing body. But those doing this task should 'not be divorced from the realities of service provision', proposing unrealistically expensive options, for example. Authorities would not be able to develop care management or assess everyone immediately, only those with complex needs. Who was to decide what was complex?

The Social Services Inspectorate made it clear that, in the government's view, 'immediate priority was to have in place by April 1993 assessment arrangements for all users, but particularly for the 110,000 or so people who would previously have accessed residential care via the social security system'. Yet this was not a particularly helpful category – such people did not come with labels on. They comprised some people entering the system from all the sources described above.

In December 1992 the Chief Inspector issued an important letter that significantly scaled down local authorities' potential duties and the potential claim on public resources (CI (92)34). Here was a real circle-squaring job. Section 47(1) of the 1990 Act had imposed a duty on authorities to assess any person who 'may b⁄ in need' of community care and to decide on what services to provide. This appeared to put heavy responsibilities on social service departments. Do not despair, said the Chief Inspector,

Two important points should be noted about this [section of the Act]:
- first, authorities do not have a duty to assess on request, but only where they think that the person may be in need of services they provide;
- second, the assessment of need and decisions about the services to be provided are separate stages in the process.

(CI (92)34)

In short, a judgement of need can be made before an assessment of need and even though a person may be judged in need the legislation does not require action to meet it. Any apprentices in circle squaring should take careful note. This is a masterpiece of the art form.

There was, however, another worry that local authorities had. Guidance circulated by the Social Services Inspectorate but drawn up by Price Waterhouse suggested that ideally a full needs assessment should be undertaken but then the care manager would have to take account of resource constraints and arrange a care package tailored to the services and the cash that existed (Department of Health *et al.* 1992). There would then be an 'ideal' measure of need as defined by the professional assessment team and the actual services a care manager would be able to provide. The first should be written down and passed to those doing the planning for future services while the client would get the latter. There could be no clearer statement of the rationing process. But authorities wondered whether they might be legally required to provide the service level set in the first, 'ideal' assessment. Only too true, the Chief Inspector said: 'Once the authority has indicated that a service should be provided to meet an individual's need the authority is under a legal obligation to provide it or arrange for its provision' (para. 5). The authority may not be able to provide what the needs assessors think necessary. So:

> If individual feedback is recorded, it should be borne in mind that, even though it may not form part of the user's assessment or care plan, it might still be accessed by users, under the terms of the access to information legislation, if the data identifiably relates to them. Practitioners will, therefore, have to be sensitive to the need not to raise unrealistic expectations on the part of users and carers.

(para. 25)

In short, do not tell clients what their real needs are and make sure you do not write them down in case you get found out and have to provide for them.

Joint commissioning and planning with the NHS

The longest-awaited guidance was that on joint commissioning between the NHS and social services departments, which had still not appeared by April 1995 and was still being discussed at regional workshops. There was, however, a paper produced jointly by the Personal Social Services Research Unit at the University of Kent and the Nuffield Institute at the University of Leeds and presented at the Metropolitan Hotel in London in July 1992 . This document, reflecting the government's intentions, was the nearest thing to guidance on the topic to appear before 1995. It set out what local authorities and the NHS should do jointly to commission services for those who needed closely integrated or at least matched services. They would need to undertake 'away days' to gain a 'shared understanding'; they would need a 'shared vision' and a 'shared mission statement'. These would need to include 'statements that express broadly what we are trying to achieve together'. 'A common understanding' would need to be generated, the services goals written down and 'shared'. The paper drew on pilot examples of attempts to work together on joint commissioning in four areas.

As these quotations illustrate, there was at the heart of this approach an intellectual model, a paradigm, that the central department had long held dear (Glennerster 1983). It was the view that local authorities and the NHS shared a common purpose and common interests in doing the best they could for old people or the mentally ill. Rational people of good will could therefore sit down together and sort out the best way of collaborating. A lot of political science literature and pure day-to-day experience suggests that this is a fallacy. There were deep clashes of organisational, personal and professional interest at work here. This explains the length of time needed to agree these guidelines. The NHS officers saw the new Act's clear identification of the social services departments as the *lead* community agencies as good grounds for getting rid of their long-term care responsibilities as soon as possible. This became evident in the actions of local health authorities during the period of this study and it led to court action and a hurried circular from Mrs Bottomley. But in the early stages these conflicts were hidden in motherhood-like statements about shared visions.

These then were the explicit and more hidden goals of government policy.

The book

In the rest of this book we shall take each of the main issues and government objectives we have identified and tell the story of how the authorities tried to interpret what the government actually wanted them to do and applied their own political and professional values to inform their actions. Before doing so we take a step back to explain how we went about the study and what theoretical frameworks we used to make sense of what we saw.

2

From high politics to local practice

In the following chapters . . . we will focus not so much on 'high politics' as on the level where reform seems most frequently to come to grief – the month-by-month, year-by-year management of the service.

(Harrison *et al.* 1992: 1)

This study, too, focuses on the day-to-day problems that arose in trying to implement the government's community care policy. But why is it so important to look at the day-to-day life of an agency? Why can we not simply look at what the White Paper said in 1989 and at the numbers of old people and others who were cared for after the legislation came into force, and draw conclusions? It is an approach that underlies some of the 'new management' techniques: define a measurable objective and see whether it is delivered. Has the performance indicator gone up or down?

There are difficulties with this approach, however. Where the objectives are clear, performance indicators can be good tools. If all pensioners are to receive a Christmas bonus, count how many do so. If they fail to receive their bonus, find out why. Much social policy, and especially the delivery of human services, poses much more subtle and difficult research and management questions.

To begin with, should we believe what politicians tell us in their white papers? These are political documents designed to win support and hide unpopular purposes, and can be used to obfuscate rather than clarify policy objectives. Trying to decide what policy the government was actually aiming to pursue is in itself a controversial matter. One approach is to examine what appear to be the precipitating factors that sparked off the policy change and deduce the main policy goals. Historians can examine the government papers of 30 years ago, as they become open to scrutiny. The current policy analyst has only more fragmentary and circumstantial evidence. In the previous chapter we tried to use such material to build up a picture of what the government's 'true' priorities were in this case and we concluded that the financial goals were paramount. This is, of course, a contestable conclusion, but in the next chapter we look at the financial outcomes both nationally and in the local authorities concerned. Even this is less than straightforward. There are innumerable ways of expressing what resources are devoted to what purpose in any organisation.

The real difficulty presented by human services, however, is that they are delivered by front-line professionals who have a great deal of independence and discretion in their work, being able to modify, transform and initiate policy themselves. They are no mere deliverers of service goals set by politicians. Lipsky (1980) has made the point very effectively in the US context, but Donnison (1965), Hill (1972), Hunter (1980), Billis (1984) and others have made similar points in the UK.

It is not merely that power tends to lie at the bottom of human service organisation hierarchies. After all, public services are ultimately accountable to the taxpayer and the politicians are there to act on the taxpayers' behalf. They should be able to get professionals to do what they want. This logic has lain behind the National Curriculum and other government attempts to control professionals in the past decade.

This top-down model of thinking presumes that the central planner or politician actually has a clear and scientifically based blueprint for what he or she wants done. This is the architectural plan or engineering blueprint model of policy implementation. It was explicitly expounded by Dunsire (1978a, b) in an early study. He, too, recognised the effect lower levels in an agency could have. Yet they were not viewed positively. The engineer has a blueprint of the iron bridge he designed. Armed with this he can go out from time to time to inspect whether the girders of the appropriate length are being used and assembled in the right way. If not, his science tells him, the bridge will fall down. The Social Work Inspectorate can tell a local authority that its 'girders' are too short.

The analogy, of course, breaks down, partly because the centre knows so little about the local circumstances or indeed about how to construct bridges at all. Nevertheless, this was the implicit model used by early analysts in studying policy implementation. They tended to say, for example: the US federal government said this programme should be implemented in the following way, it was not, therefore the programme is deficient (Derthick 1972; Pressman and Wildavsky 1973). A secondary conclusion was: governments are no good at implementing policies, so stop giving them the resources to fail. More sympathetic observers who followed tended to say, hold on, perhaps the locals were not so stupid after all. Perhaps they knew things the feds did not. They may have modified the detail of the original programme to suit what Congress wanted and did so in ways that met local circumstances better (Elmore 1978, 1982).

In the UK, Hill (1981) and Barrett and Fudge (1981) took a very similar line.

This line of argument, and the research methods that followed it, came to be called 'bottom-up' implementation research. Authors insisted that their research must be sensitive to the ways in which local actors constructively adapt the original policy guidelines to local circumstances. It must be sensitive, too, to the valid conflicts between local and central political legitimacy. There may be conflict not just on the means but on the ends of the new policy and a compromise may emerge from local resistance to those aims. In a pluralistic society that may be a gain, not a deficit. At the very least the research should map these conflicts without taking sides on the outcome.

For other authors this was simply too relativistic, a retreat from the original purpose of an implementation study. Sabatier (1986) advocated a synthesis of the two approaches. He distinguished what he called the 'deep normative core' of a policy, the 'near core', and secondary aspects. Secondary matters can be changed by local actors and the policy still achieve the basic objectives of the policy. Some more fundamental aspects of the policy may be changed without seriously affecting the basic goals, but some local changes will involve fundamental policy failure. Research must distinguish just which objectives are achieved and which less important ones are modified.

In the context of the present study we have already argued that checking the growing state social security spending was, in Sabatier's terms, the normative core, the real heart of the government's policy, with which one may agree or disagree. Creating a mixed market, where the local authorities moved from their dominant provider role to an enabling role and encouraging collaboration between health and social services were near-core policies, in the sense that the government could be somewhat relaxed about the way they were implemented. Forms of assessment and care management were, we would suggest, secondary to the government's main purposes.

On this analysis we might hypothesise that the government would try to ensure it won on expenditure, compromise slightly on the purchaser–provider split, but leave the care management issues more open to local determination.

Variety no bad thing

Sabatier is an American, however, and the hard ideological conflicts between central and local government, about markets and public and private provision that you find in the UK, are less evident in the US. In our study we had to take account of party politics as a variable, although, as it transpired, it was not possible to read off an authority's enthusiasm for implementing the legislation solely by its political stripe. Again, we make no judgement about the actions of individual authorities but merely reflect that a variety of means of implementation, which reflects the real politics of those doing the work, is more likely to get a good job done than not.

Does the centre know what it is doing?

Another difficulty with the top-down model of implementation research is that it tends to assume that, if not the local detail, then at least the broad intellectual rationale for the policy is rightly conceived by the centre. This is frequently not the case or is at least questionable.

In a study of the 1974 Labour government's attempt to redirect local health and social service resources to the elderly and other priority groups one of the present authors (Glennerster 1983) concluded that the government had not succeeded above all because the intellectual model for achieving change was simply inappropriate. It tried to adopt centralised rational comprehensive planning. The government produced a national budget and planning guidelines, and local districts and social services departments were intended to plan jointly to implement these guidelines. In practice, power in the NHS and local authorities was so diverse and the competing bureaucratic interests so entrenched that such a model had little hope of success. It was only by watching this initiative play itself out at local level that this became clear.

In their study of the 1979 Conservative government's introduction of general management into the NHS, Harrison *et al.* (1992) came to much the same conclusion so far as that reform was concerned. Would the 1990 community care reforms be any different?

Certainly the Thatcher government had given up all ideas of central planning in the early 1980s. Planning guidelines had disappeared. The language changed. But in 1990 something remarkably like the old model re-emerged, at least as far as the relations between central and local government were concerned. The Conservative government was frustrated by Labour local authorities. They would not follow the route prescribed for them. They insisted on finding ways round central attempts to curb spending. Mrs Thatcher concluded that the only true mandate of the people was held by her Westminster government. Effective taxing powers were withdrawn from local government in successive steps through the 1980s and 1990s. Local government came to be viewed even more as the agent of central government than it had been in the 1960s (Glennerster *et al.* 1989).

If central government had taken more powers over local government, did it know what it wanted to do? Was it working with a realistic model of the world? The goal of stopping the social security payments to old people in private homes could be achieved, technically speaking, at the flick of a switch. Here was top-down implementation in its pure form. Local social security offices were under the direct control of the central department, not local authorities. The officials concerned who actually made the payments had no discretion in the matter. Nor did they have any professional status. There might be political repercussions but a clear command and control structure was in operation. A specialist bureaucracy with power clearly residing at the top could be expected to do its job. The hypothesis would be that it would succeed, though the private nursing home lobby might resist and slow or change the policy at the top.

Yet the government was expecting to achieve more than this. As we saw in the previous chapter, it was aiming to change the way local councils organised their internal operations and the way social workers went about their jobs. Indeed, the aim was to redesign the social work task.

This created quite a different level of implementation problem, where previous research and knowledge of the services might have given pause for thought. In the NHS, general managers had indeed been appointed but the extent to which the balance of power between managers and doctors had altered was questioned by most academic studies. Power in the NHS is widely dispersed. The professions lay claim to bodies of knowledge that it is difficult for managers or politicians to challenge. However, this applies more to some professions than others. Social work's knowledge base and its public esteem is far weaker. The government no doubt felt that social workers would be an easier target. Yet to succeed the government had to have a clear idea of what it wanted to achieve. In its absence local authority officers would suffer from what Harrison *et al.* (1992) called 'puzzlement'. They were genuinely unclear about what they are expected to do. We shall find clear evidence of puzzlement in this study too!

The deeper assumptions

The government repeatedly said that its aim was to create a 'needs-led' service. Why was it not needs led already? Various strands of writing had helped underpin this critical view. One influential study of the way social workers went about their task, by Gilbert Smith (1980), suggested that social workers did not, as their textbooks suggested, identify the unique attributes of their clients' condition and then put together a tailored mix of services to meet these needs. What in fact happened was that clients were placed in or directed to whatever facilities the local authority had available. A predetermined and standard package was allocated to the client unmatched to the subtleties of the individual case.

The American politics of budgeting literature, from Wildavsky (1964) and Niskanen (1971) onwards, suggested why. Organisations' senior managers negotiated to sustain or expand their own empires. Their incomes and status derived from the size of those budgets. Since there were no paying customers there was no reason why the organisation should respond to consumers' wishes. It then became the social workers' job to fit the clients into the services which this internal budgetary politics had produced. This analysis was largely adopted as a fair description of the world by Conservative politicians. In what became one of the best-known pieces of research on the subject, academics at the Personal Social Services Research Unit at the University of Kent claimed that it was possible to reverse this incentive structure by taking the budgets away from the service-providing sections of the local authority social services department and giving the spending power to the social workers who were closest to their clients and making the rationing decisions – the care managers. These workers should have a budget and be able to spend it on whatever services they agreed with their clients were necessary, so long as they kept within their budget. Their own research with authorities that were doing this, albeit only with those old people on the verge of entering an old persons' home, suggested that this new way of allocating services did produce a more flexible mix of non-residential services for such people. But of course it implied a huge shift in the power structure within the departments, especially if the idea were generalised beyond the group of elderly people on the margins of residential care with which their research was concerned. If senior bureaucrats gained so much power by wielding budgetary power why should they give it up? Instead of budgets and departmental allocations being determined by senior management they would be determined by the day-to-day decisions of front-line and junior staff. Dunleavy (1986, 1991) points out that the most senior managers *might* not mind such a change so long as they remained in charge of total spending and could shape the structure of their own departments. They might even be pleased to be free of the day-to-day worries of managing a service in times of expenditure constraint. The day-to-day rationing problems could be left to the new privatised or hived off agencies. The less senior managers and lower-level staff would have much more to fear. They would struggle to retain their power. This kind of analysis suggested both reasons for the change and many good reasons why it might go astray (Glennerster and Le Grand 1995).

Changing organisational cultures

It was not merely power relations that would pose a problem. The culture of the social services departments reflected the training its workers had received. They were steeped in public service attitudes – belief that competition was a destructive force, that care and competition did not go together, that care and cash should not be mixed. These had been central tenets of social work training and values since 1948 at least. 'Changing organisational culture' became the buzz words for both NHS managers and local directors of social services. Yet for the government to change the culture of organisations it did not own and whose political masters did not favour change was more than a 'managerial' task. These changes were going to succeed or fail at the local level. They were likely to be modified in whole or part in the normative core, the near core or the secondary aspects of the reforms.

Success?

As we have suggested already, past reforms in this area have worked to models of the world that have proved less than helpful in practice. A reform may succeed in forcing change through, getting local actors to do what you want or to pretend to, but the core intentions are not achieved because the world does not work the way the reformers think it works. Colleagues at the London School of Economics (LSE) have expressed this well:

> We noted earlier that one of the perennial problems of reform in public management is pervasive pressure for across-the-board obeisance to fashionable management models, and for non market organisations to measure their success or otherwise by blanket adoption of the kinds of ritual and rhetoric that important people are assumed to want. If the history of public management reform tells us anything, it is that much of this cloning and imprinting will be deeply inappropriate to particular cases. Perhaps policy-makers need more counter-fashion consultants; at least, they must go beyond simple mantras of the 'four legs good, two legs bad' variety about alternative models of public management and make much more discriminating effort to identify the *circumstances* in which two legs are better than four, or vice versa.
>
> (Dunleavy and Hood 1994)

In our terms this means being sensitive to the fact that private agencies may be available and appropriate in some areas and for some purposes and not be in others. The fact that not all our authorities took the same view of purchasing and providing is as likely to suggest success as it does failure for the policy in the long run, free from the fashionable mantras of the time.

For the most part, in this study we are not concerned with making final judgements about the success or failure of the changes. It is far too early to do that. We are primarily concerned to show why different authorities came to do different things within the framework of a single new piece of legislation following a lot of central guidance. Yet at the heart of the changes was the idea that consumers would find services more tailor-made to their needs. It should be possible for Mrs Smith to be helped into bed when she wants to be, not when the trade union or bureaucratic rules say she should be. Had the changes made any difference to Mrs Smith in this regard? We did try this litmus test on the resulting services to see what it produced.

Contiguous system changes

It is important for the reader to remember that although we are primarily going to focus on changes to the services we call community care, and departments called social services departments, these changes were not taking place in isolation. Similar ideological policy thrusts were affecting and already had affected other local authority services and the NHS, with which these authorities had to work closely. All were affected by tight restraints on public spending. Since the early 1980s local authorities had been required to offer to open tender services they had previously provided. Refuse and street cleaning, housing repairs and maintenance and school meals had all been opened up to privatisation. Community care services were only the last in this line. Many authorities had for many years relied on voluntary agencies for services though without a strict contractual basis. The NHS was also being reorganised and a purchaser–provider split was being imposed. Many officials in the NHS were reapplying for their own or others' jobs. This was not the best time to produce collaborative long-term joint plans.

The study

We can see that the government had chosen particularly difficult terrain for its community care changes. There was plenty of scope for local battles, resistance and more subtle changes by staff as the cascade of change washed down the system. How best should the outcome be studied?

One way to do so was to ignore the internal politics of the changes and look merely at the impact on consumers. This was a legitimate approach but others were doing this and we were interested in how social services departments, especially, adapted to and adapted the changes. We could have taken a large sample of local authorities and interviewed staff at regular intervals to see what they made of the changes. Other studies, too, were doing this and our previous experience led us to be suspicious of this approach. Formal interviews undertaken at, say, six-month intervals, especially with senior staff, tend to elicit the kind of official replies officials think they are supposed to make. The replies also tend to give the impression that the senior person is part of a smoothly operating machine, and that her or his role had been a rational one. As the official reflects on and tries to make sense of his or her life over the past months it is put in a rational adaptive mode. We all try to make our messy lives look rational to friends and colleagues, let alone outsiders.

In line with previous studies (Glennerster 1983), we took the view that a lot more can be gained by watching day to day, or at least weekly, what is happening in an organisation with frequent interviews, informal conversations and observations of life and meetings as they happen. This softer material can then be checked against council documents, policy statements, minutes of meetings and budgets and contracts. We have described this approach as 'administrative anthropology' elsewhere (Glennerster 1983) and many ethnographic studies adopt some of the same techniques.

The disadvantages of such an approach are that only a few organisations can be looked at in this sort of depth at any one time, given budget and research management constraints. We were fortunate that the ESRC did give us a grant that enabled us to study five authorities in this depth over the period from the end of 1992 to the autumn of 1994. We were able to take the story back retrospectively to some extent in our interviews and documentary study. We were on site during the crucial period before and after the reforms came into full operation in April 1993. We were fortunate, too, that three of the authorities had been the subject of previous studies by the authors so that there was more continuity and opportunity to have an in-depth understanding than is often the case. It also gave the opportunity to compare the community care changes with the authorities' longer institutional histories.

The staff we interviewed most frequently and the meetings we attended regularly were with senior staff, next with middle managers and least with front-line staff. This partly reflected the 'cascade of change'. It was mainly the senior staff at the outset who were trying to make sense of the changes and decide what to do. Our focus was on that process, not on the day-to-day work of social work staff. We did interview and observe some front-line work in progress but it was never intended to be our primary research focus. What this did tell was that the staff at the bottom had a very different picture of what was happening to the more optimistic view held, in many cases, at the top of the organisation. It may well be, as some senior staff expressed it in our feedback sessions, that change takes a long time to become accepted and understood lower down an organisation. We were taking a slice through an agency only part way to ultimate implementation. The junior staff may well feel better about the changes later. However, any study of this kind can only try to describe the slice of life as it finds it.

The authorities

These were chosen to reflect a cross-section of authorities politically – some strongly supportive of the government's changes, others more traditional, and some marginal politically and in terms of their adherence to the mixed-economy model at the outset. They were based in London and the home counties. One authority was a county and four were boroughs (Table 2.1). We make no claim that our study is geographically representative. We have agreed that the authorities should remain anonymous to preserve the anonymity of the leading actors.

The authority we call the 'county' was typical of a growing and prosperous area in the 1980s. It had a rapidly growing elderly population – the result of inward migration. Overall the social indicators were average for its type, broadly average housing tenure and conditions, the average number of children with single-headed households, but below average on income support. There were more households from the new Commonwealth than some other areas of its kind. Though average overall, the county was much

Table 2.1   The age profiles of the authorities' populations 1993/4 as a percentage of total population

	Under 8	*8–17*	*18–64*	*65–74*	*75+*
County	11	13	64	7	5
Borough					
A	10	11	62	9	6
B	9	8	70	7	6
C	11	12	64	7	6
D	11	12	65	7	6

Source: Registrar General.

more varied than these statistics suggest. There were very varied communities. There were rural areas matched by urban concentrations with very different political representation. The council was Conservative and then moved to being governed by an alliance of non-Conservative parties moving to the left as elections failed to go the Conservative way. In all this it was a median council.

The borough we shall call A was Conservative throughout. Like many equivalent boroughs it supported a considerable commuter population and was also prosperous in its own right. Its social indicators were also typical of its kind – below average levels of housing deprivation, rates of claimants for social security, and very few people from ethnic minorities. The proportion of its population over 65 was above average for its type.

Borough B was more typical of an inner-city deprived area though like most of its kind this was only true of part of the borough. It had an above average level of social deprivation indicators such as housing and numbers of claimants and a large public housing stock. Its age composition was about average. It had a Labour majority.

Borough C was also Labour, and had been for many years. It was much like many old-style county boroughs of the 1960s with a tradition of support for public social services, which it provided to a high standard, if of a traditional type. As in borough B, there was a very poorly developed private sector. In many ways its social indicators mirrored the national ones. It did have an above average number of residents from ethnic minorities. Its claimant rates were somewhat below the average, reflecting reasonable job opportunities. Its proportion of people over 65 was also slightly below average and its proportion of overcrowded households slightly above.

Borough D was also mixed socially and ethnically; it had higher than average rates of elderly people on income support and single parents. It had more children from non-Commonwealth homes than most boroughs and had a mixed political history.

These were not the quiet Conservative shires where policy could be slipped into gear. There were traditions and values in the organisations that were resistant to what the government wanted to do and some members of staff were very enthusiastic. It is now time to venture out of the academic cloisters and into the difficult terrain of day-to-day life in social services departments.

3

Paying for community care

We have seen that containing the growth of public spending lay at the heart of these reforms. In this chapter we review how far the government did succeed in restraining that growth in spending and how the new arrangements for a specific community care grant worked.

Checking explosive growth

The social security budget had pumped well over £2000 million extra a year into long-term care, mainly of old people, in the decade before 1992. What would happen when that ended? Groups representing the elderly and the local authority associations were afraid that only part of that spending would be transferred to the local authorities. It would be lost in the complex general grant local councils received. Moreover, insofar as it was transferred, it would never find its way to social services departments or the elderly or community care services. Local authorities would be left with the extra responsibility and no cash. These views were also put strongly by the owners of private residential homes, who worried that the money would not be spent on their facilities either.

This pressure paid off and led the government to compromise, at least in the transitional phase. The sum of money to be transferred would be separately identified and for a period it would be ring-fenced, to be spent only on community care services. A group of civil servants and representatives of the local-authority associations formed a joint technical team, which came to be called the Algebra group. Its terms of reference were: 'To explore the factors which might influence the transfer of central Government finance to local authorities for the full implementation of community care in 1993/4 and other related matters' (Department of Health 1992).

The group set out to estimate the rate of growth in the number of new

Table 3.1   Community care transfer money

	Annual increase	Cumulative amount
1993/4	£399 million	£399 million
1994/5	£651 million	£1050 million
1995/6	£518 million	£1568 million

Source: Department of Health (1992).

people who would have received social security support for nursing home care if the changes had not been made, the amounts that would have been spent on them, the decline in the number of people already receiving benefits under the old policy, and what would have to be spent on ordinary income support for those coming into care under the new policy.

It was assumed that the number of claimants entering independent homes would have gone on rising by 30,000 a year. This was in line with increases in the previous decade. The next step involved making assumptions about how much the old benefit limits would have been raised. This was pure guesswork. Returns from homes enabled them to make some estimate of the number of old people on support who might die or move from these homes in any one year. The minimum estimate here was 13 per cent.

From this it is reasonable to expect that the Department of Social Security and the Treasury were hoping that the social security budget of £2500 million would decline at a cumulative rate of about 13 per cent a year once there were no more new recipients of support. In the first year or two this would amount to an annual reduction of about £325 million a year. On top of this the Treasury would be saving the annual *increases* in support that they had to pay for in the past decade. In the two years before the reforms took effect the Treasury had to pay out an additional £300 million extra on the base budget each year. In short, if the Treasury managed to give local authorities anything less than £625 million a year in the early years of the scheme it would be saving money on what it would have had to pay under the old arrangements. In the end the amounts transferred from the social security budget to local authorities in England were pitched somewhere between the £325 million and the £625 million figure, as befits a Whitehall bargain. The actual figures agreed on are shown in Table 3.1. These figures were to change slightly in later public-spending rounds.

In 1993/4 local authorities were paid another £140 million to cover the costs of setting up new systems of assessment and administration to cope with the changes. The impact on local authority social services departments' resources in real terms can be seen from Figure 3.1.

All in all, these were not ungenerous settlements. The sting was in the tail. There was no promise to increase the cumulative transfers beyond 1996. The

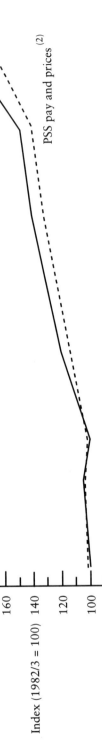

Figure 3.1 Growth in real terms in local authority net current expenditure on personal social services (PSS). (1) Revalued to average 1993/4 prices using gross domestic product deflator. (2) Revalued to average 1993/4 prices using PSS pay and prices deflator.

Source: The Department of Health (1995).

ring-fenced grant was only transitional. The special earmarked grant of nearly £400 million in 1993/4 would be absorbed into the local authority grant system and distributed as part of the normal standard spending assessment. The next year's extra £650 million would be absorbed the subsequent year. After 1996 the special grant would disappear altogether. How far the extra added to the base grant in these years would be sustained no one could be sure.

The transitional grant

We have seen that the government gave way to pressure to give local authorities, for a temporary period, a specific grant that had to be spent on their new community care responsibilities. It also gave way to pressure from the private nursing home lobby to ensure that public money to these homes was not cut off overnight. Government thus required local authorities to spend a large part of the grant on services provided by the independent sector. This was defined to include voluntary organisations and trust hospitals, not just private for-profit providers. Eighty-five per cent of the social security transfer element of the grant had to be spent on the independent sector:

> As the Government is committed to the development of a mixed economy of care, it has been decided that local authorities must also spend 85% of the social security transfer element of their grants in the independent sector. This must also be spent on community care *services*, and the local authorities must be able to demonstrate that their spending in the independent sector has risen by the amount shown in column 3 . . . compared with 1992/3.
> (Circular LASSL (92) 12 (amended), 14 December 1992, para. 12).

Independent meant 'any provider organisation which is not owned, managed or controlled by a local authority'.

In addition, special grants to fund new initiatives in mental health services, alcohol and drug abuse and AIDS were introduced. The total amount local authorities were expected to spend on their social services in 1995/6 was £6250 million. Of this, about £1200 million was to be spent on the new community care responsibilities funded through transferred money. The remaining £5000 million would go on their other responsibilities, many of which could be described as community care too, of course.

Having settled the conditions of the grant, the question was how to allocate it between authorities? To minimise the disruption to the private-sector homes the initial intention was that the grant should be recycled to those areas that had benefited from social security spending. This would have defeated much of the argument for the change. The Audit Commission had originally complained that public money was being spent in areas with private homes, not those areas with greatest need. However, there was a political constituency to meet – the private-home owners.

In the end the government decided to allocate half the transfer element in the first year according to the pattern of past social security spending. The other half would be allocated according to the standard spending assessments (SSAs) used by the government to set grant levels to local authorities for social service purposes. This formula gives heavy emphasis to the numbers of old people in the population. The government was then subject to pressure from the local authorities that were gaining very little but who had large elderly populations. In 1994/5 the government agreed to allocate all the transferred money between authorities according to the SSA formula, which gave a heavy weighting for the numbers of elderly people (LASSL (93), 19 December 1993). As this happened, authorities with high levels of social security spending under the old regime began to lose relative to those with few private nursing homes and many old people.

Our borough C was in the latter position. In 1993/4 it received only a negligible sum under the part of the formula that gave authorities money in relation to the past sums spent by social security on old people's homes in its area. This borough gained no more than about £1 million from the transitional grant in 1993/4. By 1995/6 it ended up with nearly three times that amount. By contrast those that had done particularly well out of the social security system and hence had an initially high grant could end up gaining relatively little extra over the next two years. Our borough A was in this position. Overall, however, the special transitional grant (STG) was to be a significant additional income for all the authorities.

In 1991/2 total spending on local authority personal social services was £5.1 billion expressed in 1993/4 prices. By 1993/4 the total had reached over £5.7 billion. By 1995/6 the total would rise to about £7 billion. This was one reason why the NHS took the view that it should be able to off-load its responsibilities to some extent.

Spending the transitional grant

None of the authorities knew exactly how much they would receive in grant until late February 1993, only a month or so before their new responsibilities began. Indicative amounts had been announced in December 1992. This made it difficult to plan, and all the authorities were very cautious in the first year.

The county

The county received roughly £6 million in additional grant in its first year. Of that, just over £1.5 million was the one-off sum given to authorities to pay for transitional administrative costs. There was the small sum to replace the benefits of the Independent Living Fund, but roughly £4 million came as replacement for the social security spending in the area, and of that about £3.5 million had to be spent with the independent sector.

The Department of Social Security (DSS) had undertaken a count of all those receiving help from them with their residential-care costs in the county in July 1992. There were well over 2000 such people. Of these, 1300 were in residential homes and over 700 in nursing homes. The officers calculated that, even without taking into account growing demand, this figure would translate into 775 or so new assessments for care each year that were likely to require some form of major care package. As a working hypothesis, the planners decided to assume that the balance of need as between client groups and type of care would remain much the same as that met by social security funds in the first year. This meant that £3.7 million would go to elderly people out of the £4 million total. This would be split roughly into £2.6 million to nursing-home care and £1 million to residential care. The estimates for 1993/4 were that 735 placements for the elderly would be needed in residential or nursing homes. The potential demands for care of an intense nature seemed so great that the authority did not envisage that there would be much scope for shifting away from residential care to a significant extent. In order to provide some extra resources for non-residential care the authority thought it need not spend the full £1.6 million on administration and perhaps a third of that sum could be devoted to service provision. The remaining sum, roughly £400,000, would be split between those with learning disabilities, physical disabilities, mental health problems and drug and alcohol abuse. This illustrates very clearly how driven the whole initial policy was by providing alternative care for the elderly.

These sums were then divided up and allocated to the 16 locality teams, who would be given the authority to purchase within those limits. This county was fortunate to have already in place a form of devolved budgetary authority. The 'new' money would be added to the old money these teams had available for spending on private and non-profit agency placements. This would give them new and enhanced purchasing budgets to spend on the independent sector and in less traditional ways.

Would the money be enough and what would happen to it in future years? The authority's officers calculated that to purchase care to replace the services the DSS had been paying for would require, in the first year, an additional £2.5 million. There was little chance of that happening given the squeeze on the authority's budget. Yet in future years the 'care gap' would grow. The officials' paper to the Social Services Committee pointed out that well over half the sums paid for by the DSS had been for care in *nursing* homes. That was a health responsibility. If the transferred moneys were not enough to meet the extra demands it was the NHS that should be asked to meet the extra demands for nursing/continuing care. The NHS, however, tended to think that the local authority was now responsible and had been given the money to provide community care for the elderly.

Even if the health authority had increased its spending to cover the costs of nursing home provision, which it could not do, the local authority was still £1.3 million short, the officers thought. The authority estimated that by 1995/6 it would be many places short of the numbers that would have been supported under the old arrangements and in cash terms this would amount to a cumulative shortfall over the years since the new scheme came in of nearly £23 million. Such were the relatively fearful thoughts the social services department had about the whole transfer and the resources that were being made available to cope with it.

With the money it did have, the authority thought it could afford to buy over 700 new places in homes. But that would increase the requirement to spend for subsequent years, too. It would be irresponsible to offer to place an old person this year and then find the authority could not do so next year. The social services committee therefore asked for a pledge that the council would agree to add the extra funds transferred in the revenue support grant to the social services department's budget in future years. No such understanding could ever be binding, however.

Despite the fact that so much attention had focused on the elderly it soon became obvious that there were other groups being affected. The open-ended cash available from the DSS had encouraged various innovative schemes, for example a drug and alcohol resettlement centre which depended on funds from the DSS, and there were growing numbers of people with learning difficulties who had benefited. The end of DSS support would threaten these new organisations and services and might result in growing demands on the council for financial support in the future.

This was a bleak picture. But when the new day dawned, before long it became clear that care managers were being unexpectedly innovative and were arranging more domiciliary care packages for people outside residential care than had been expected. In particular the uptake of nursing home care was nothing like what had been predicted.

The greater use of domiciliary care was just what the government had advocated. Yet the government's rules were creating difficulties for the care managers. They were required to spend 85 per cent of their extra cash in the independent sector, but the independent sector did not offer good quality home support services, not yet at any rate. The managers found themselves unable to pay for the home care they had negotiated with clients despite the fact that they had spare money because of the 85 per cent rule. They could not spend the grant on the council's own services, which were well developed and respected for their high quality.

By August of the first year it was clear that the expected budgets for residential care were being underspent. A decision was taken to reduce them and transfer £500,000 to fund purchases from independent home care agencies and another £250,000 was allocated to fund private home nursing care with the support of the NHS. The withdrawal of DSS support from those with learning difficulties and others also meant that the Social Services Department had to meet more of the costs of their care in voluntary agencies. This proved an unexpectedly large addition to be met out of the STG money.

When the total reconciliation was done for the first year of post-reform spending, i.e. 1993/4, some interesting facts emerged. The total purchasing budget for the year from external agencies was roughly £1.5 million below the expected budget of £8.5 million. But the in-house budgets were higher than expected. On the other hand the external purchases for the learning disabled group were well up, as was spending on children. The original estimates had been that there would be 725 placements in nursing homes and residential homes. In the event there had been 540. About £800,000 more had been spent on home care services. Some of the savings were carried forward to the next year, the authority being very worried about its capacity to maintain its purchases for the new clients in an uncertain financial climate.

Based on this experience the authority planned for year two. It did not dramatically change its targets from the previous year in case there was an upsurge in demand. It assumed that by the end of 1994/5 there would be about 500 placements in residential care. Care managers had made well over 200 placements in nursing homes, though 27 per cent of the clients had died in the year. The total demand for places was not as great as had been feared and care managers were making non-institutional provision in an encouraging way. The demand for nursing home places was assumed to grow slightly. About 200 placements were agreed, the higher turnover enabling any higher demand to be accommodated. More respite care in nursing homes was planned and a joint agreement with the health authority enabled the council to buy some places in nursing homes more cheaply than the authority could provide. The authority was keen to respond to the care managers' wish to arrange more home care provision, which had to be provided in the private sector. The purchasing arm of the authority would do its best to develop more good private or independent provision of home services.

It was also recognised that the learning disabled group were going to need far more than had been recognised in the early plans. There was far less 'turnover', deaths to be blunt, in this group and the long-term costs of the new placements were going to be much higher than for the elderly. As a result of modelling these demands it was proposed to increase the allocation to this group to £1.3 million.

The overall impact of these spending decisions on the authority's budget is worth noting. Much of the discussion about community care takes place in a vacuum. The effects on the social services departments of other factors tend to be forgotten. Yet, they were also trying to cope with the persistent public concern about children at risk and to implement the Children Act 1989. The effect on this county's budget over the years was striking. In 1987/8 only 21 per cent of the social services committee's budget was devoted to children. By 1992/3 this figure had risen to 30 per cent. The learning disabled group also took more of the budget. The consequence was that over the same period the share of spending on the elderly fell from 51 per cent of the budget to 35 per cent. This was despite the fact that the numbers of over-85s had risen by 10 per cent and would rise by 18 per cent by 1994.

Did the new money change this situation? It did arrest the decline in the share of spending taken by the elderly but it did not stop it, as a paper to the committee pointed out. In 1993/4 the elderly's share of the social services department's budget fell again, from 35 per cent to 33 per cent. The committee paper concluded:

- Expenditure on services for the elderly was not keeping pace with demographic growth.
- Expenditure on services for people with learning difficulties needed to grow year on year by £0.75 million.
- The STG cut off in 1995/6 did not recognise 'the slow ticking time bomb of the needs of people with learning disabilities'.

In short, this social services department had much more on its mind than the 'community care' changes. The other pressures were considerable. Moreover, the rules of the game meant that the most obvious response, expanding its own in-house domiciliary services, which were of a high standard, was not easy to do. It involved some budget manipulation.

The experience of 1994/5 turned out to follow the same trends as in the first year. Care managers were able to move from using residential and especially nursing home care to home care, and independent provision for home care began to develop.

The fact that the authority made the very sensible decision to pool STG money with its other external purchasing budgets made monitoring the use of the STG money less than straightforward. But taking all community care spending in the independent sector together at the end of 1994/5, only a minority was being spent on traditional nursing home or residential care for the elderly. Much more was being spent on other client groups, such as the learning disabled, where a well developed independent sector existed, and a growing amount on domiciliary care services for the elderly that was being offered by the independent sector. No fewer than 31 different agencies were providing services for probably well over 1000 clients in 1994. Spending varied substantially between localities, however, reflecting the availability of non-statutory provision in different areas. Hitting the 85 per cent target therefore involved some careful monitoring and juggling in a decentralised system. Nevertheless, overall the private and voluntary sectors were well enough established and growing for this not to present too much of a problem. This was in marked contrast to the situation faced by some of our poorer urban authorities, as we shall see. The transition had been smoother than the officials had first feared and the demand for residential care services from the elderly less than had been expected. What would happen when the transitional funds ceased and were fully incorporated into the revenue support grant for the authority was much less clear. When our field work ended demands were growing and the local authority grant settlements were becoming very tight.

The boroughs

Borough A received over £2 million in transferred money and nearly another £1 million or so for transitional support services. The borough adopted a cautious approach to the expenditure of its STG money. A special community care group was formed involving the borough treasurer and the chief executive to monitor STG expenditure, and the bulk of it was initially allocated to the purchase of residential and nursing home care. Just as in the county's case, it was evident by August 1993 that spending on places in nursing and residential homes was well below the estimates. One reason for this was the drive before April 1993 to use the private sector and social security support to the maximum. This had led to an initial lull in demand for places. Applications for assessment began to grow after a few months. Even so, the take-up of places in homes was lagging behind the original estimates.

The borough had set up multidisciplinary panels to check the initial assessments of care managers – one for older people and one for non-elderly adults. Home care spending was above expectations and the new demand had to be met by in-house services. The authority did not believe the commercial sector was sufficiently developed but it hoped to encourage development of the private market by promoting the establishment of the voluntary registration scheme for domiciliary care providers in London. Officers also developed a specification for an intensive home care scheme under which care could be purchased from the independent sector. However, the committee were reluctant to go ahead. There had been a number of unfortunate experiences with previous attempts to contract domiciliary services that affected this decision. The service eventually developed in-house.

It was decided to spend some of the savings on short-term projects – a business manager was appointed to review the assessment process and some short-term help with care management was bought in to speed assessment and clear the backlog. It soon became evident, however, that the underspend was going to be a two-year problem after which, on current trends, the authority would be overspending. In the short term it was in danger of having to return money to the government. This created the chance to fund the voluntary sector by approving some one-off projects – equipment for day centres, information technology equipment, a new vehicle for a local

MIND group, and other small items. Spending on an adult placement group was above estimate but the rest remained below target. It looked, in January 1994, as if there would be an £850,000 underspend on the 1993/4 grant. The turnover in places had proved higher than the council had expected, which meant that it was costing less to sustain the long-term costs of placing people in a home than had been expected. Moreover, many people who were assessed as needing a residential place were subsequently found to have savings over the new capital limits the government had set. They had capital worth more than £8000 and would have to finance their own care. The social services committee was asked to delegate authority to a subgroup of members to consider bids from the voluntary sector for once-only expenditure to meet the continuing shortfall in expenditure, 'thus avoiding the possible need to pay back this sum to the Government'. This they did.

The STG was to be higher in 1994/5 and estimates for the next year suggested a bigger failure to meet the independent-sector target unless corrective action was taken. Nearly £1.5 million was set aside as a contingency to support strategic developments in the independent sector. These were, first, services for people with disability, particularly physical disabilities and sensory impairment, and second, services for people with mental health problems. The funds were used to develop alternatives to residential care to sustain people longer in the community.

Borough B was in almost the opposite situation. It had to make considerable cuts in its overall spending to avoid capping and for other reasons, and the social services committee had its budget cut by over £4 million in 1990/1. The budget was tight in 1991/2 and was below the levels implied in the government's SSA for social services. However, for 1992/3 the council agreed to an increase for the year of over £¾ million to prepare for the new demands of the community care legislation.

Nor had this area done well under the formula. It had very few private homes and therefore only a small element of social security funding. Since the early grant formula reflected a high weighting for existing spending, the STG was not high. For the first year of the new grant it got only about £1 million. The authority assumed that, of that £1 million, £850,000 would be spent on placements in nursing and residential homes, about £50,000 on domiciliary care, and the remaining £100,000 on those with learning disability, mental health needs, physical disability and drug and drink dependency. These were simply allocated in line with the government guidelines. They translated into only 30 places in nursing and residential homes for elderly people. The infrastructure element of the grant was mainly used up in paying for new care management and assessment posts, with some money for computers.

After these estimates had been drawn up, the government's new capping rules required the council to make more cuts in the base budget for the social services department. What was more, a revision to the calculations for the authority's SSA was made necessary by the results of the 1991 census, which showed that the borough had fewer people over 85 than had been thought. General practitioners in the area had more people over 86 on their registers than the census had counted. Who was right is not clear, but it did not alter the fact that the basic local-authority grant was reduced. This led to more savings being demanded from the social services department.

It was in this climate that the use of 'extra' funds should be viewed. The department aimed to ring-fence the new community-care money, add to it the money it had always used to buy services from other agencies, and use it all to purchase services for defined categories of client.

The department decided to establish panels to allocate each element of this new money, with a budget for each client group. Thus a panel and a budget holder were appointed to decide on the allocation of the bids from care managers for placements in residential and nursing homes for elderly people and one bid for claims to buy in externally provided domiciliary care. It was only in cases where such care involved calls on external agencies, for example to provide care at the weekends or evenings, that bids would go to this group.

The department's initial estimate that it would need to make about 120 new residential placements in the first year after the new arrangements came in proved about right. These were made throughout the year, placements beginning more slowly. This meant that they were able to keep within their target spend. However, in the next year they would have not only to continue to support most of these residents, at an uncertain price, but also place more residents.

In the autumn of 1993 the council learned that because of changes the government was making in the allocation of the revenue support grant for all their services, it would be getting less grant the following year. The council would have to make cuts of £13 million and the social services department cuts of £2.5 million. Even if the community care money remained the same, the previous year's commitments meant that only about 60–70 beds could be supported for the whole year. Severe pressure was being felt, too, on places for the severely mentally ill. There was a waiting list.

Though most of the initial budget had been allocated to residential placements, demands for alternative, domiciliary care from the independent sector began to be developed that ran ahead of the estimated budget. This was viewed positively and money moved across from the residential budget.

This extreme tightness had one positive result. The NHS realised that the social services department was in no position to be able to relieve it of much burden and an agreement was reached to enable the department to have access to 50 nursing home beds for very dependent old people. These would be allocated through the care management process. If the STG had been bigger the pressure to work together might have been less.

In the next year, however, the STG was increased quite sharply when the new formula provided the basis of allocation. The grant tripled. The authority pooled both the new grant for the year and the element in the basic grant that reflected the carry forward of the previous year's community care money and a carry forward of the department's original external commissioning budget. This total pot was then divided into separate placement budgets for each client group: older people, those with learning difficulties, residential and day care, mental health placements, places for those with disabilities, and drug and alcohol abuse, with a larger element for domiciliary care. A significant contingency fund was set aside to see how the demands turned out.

The change in allocation formula of the transitional money had saved the authority from a very difficult situation. Its allocation of money to distinct budgets for external commissioning for each client group meant that a picture of what was happening could be followed and adjusted as necessary.

In contrast, borough C chose not to consider the use of the transferred money as a separate entity. The community-care plan did not discuss the use of the money nor did the social services committee get distinct proposals for its use. As the director put it in a communication, 'The expectation was that the money was available to meet individual need as assessed.' This is difficult to fault in theoretical terms but it made the impact of the change in funding difficult to identify. In 1994/5 a severe overspend on services for elderly people was identified within the STG budget and corrective action had to be taken. The authority had to cut back severely to keep within capping limits. It had received an even lower allocation of transfer funds in the first year than borough B because of the very small take-up of social security money. It had one of the lowest levels of grant per head of the elderly population in the country. Thus a very tight rein was kept on new placements.

There was a slow pick up in numbers applying and being assessed and placed in the first few months. Tight limits were put on private-sector price levels the council would accept and the council would not guarantee the resettlement costs of people with learning difficulties that the social security system had given. (This policy was later relaxed.) About £90,000 of home care was purchased from the independent sector in 1993/4.

In the next financial year, 1994/5, the size of the transitional grant rose because of the formula change. The authority continued its cautious approach. One official said,

> The truth is that caution has won out over excitement, and we are rolling towards a significant underspend on STG this year on our current levels of activity. We will make adjustments as necessary in order to claim our grant . . . there are obviously two processes at work. The truth is that we will lose another £2 million out of base budget again this winter, and therefore we have to concentrate on what budget capacity we will have next April, that is our key job.

The additional revenue was essentially helping to offset the reduction in base budget produced by government cuts to the general grant.

Our final borough, D, was in yet a different position. It had done unexpectedly well out of the first year's grant because of the large number of old people's homes it had and the high original social security spend. It decided to spend virtually all its transferred money on residential care, initially. Before long it became apparent that there was an urgent need to provide some support services, notably to meet the increased pressure of assessment from the new applicants for care. There were just two NHS staff engaged on this duty. It was agreed that three extra staff were needed with nursing, health visiting and community nursing qualifications. This choice of nursing as the key qualification was an interesting one in itself but the NHS said that it was not in a position to employ the extra staff. The social services department undertook to do so out of the transferred money. It was also argued that additional accounting assistance was necessary to monitor the large new payments to private homes that would be necessary. Eleven separate budgets were created to cover placements in residential homes and nursing homes for distinct client groups. The department and the health authority agreed the number of people they thought would need care in each category and the anticipated weekly cost. The outcome at the end of the first year shows some similarity with experience in other areas. The overall total was down on expectations – nursing home take-up had been greater and residential home care less than expected.

Some unspent money was used from the 15 per cent available to fund the costs of those placed in local authority homes once the required level of independent-sector funding had been achieved.

An overview

Overall, then, the financial pressures on the authorities by the end of the second year that derived from the community care reforms alone were far less than most authorities had feared. The pressures some were under derived from the cuts in their base grant. The authorities that suffered most initially were those that received far less than their numbers of old people justified because of the government's desire not to hurt the private-homes sector too much. Once the grants were allocated in relation to the new community care formula, most authorities found they could meet the extra demands. Care managers were beginning to put together domiciliary care packages that were calling on the services of the private sector. All this reflected the expectations of the reformers. Nevertheless, this last development was still very slow. Sufficiently good care, especially for the very vulnerable, was still hard to find. Local authorities could have provided more themselves but that was prohibited by the 85 per cent rule. This reflected the conflict between the efficiency goal of the reforms and the mixed-economy goal, at least in the short run.

The long-term impact is more difficult to foresee. By 1995 some of our authorities were under severe budgetary pressure caused by the reduction in revenue support grant. This was even more true in a number of authorities we were not studying. The situation in the Isle of Wight and Gloucestershire hit the national headlines in 1995. The government acknowledged the difficulties of some 20 authorities, and allowed them to carry forward their savings in 1993/4 into 1994/5. Education budgets were being cut in 1995/6 and in the normal laws of budget setting social services departments were likely to feel even more pressure in the next round. The fate of the community-care services would depend on the scale of the general local-government finance settlements after 1996. These prospects were not looking good.

4

Changes in the structure of social services departments

Though a social care market was a near-core objective of the reforms, the precise restructuring of departments was not. Historically a lot has been expected of restructuring within social services departments. Restructuring has been seen as a means of achieving change, most notably so at the time of the Seebohm reforms. The 1989 white paper on community care indicated that the emphasis would be on process not on structure. However, given what social services departments were being asked to do, particularly in terms of becoming enablers, it was highly likely that there would have to be reorganisation. Nevertheless, government was concerned to get away from what might be termed the 'technical fix' mentality, whereby it was believed that once reorganisation had taken place the desired changes would automatically follow. This kind of thinking had been the hallmark of the changes in both health and social services in the 1970s. However, when reorganisation takes place, it tends to dominate the stage and it inevitably has consequences, not always foreseen, of its own. Local authorities were given copious guidance on how to achieve particular aspects of the changes, especially enabling and care management, but none on departmental reorganisation. Nor has the changing structure of departments been a focus of attention in the academic literature, and yet we are almost certainly seeing the end of the 'Seebohm departments'.[1]

In our sample of authorities, very different approaches were taken to the issue of departmental reorganisation. Two restructured very early, at the end of 1991 and the beginning of 1992. The other three authorities proceeded more slowly, but interestingly all have evolved towards creating what might be termed a 'high and firm' functional split between purchasing and providing divisions, beginning at assistant director level. Thus it seems that what government asked social services departments (SSDs) to do in the end required a fundamental reorganisation, notwithstanding the reassurances in the white paper to the contrary. We suggest in this chapter that the reasons for the very different pace of reorganisation in the different authorities had much to do with local circumstances, cultures and personalities, and that the new structures have given rise to particular organisational issues that have implications for implementing the legislation. The changes have been radical but some of the resulting tensions nevertheless exhibit traces of problems that were familiar in the old departments.

The response of the authorities we researched to the passing of the 1990 community care legislation in terms of restructuring their departments varied widely. It seems obvious to try to explain this in terms of degrees of resistance to the new legislation or difficulties in implementation. In fact, there was little overt resistance among senior managers, although there was considerable foot dragging in some places, certainly until the result of the 1993 general election made it clear that the legislation would be fully implemented. All authorities faced enormous difficulties in implementation. The differences in the pace and nature of restructuring related more specifically: to the way in which senior managers interpreted the changes; to their particular preoccupations, which were in large part dictated by local circumstances; and to the strengths or weakness of the strategic capacity of departments.

Reorganisation in the research authorities

The Seebohm departments set up in the early 1970s were about liberating social work from medical domination and providing universal access through a single port of entry. The Seebohm proposals represented the culmination of the social administrators' determination to use the concept of generic social work to overcome fragmentation of the personal social services, together with their more general faith in the power of an administrative reorganisation to achieve a change in principle and purpose. Expressing optimism about the preventive properties of social work, the Seebohm report (Cmnd. 3703, 1968) aimed to make social work accessible to all families and to create unified social work departments. In principle, then, the report tended towards universality and genericism, but it is not clear whether the Seebohm Committee made the connection between the creation of a unified service that was universal rather than for families and the implications of universal access for the practise of social work. While the personal social services remained highly residual, the creation of a single-door service nevertheless had the effect of dramatically increasing the number of clients.

The principle of genericism proved notoriously ambiguous. The Seebohm Committee recommended that the basic field social worker should move towards taking responsibility 'for the whole range of individual and family social problems, drawing on support in this from consultants within the social services department' (Cmnd. 3703, 1968, para. 18). This made it sound as though the basic-grade social worker would be expected to deal with the whole gamut of presenting problems, calling on the help of specialists in the department. However, later on in the report, the Committee recommended that 'nevertheless subject to certain provisos . . . we consider that a family or individual in need of social care should as far as possible, be served by a single social worker' (para. 516), which made it sound more as though one worker was intended to take responsibility for a client on the lines of a key worker or possibly a care manager, but that a range of workers might be involved in providing care. The Seebohm Committee paid very little attention to defining the role and tasks of social workers compared with that given to the structures necessary for service delivery, which may be seen as further evidence of the Committee's preoccupation with genericism as a means to achieve administrative unification.

The goal of the administrative unification of social work resulted in social work values predominating in the new social services departments, even though, as Wistow (1992) has pointed out, only 12 per cent of the staff were qualified social workers. The goals of the early 1970s reforms stand in stark contrast to those of 20 years later, when the emphasis was put on reducing the role of SSDs in the direct provision of social care and on more efficient and effective ways of undertaking social work practice via care management. We might therefore expect that SSDs were bound to be subjected to profound organisational and cultural change.

The Seebohm departments organised themselves according to a variety of divisions on the basis of geography, function and client group (Challis 1990). The first two of these tended to predominate because of the desire to promote generic practice. However, as Stevenson and Parsloe (1978) and Challis and Ferlie (1987) have shown, informal specialisation became increasingly popular as social workers struggled to stop deskilling in the face of crisis management. There was tension between the nature of the divisions determining the structure of SSDs, together with tensions between field and residential social workers, specialist versus generic practice (primarily a field work tension), professional domination versus participation, and between centralisation and decentralisation. It is probably fair to say that none of these tensions was ever wholly resolved in the old SSDs.

The county

Following a period of extensive consultation between 1990 and 1991, the SSD restructured in September 1991 into three 'streams': purchasing, providing, and strategy and quality assurance. Reorganisation was profound, affecting most levels of the department and work with children as well as adults. The county did not simply reposition existing staff within new divisions/streams, but rather created: a new geographical alignment (whereas the pre-1991 structure had divided the department into six geographical divisions, the new structure created 16 localities within the purchasing

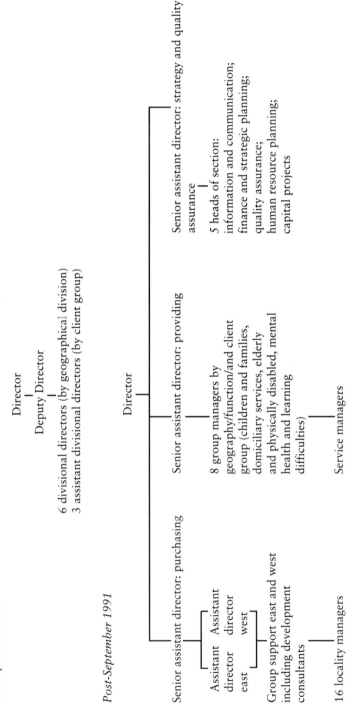

Pre-September 1991

Director
|
Deputy Director
|
6 divisional directors (by geographical division)
3 assistant divisional directors (by client group)

Post-September 1991

Director

Senior assistant director: purchasing

Assistant director east   Assistant director west

Group support east and west including development consultants

16 locality managers

Senior assistant director: providing

8 group managers by geography/function/and client group (children and families, domiciliary services, elderly and physically disabled, mental health and learning difficulties)

Service managers

Senior assistant director: strategy and quality assurance

5 heads of section: information and communication; finance and strategic planning; quality assurance; human resource planning; capital projects

Figure 4.1 Restructuring of the county's SSD, 1991

division – see Figure 4.1); new posts, especially care managers, who were recruited from social work, occupational therapy and home care; and new ways of interrelating between purchasers and providers.

The county's reorganisation was thus both early and dramatic. Offices, jobs and systems were changed over one weekend and 1200 staff were transferred to new posts. Some of the sensitive operational details were not worked out in advance, for example where purchasers and providers shared offices budgetary responsibility for office overheads had not been decided, which, according to one third-tier provider, resulted in considerable tension. One particularly disillusioned third-tier purchaser commented: 'The whole thing was turned upside down, the localities were brought into play, and there were no procedures, no policies, nothing. It was absolute total confusion. So people made up procedures and fell back on old ones.' Yet staff were told that the majority would find themselves doing the same job in the same place and there was considerable truth in this; many of the provider units remained much the same while the bulk of the change was borne by purchasers. Establishing the purchasing function was the more difficult task because it was so new, and stability in the division also proved difficult to achieve. There was complete staff turnover at second and third tier in 1992/3.

While the new purchasing stream experienced the most radical change, the whole department was to be profoundly affected by the change in organis- ational culture that resulted from implementing a firm purchaser–provider split. As a senior manager in the strategy and quality assurance stream reflected late in 1994, 'I think also you have to look at people who are in jobs as well. It's not as simple as just creating a structure and a job and putting someone in it and expecting them to do it', which sounds very much like some of the comments about the difficulties of putting old wine in new bottles that accompanied NHS reorganisation in the early 1970s (Brown 1973). In fact, the county displayed a willingness to bring in new people to fill senior posts rather than just rearranging existing staff, as happened in two of the boroughs.

The county's 'big bang' approach to reorganisation proved difficult for many staff, but may have been justified insofar as all the research authorities have moved steadily towards the model the county adopted very early on. Given that our field work began in January 1993, we have had to rely chiefly on respondents' memories and somewhat on documentary materials in our effort to explain why the county opted for root and branch reorganisation. First, in the late 1980s the Conservative-controlled county had seized on a radical enabling model of local government that involved 'externalising' what had hitherto been in-house services such as highways and planning, property services and the treasurer's department. This involved setting up these services in a trading relationship with the 'client regulator, facilitator centre'.

It seemed to senior staff in social services that it was only a matter of time before their department was also subjected to a similar process. The introduction of a purchaser–provider configuration offered a way of stopping this happening wholesale and in particular offered a way of protecting social work services by introducing care management and locating it in the purchasing stream. The county was also moving in the late 1980s towards decentralised, localised cost centres and devolved budgetary responsibilities. The creation of 16 localities in place of the six divisions that had existed previously was based on the principles of local access and accountability, and keyed into these particular preoccupations of members and senior officers in the authority. It was also strongly favoured by at least one senior manager in the SSD.

We would therefore emphasise the particular local circumstances that characterised the position of the county in explaining the radical restructuring; however, there does also appear to have been a genuine desire on the part of senior officers to implement the community care changes and a belief that they would prove positive. Thus restructuring was not conceived of in isolation, but was considered as part of a whole array of changes with the move to a more mixed economy of care, and the establishment of care management, more rigorous needs-based planning and resource allocation. The county established a range of task groups to take forward the implementation of the changes, including a community care implementation group, which deliberately brought all senior managers together on a regular basis to address the array of issues involved in implementation.

The views of staff about the way in which the reorganisation was handled varied considerably. There was an elaborate process of consultation involving the use of videos, roadshows, broadsheets and staff surveys. But inevitably there were losers as well as winners in the exercise. Most notably, of the six divisional directors in the pre-1991 structure, only one secured a senior assistant directorship. One 'loser' in the restructuring process commented that senior managers had communicated, but had done less well on listening. Some third- and fourth-tier staff also felt that what happened was not so much a consultation as a public relations exercise. But there was undoubtedly a clear commitment on the part of very senior staff both to the new structure and to communicating it in the broader context of enabling and the drive towards needs-led social care in order to take staff with them. Consensus was hard to achieve in such a large department, which had in any case been prone to internal division (between the six geographical 'fiefdoms').

With regard to the formation of 16 localities (which became 15 when two amalgamated at the end of 1993) in the new purchasing stream, a second-tier manager spoke of 'a scorched earth' policy whereby the people in the old divisions walked out and the new locality members were left to find their way. A fourth-tier officer in the strategy and quality assurance stream commented that it was initially very difficult to know what the different streams were doing. The large number of localities meant that communication with shire hall became more complicated, there being something of a bottleneck at assistant director level. Locality managers developed quite different styles and patterns of work. The small size of localities posed further difficulties. For example, the problem of adequate staffing levels was not addressed until 1994, when a process of 'twinning' was introduced to provide more cover at times of staff shortage.

The position of the development consultants supporting the assistant directors also proved somewhat problematic. One referred to feeling like 'piggy in the middle', while a senior manager in the stream spoke of having 'this box on the side of the structure where they were and . . . more and more things kept going into this magic box so that the development consultants' workload has developed in a rather *ad hoc* way'. Purchasing was the only stream to experience a significant change in structure after September 1991, when the contracts and budgets unit was added in the summer of 1993 in an effort to develop and give more coherence to the purchasing function in the authority.

The formation of the strategy and quality assurance (SQA) division was important for consolidating the county's crucial strategic centre. For example, the role of the planning section, which had existed in the SSD since 1987, became increasingly significant, not in terms of traditional service development, but in relation to the growing demands of strategic purchasing, including the determination of principles to underpin resource allocation, eligibility criteria and needs analysis. The SQA division continued to hold a large number of central functions: finance, information and information technology, quality assurance, human resource planning, and, until it was moved to the providing division in the summer of 1993, capital projects. The SQA stream was perceived initially as having a 'ring-holding function', a neutral role between providing and purchasing, but increasingly it developed closer relations with purchasing, such that a senior manager in purchasing agreed in late 1994 that there was 'a fudge' between the two streams: 'Strategy and quality assurance find it increasingly difficult to say something or plan something which isn't about purchasing.' That this was not without tension was revealed by a fourth-tier officer in SQA, who said 'very few organisations function well if they employ a donkey as a guru'.

Comparing the new structure to the old it is possible to see that, in certain respects, purchasing subsumed the old field work teams (teams of care managers were placed in the localities), while providing subsumed the old day care and residential teams. Thus the new overarching orientation of purchasing and providing contained within it traces of the old divide between field work and residential care. The client group split moved in different directions within the purchasing and providing streams. In providing it moved up from fourth to third tier, where it sat alongside a geographical split. But in purchasing, the client group split moved down the hierarchy to below the locality managers, although a client group lead role was later given to

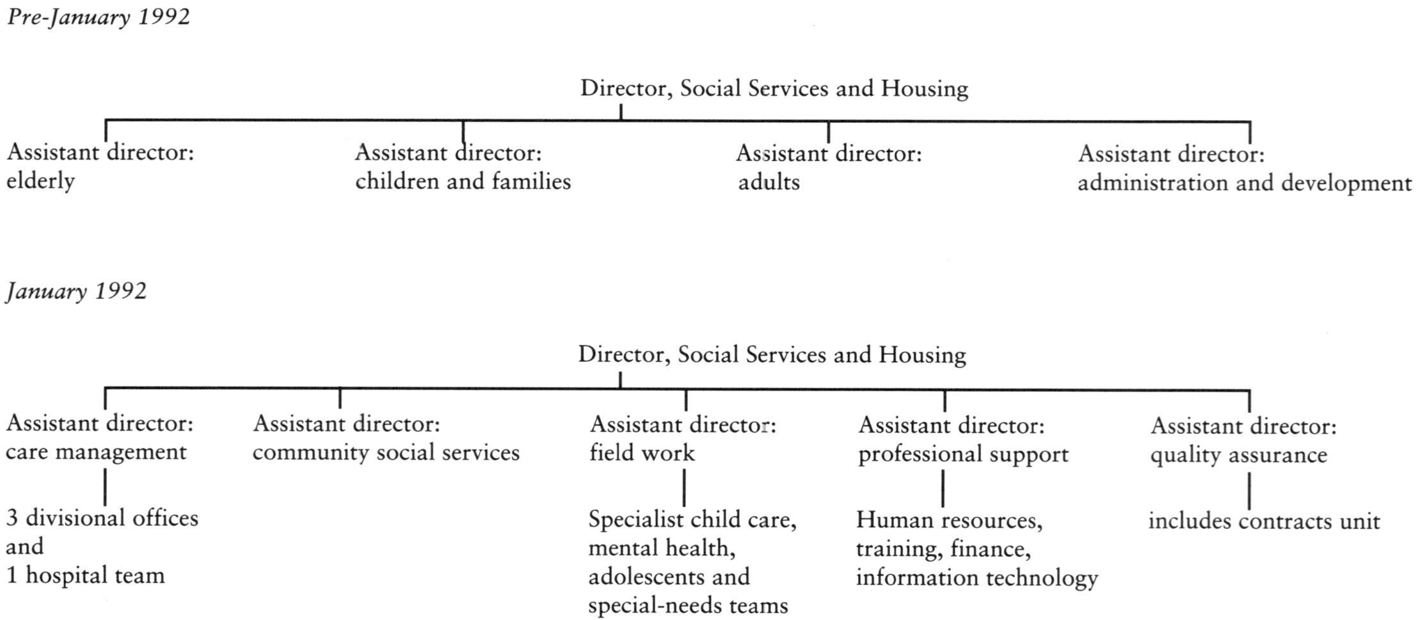

Pre-January 1992

Director, Social Services and Housing

- Assistant director: elderly
- Assistant director: children and families
- Assistant director: adults
- Assistant director: administration and development

January 1992

Director, Social Services and Housing

- Assistant director: care management

  3 divisional offices and 1 hospital team

- Assistant director: community social services

- Assistant director: field work

  Specialist child care, mental health, adolescents and special-needs teams

- Assistant director: professional support

  Human resources, training, finance, information technology

- Assistant director: quality assurance

  includes contracts unit

Figure 4.2 Restructuring of borough A's SSD, 1992

individual locality managers and was also maintained at group support level. However, in autumn 1993 a client group lead role was given to assistant directors, moving the client group split back up to third-tier level.

Challis (1990) suggested that departments with divisions based on client groups would be the most disadvantaged in respect of the functional split demanded by the new community care legislation. The county had a primary division based on geography before 1991 and client divisions existed below that, but the changes in the purchasing stream since 1991 suggest that it has remained difficult for departments to juggle functional and client-based divisions.

The county experienced two forms of reorganisation: the establishment of the purchaser–provider split and at the same time decentralisation within the purchasing stream, with the formation of the localities. This helps to explain why the changes posed particular difficulties for the purchasing stream. However, by the second year considerable adjustment to the new roles and relationships had been made by staff, who by then had, on the whole, accepted the new structure and were showing determination to develop their new roles. In contrast to this, most of the boroughs had yet either fully to establish or to settle into new structures.

Borough A

Borough A also set out explicitly to establish a purchaser–provider split at second-tier level, early in January 1992. A paper that went to the social services committee in the middle of 1990 referred to the need for two clearly demarcated divisions in the SSD, one dealing with assessment, the other with provision.

Before January 1992 the department had three divisions based on client groups. These were replaced in the reorganisation by a set of functional divisions (Figure 4.2), albeit that in the event the purchaser–provider split was not as clear as had been implied in the documents issued before reorganisation.

In the new structure the community social services division became a clear providing division and care management a clear purchasing division, although the job description for the assistant director of community social services referred to the capacity to manage 'a purchaser or provider function of the department'. The field work division was effectively defined as both a purchaser and a provider. Also, the contracts unit was not located in the main purchasing division but in operational support. In part, this was because it was believed that it would be purchasing services for both the field work and care management divisions, and in part because of the rather narrow definition of the work of the unit in line with the kind of competitive compulsory tendering that the Conservative administration had long been keen to promote. In mid-1994 the work of the contracts unit was devolved to the purchasing divisions, which may be seen as the last step in the shift from seeing purchasing simply in terms of contracting out to using it as a vehicle for enhancing user choice. It took some time before the rather different style of purchasing associated with community care was fully understood in the borough.

Furthermore, the boundary between care management and field work was not clear. Having opted for a multi-occupational care management division identified as purchasing, the department faced the problem of what to do with statutory social work. Hence the creation of the field work division, which consisted of a number of specialist teams including child care, mental health, special needs and an adolescent resource team. The intention was that the care management division should be the 'front door' to the department. All clients would enter through this door and those in need of statutory social work, for example under the Mental Health Act 1983, would be passed to the field work division. The problem was that considerable confusion arose as to when a care management case became a field work case. Field work had a limited number of teams and was often unwilling to take on clients, which resulted in clients with similar problems being dealt with by workers from two different divisions. It seems that with the move to care management and the separation of assessment from the provision of service there were a number of issues that were not easy to resolve.

The reorganisation resulted in a reduction of staff, from 540 to 527. In keeping with the council's expressed objectives, the department put in place a flattened hierarchy, which it considered would aid devolved decision making. In the care management and field work divisions the fourth-tier team leader grade was taken out and third-tier service managers took on the responsibility for managing 14 people rather than the eight managed by the old team leaders. Reflecting on this in the middle of 1993, the new director said:

> the bit that I think was difficult was removing the team leaders . . . the effect that I can see is that the assistant director spends lots of time on operational issues and is very much alone, instead of working on strategic issues. I don't know that any other authority has flattened the hierarchy quite so much.

Borough A emerged from reorganisation with only care managers, service managers and an assistant director in its care management division, whereas most other authorities had at least five layers of staff. However, borough A moved relatively quickly to extend the structure. As a second-tier manager put it:

> They took team managers out and created service managers; the trouble with service managers is that the concept is fine, but they get dragged down to being glorified team managers instead of being dragged up, so

we have put more practice managers into the structure, which is team managers by another name . . .

By March 1994, there were five layers of staff in the community care division: an assistant director, principal service manager, service manager, practice manager, and senior care managers/care managers/social services officers.

Borough A's desire to move quickly towards a purchaser–provider split must also be related to local circumstances. There was a push within the authority to implement client–contractor splits in all departments as a continuation of government's late-1980s policy of exerting pressure on local authorities to put non-human services out to compulsory competitive tender (see, for example, Ascher 1987).

This interpretation of enabling was strengthened by the way in which the 1989 white paper held out the promise of revenue savings to local authorities that externalised their residential care homes. In the end, these revenue savings did not materialise, but many authorities transferred the ownership of at least some of their homes (Wistow *et al.* 1994). Borough A, which was anxious to be seen as a Conservative 'flagship' borough, was among them. One second-tier manager commented that the director was looking for something 'that was fairly radical'. Another second-tier manager commented that there was recognition within the department that restructuring would have to take place in the wake of the community care legislation, the emphasis being put on the need to introduce care management: 'It also fitted with, at that time, the authority's drive for a purchaser–provider split, and that was almost more of a driving force than care management itself, and it made sense to put the two together.' This manager felt that the reorganisation had been widely discussed in the department, but the balance of views expressed to us tilted in the opposite direction. A second-tier manager referred to the 'slap, bang, wallop' management style of the department at that time and a third-tier manager said:

> I mean, when I first joined it was like we have to have a purchaser–provider split, before you knew where you were, how you were going to do it, there was a date it had to be done by, and you were left to work out how to do it without having any guidance and that has been the style of the Department I think.

The sense of third-tier managers in general was that 'they were just told how the new structure would be'.

Just after the reorganisation took place, the director resigned. The borough had an acting director from February 1992 to March 1993. The SSD also had a number of vacancies in strategic planning/research posts during the period, which meant that the assistant director in charge of care management – the

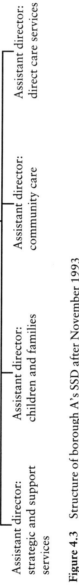

Figure 4.3 Structure of borough A's SSD after November 1993

pivotal new division – had very little support to draw on during this crucial period.

The reorganisation brought into being two support divisions (professional support and quality assurance); however, these were rather depleted in terms of personnel. One of the assistant directors was absent from his post and has since left the department. In March 1993 these divisions were merged into one division, operational support services, and a new assistant director was appointed. The contracts unit, previously located at tier three of the department (see Figure 4.2), was made accountable to the head of finance, administration and contracts within the new division and therefore was effectively downgraded to fourth tier. Its role was described more in terms of monitoring and enforcing existing contracts, and less in terms of creating opportunities for the further externalisation of services, which was identified as a responsibility of all senior managers within the department. The head of the contracts unit had come from one of the public utilities and was strongly associated with the commitment of the authority to introducing client–contractor relationships.

The community social services provider division brought together a range of services including personal care, the family placement service, meals, special sheltered housing, residential care and transport, which would previously have been managed by the appropriate client group division. It was not therefore a case of providers 'just carrying on', as is sometimes thought. Yet the provider division did manage to develop a firm identity.

The position of the care management division proved more difficult because of the lack of clarity regarding its relationship with field work and because overnight it began to operate a generic system of assessment for clients, including children and families, rather than using specialist intake teams, as had been the case under the pre-1992 structure. In November 1993 it was decided to undertake a further major reorganisation, whereby two divisions – children and families, and community care – were created, reflecting the two major client groups, adults and children (Figure 4.3). According to the same staff who commented on the January 1992 restructuring, 'the whole atmosphere' surrounding this reorganisation was different, with staff feeling 'consulted rather than imposed upon', although one fourth-tier manager still questioned the extent to which front-line staff were consulted.

Effectively field work became the children and families division, with staff in this division retaining the title 'social worker', while care management was renamed community care and continued to employ care managers to work with adults and elderly people; two social work teams, one for people with mental health problems and another for people with special needs, were transferred to this division. The remaining divisions were renamed: community social services became direct care and the operational support services division created in March 1993 became strategic and support services. This reorganisation was thus driven primarily by operational concerns. The

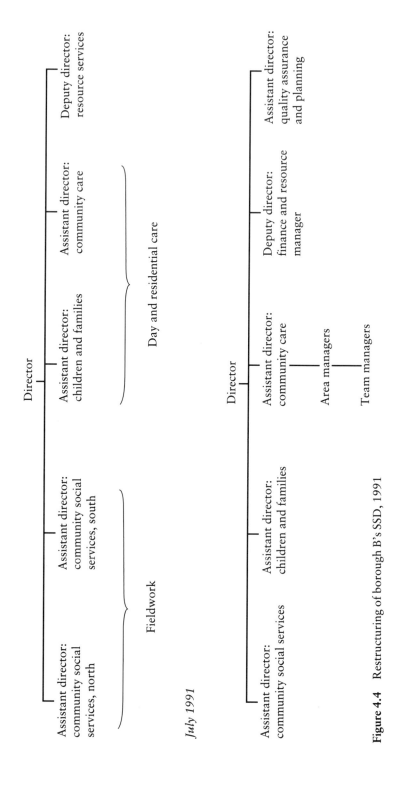

Figure 4.4 Restructuring of borough B's SSD, 1991

Pre-July 1991

Director

Assistant director: community social services, north

Assistant director: community social services, south

Assistant director: children and families

Assistant director: community care

Deputy director: resource services

Fieldwork

Day and residential care

July 1991

Director

Assistant director: community social services

Assistant director: children and families

Assistant director: community care

Area managers

Team managers

Deputy director: finance and resource manager

Assistant director: quality assurance and planning

tendency to leave work with children largely outside the ambit of restructuring has been the pattern in all the London boroughs to date. It is therefore possible to see the re-emergence of separate children's divisions on the pre-Seebohm model, albeit that, as a result of the purchaser–provider split, the provider division (direct care), provides services such as fostering and adoption.

Borough A was quick to reorganise and to introduce the labels of purchasing and providing, and of care management. But the evidence suggests that the processes attaching to these new functions and activities were not thoroughly thought through in 1991. There was no evidence of any pan-departmental implementation group, as in the county or borough B. It is therefore not surprising that, unlike in the county, the borough has experienced significant further reorganisation.

Borough B

Borough B reorganised in response to the new policy of community care for the first time in July 1991, but at that stage the SSD's concern was to recognise structurally the two major pieces of legislation affecting children (in 1989) and community care (in 1990). Thus a set of divisions that encompassed both a field work/residential–client group split was replaced by a primary division on the basis of client group. The idea of introducing a purchaser–provider split was not explicitly discussed in 1991, although arguably the new structure provided a basis for one.

Early in 1991 the department had moved towards the specialist delivery of social work services, a popular move with staff, albeit that it was undertaken at a time of budgetary cutbacks. The July reorganisation was thus the second in that same year (see Figure 4.4). The second reorganisation merged the community services north and south into a single community social services division, which involved the removal of an assistant directorship and several principal officer posts. The new division was identified as being responsible for access, assessment and care management, and advice and information. Domiciliary care also continued to be located in this division. At the end of 1992 domiciliary care services were taken out of the teams to be managed by a principal officer, which made the service easier to transfer to a provider division early in 1993. Thus the community social services division was by no means clearly identified as a purchasing division. Children and families and community care were identified as 'essentially provider divisions'.

Two new strategic divisions were created, replacing what was the resource services division. The assistant director post freed up by the merging of the two social work divisions was used to create the new assistant directorship for quality assurance and planning. Located within this new division were inspection and registration, complaints, race equality, strategic planning and consultation, and purchase of services and management of service-level agreements. The description of what the last of these sections might do was quite limited in the policy paper that went to the social services committee in July 1991:

> The new 'commissioning unit' would assume the role of managing the contracts with the department's residential care when transferred, service level agreements where they exist with the voluntary sector, competitive compulsory tender contracts and any other commissioning of service which might take place in the future.

At this point only the voluntary sector was mentioned as a possible contractor. In fact the commissioning unit remained an idea confined to paper until late in 1992.

It was during 1992 that borough B made considerable headway in evolving the purchaser–provider split. In large measure this was due to the arrival of a new and energetic assistant director to head the quality assurance and planning (QAP) division in July. She found that many of the functions of her division existed only on paper, most notably commissioning. In October 1992 a commissioning unit was formed, headed by the staff member who had been the head of the HIV commissioning unit in the department. It was expected that the new unit would employ six commissioning officers, but some of these posts remained vacant throughout 1993 because of difficulty in recruitment. The development of the new QAP division continued with the rebuilding of the strategic planning unit in late 1992 and the establishment of a quality standards section early in 1993. The new assistant director appointed staff to the race equality posts, which were vacant when she arrived, and then transferred them into the quality standards section. The assistant director was critical of the existing social services' approach to planning, which she felt stifled initiative, and was committed to filling posts with staff who had the vision to develop positive and imaginative interpretations of the new legislation. Thus the new division grew at enormous speed and underwent considerable change in 1992.

The reasons for this were related not only to the personality of the new assistant director, but also to a change in thinking on the part of senior management in the department. The SSD began with a determination to implement the new legislation in a user-centred fashion and focused initially on care management. But early in 1993 the director acknowledged that during 1992 senior managers had begun to recognise that commissioning 'is more than contract management, it is trying to think through what we commission, why, where from and for what purpose'. The borough went on to draw up a statement on ethical commissioning, which talked about the way the process could be used to enhance equal opportunities and to stimulate new provision for those whose experience of traditional services had been negative, particularly black and ethnic minority users. A market mapping exercise had shown that a number of clients were badly placed and had had little choice, and as a result the director began to feel that enabling could enhance the position of the user. The new assistant director of QAP was also convinced that equal opportunities could be enhanced by clear agreements on quality and by the development of a portfolio of more relevant services from the independent sector. These views pointed towards the need to develop a macro-purchasing function in the department. There were also practical reasons to concentrate more on developing a purchasing function during 1992. The SSD had a shortfall in both the independent provision of beds in the borough and in its STG moneys.

The rapid development of the new QAP division was not without tensions. The view from elsewhere in the department tended to be that the commissioning unit had been 'like an avalanche coming from nowhere'. Even though the groundwork for the unit had been laid in the reorganisation document of July 1991, no real consultation about its form took place. This was important because the unit was very different from the contracts management unit established in borough A. Those involved in it expected that it would drive policy in the department. There have been tensions between QAP and providers, and between QAP and the community social services division, some of whom would have preferred to see the unit established within that division, rather than the development of what was effectively a micro- and macro-purchasing structure. In its early days the commissioning unit adopted a rather bullish tone, making it clear that its staff were committed to purchasing the best service irrespective of the nature of the supplier. One senior provider manager felt that his division had become accountable to the QAP division as well as to the director.

Finally, in January 1994, the SSD established a firm functional purchaser–provider split by merging the children and families and community care divisions to form community care and family services, with the loss of an assistant director and four third-tier staff. At the same time, domiciliary care was transferred into this new division. The change in structure was budget driven; council members demanded the abolition of an assistant directorship. But the choice to make a clear purchaser–provider split, rather than, say, merge the finance division and QAP was the department's own. As in borough A, providers with different histories found themselves brought together. Whereas the manager of the home help service had been used to attending senior management meetings with social work managers, under the new structure she met fellow providers of, for example, children's residential units, whose concerns seemed remote.

Thus while Borough B evolved the structural purchaser–provider split over two years, it has nonetheless been radical in ways not dissimilar to the county. It did not just reshuffle staff, but created new posts and changed personnel in key positions within the department. This in turn explains in part why the shift towards a purchaser–provider split accelerated and gained real meaning. The changes in structure in this borough did not consist of relabelling,

Pre-April 1992

Director

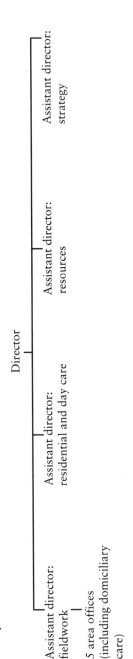

Assistant director: fieldwork

5 area offices (including domiciliary care)

Assistant director: residential and day care

Assistant director: resources

Assistant director: strategy

April 1992

Director

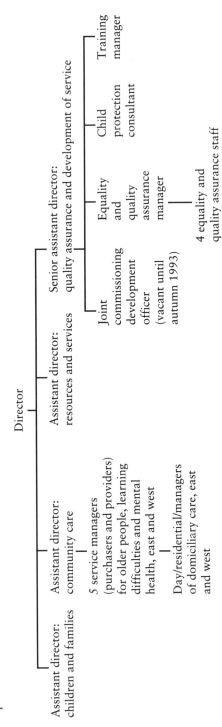

Assistant director: children and families

Assistant director: community care

5 service managers (purchasers and providers) for older people, learning difficulties and mental health, east and west

Day/residential/managers of domiciliary care, east and west

Assistant director: resources and services

Senior assistant director: quality assurance and development of service

Joint commissioning development officer (vacant until autumn 1993)

Equality and quality assurance manager

4 equality and quality assurance staff

Child protection consultant

Training manager

Figure 4.5 Restructuring of borough C's SSD, 1992

but reflected hard thinking on the part of senior managers about the nature of the changes they wished to promote.

The process of implementation in borough B was overseen by a strong project management group, established in 1990, which was similar to the county's community care implementation group. The existence of such a group signalled the strengths of the respective senior management teams. Both boroughs A and C relied much more heavily on joint groups with health personnel to tackle the work of implementation, a strategy that was not without its own advantages.

Borough C

In April 1992 the SSD in borough C reorganised primarily in order to take account of the 1989 Children Act and the 1990 NHS and Community Care Act. This resulted in a shift from a functional split based on the field work/residential care divide, to a division based on client groups (Figure 4.5).

The April 1992 reorganisation also introduced a purchaser–provider split, but only within the community care services division, at third tier. The injunction concerning 'enabling' in the community care legislation was not taken up as a priority in borough C. Instead the borough began its efforts to implement the legislation by concentrating on care management and joint working. The separation of purchasing and providing within the community care division strongly resembled the old field work/residential divide within the department, except that domiciliary care moved across from 'field work' to providing. There were grave difficulties in holding the purchaser–provider split in one division, and these were exacerbated by the resignation of one third-tier purchasing manager and the long absence of another. In addition, the department experienced problems due to the death of the director on the eve of reorganisation.

When the director introduced the changes to the social services committee he indicated that he wanted a greater synthesis of strategic work and operational work. Yet the new structures left the SSD with a continuing split between those divisions primarily devoted to direct user contact and those with a greater support or strategic role. In addition, while the division that was presumably supposed to take a strategic lead (quality assurance and development of service) had a number of designated planners and strategists, these were neither placed nor used optimally with respect to the 1990s managerial agenda. The time of the senior planning officer was swallowed up by the task of producing the community care plan, while the research team endeavoured to make a strategic impact but were tucked away alongside the equal opportunities staff.

As in the county, there were different versions of how successful the reorganisation was. The director told the social services committee that his discussions with large numbers of staff had indicated that it had been

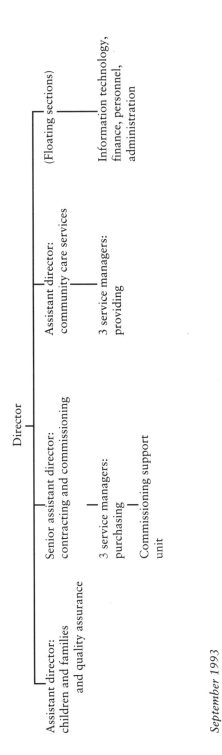

May 1993

Director

Assistant director:
children and families
and quality assurance

Senior assistant director:
contracting and commissioning

3 service managers:
purchasing

Commissioning support
unit

Assistant director:
community care services

3 service managers:
providing

(Floating sections)

Information technology,
finance, personnel,
administration

September 1993

Director

Assistant director:
children and families

Senior assistant director:
community care and
quality assurance

'Head': community care
services

(Floating sections)

Figure 4.6 Restructuring of borough C's SSD, 1993

successful, but a member of the children and families division and a member of the community care services division suggested that it had proved traumatic for many staff, involving as it had some demotions as well as changes of place and manner of working. According to this version, the demotivating effect began to wear off only early in 1993. Borough C did not mount a consultation programme like the county. There were no roadshows or newsletters and one third-tier purchaser reported that the understanding of the changes at third tier and below was poor.

In May 1993 the department underwent a second reorganisation (Figure 4.6), which was justified in terms of the need to clarify roles and relationships and which was undoubtedly pushed by the decision of central government at the end of 1992 to force SSDs to spend 85 per cent of the STG in the independent sector, thus making commissioning a more urgent task. A March consultation paper on this reorganisation elicited only 14 replies, which a fourth-tier manager believed was because staff considered the reorganisation a *fait accompli*. The consultation paper rejected the idea of a rigid demarcation between purchasing and providing, stating: 'There is no neat split between purchasing/commissioning and providing . . . the emphasis must be on "One Service: Two Tasks". Good communication will be the key.' Borough C preferred to refer to a purchaser–provider 'relationship' rather than a 'split'. The director denied that the department was merely falling into line behind the prescriptions set out in the policy guidance (Department of Health and Price Waterhouse 1991), but talked of the need to challenge providers.

The May 1993 reorganisation took place in a climate of financial cutbacks. The director had wanted to create two purchasing and two providing divisions at second tier, but one assistant director had to be made redundant and in the event this was the assistant director of resources and services. This assistant director had championed the cause of user/carer consultation and involvement, and had played an influential role in building relations with the voluntary sector and in turning joint planning structures into a joint commissioning framework. The removal of this post came as a surprise to staff, who had held its incumbent in high regard. The director spoke of the difficulty in convincing members of the considerably increased responsibilities being borne by social services in the wake of the community care legislation.

Clear purchasing and providing divisions were created as a result of this reorganisation; only the children and families division remained largely untouched. The 'floating sections' (see Figure 4.6) reported to the director and were not devolved from the centre of the department to the purchasing and providing divisions, as happened to some extent in the county. A new commissioning support unit was added to the purchasing division, but while this looks on paper like the one created in the county or in borough B, its head had previously been the head of the voluntary sector unit, thus the orientation of this unit was likely to be rather different. The purchasing division also took in those aspects of planning and strategic work that the senior assistant director had previously controlled in the quality assurance and development of services division. Thus one striking effect of this reorganisation was to increase the designated purchasing function by supplementing the existing purchasing teams with a commissioning unit, although commissioning posts within this unit remained unfilled owing to the lack of suitable candidates and the department's underselling of the posts in terms of interest and salary, together with an unwillingness to consider people without a social services background. In contrast, the community-care division became solely a providing division and thus lost staff. In September 1993 the assistant director of community care services left and the decision was taken not to fill the post. Instead, the opportunity was taken to reduce the numbers of senior managers in this division. One of the three service manager posts was removed following the resignation of a post-holder. In addition, instead of recruiting a new assistant director, a new post was created of 'head' of community care at a lower scale, thus making another cost saving. Within 18 months the number of posts at second-tier in the SSD as a whole was reduced from four to two.

Indeed, borough C has experienced considerable instability in terms of staffing. Such new posts as had been created in commissioning proved difficult to fill (as was also the case in boroughs B and D). The small research section within the purchasing division was threatened during 1993; the research manager resigned in January 1994 and was not replaced. At third tier, the service manager (purchasing) older people post was held by a staff member who was acting up for much of 1993, during which time the post itself was under threat. However, early in 1994, the post was renamed commissioning manager for older people and filled by the incumbent. A service manager (purchasing) for learning difficulties and mental health was on maternity leave and then sick leave for most of 1993 and early 1994 before leaving in the summer of 1994. Thus the borough had considerable staffing difficulties to overcome at a time of major change. There was in particular something of a purchasing vacuum which contributed to a concentration of responsibility for strategic direction and decision making in the hands of the senior assistant director.

Borough C had an elaborate structure of formal groups designed to take forward the implementation of the new community care policy, built mainly around its joint commissioning structure, although it lacked a pan-departmental group at senior level on the lines of the county's community care implementation group. In fact, decision making by informal groups seems to have been just as, if not more, important. However, the department's management hierarchy was thin and became thinner over 1992–4. Many initiatives came from two key fourth-tier managers, particularly concerning the development of assessment and 'care coordination' in the authority, but there was a perception among some middle managers that senior managers sometimes failed to provide either firm backing or clear direction. Despite a commitment to devolution, middle managers were not always given an authority commensurate with their responsibilities.

Communication generally has been a major difficulty for borough C, with lower-level staff waiting for direction and senior staff being reluctant to impose change on them. This is very different from the county, where some staff had doubts about the process of consultation, but felt that they were given clear direction.

Borough D

The pattern of restructuring in borough D has been very different from that of any of the other authorities. It was the end of 1992 before the SSD received a review of its structure, commissioned from an independent consultant. This review recommended that the department be reorganised to create a high and firm purchaser–provider split at second-tier level. The proposed changes for the second tier of the department were accepted by members at the end of 1992. The idea was to implement structural change at all levels of the department between April 1993 and April 1995, but the failure to appoint a new assistant director of commissioning until the end of 1993 substantially delayed matters. Furthermore, a change in political administration in 1994 from Conservative to Labour resulted in a decision further to delay implementing the lower tiers of the new structure.

The old structure in borough D was singular, being based on a mixture of divisions by function and by client group with no clear pattern of accountabilities (Figure 4.7). Thus the service manager for general and mental health, who managed social work assessment in the hospitals and services for the mentally ill, together with all the area managers were to be found at second tier and accountable only to the director. It was far from clear whether a home help in a particular area was accountable to an area manager or the service manager for home care, located at fourth tier in the elderly and disabilities division. In addition, two of the three assistant directors were acting up in 1992. Thus for the most part the faces of second-tier managers were firmly turned towards operational rather than strategic concerns.

The review of the old structure was initiated by members and was therefore associated in the minds of staff with members' desire for budgetary cutbacks. All three points in the terms of reference for the consultant mentioned the importance of securing cost-effectiveness. The response of staff to the review was on the whole negative, but the director recognised that 'the client–contractor split is coming in everywhere, so this department cannot be different from every other department in the council . . .'.

The review noted the strength of a professional social work culture in the department, which strives to be client centred and which cares 'passionately',

Pre-January 1993

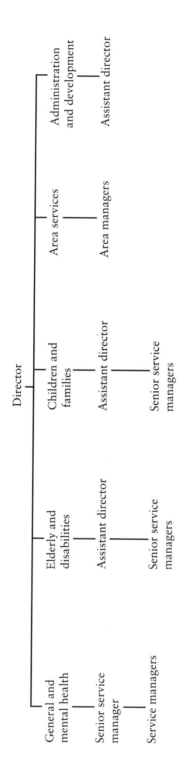

January 1993

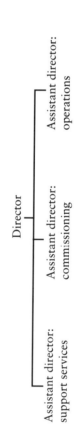

Figure 4.7 Restructuring of borough D's SSD, 1993

but which 'is not balanced by a commitment to concepts of efficiency, effectiveness, value for money or the need to ration services against available resources'. Communications in the department were also held to be poor and there seemed to the consultant to be no explicit sense of direction or shared vision. The consultant observed a tendency to try to do things by forming small working parties instead of one senior officer grasping the nettle. The principal diagnosis of the report was that too little emphasis had been given to management-related issues.

In recognition of the limited resources of the department, the review proposed that the SSD focus on protecting 'life and limb' and make services concerned with enhancing the quality of life a second priority. In order to secure a better strategic assessment of need, the range of services necessary to meet need, and the more entrepreneurial spirit among staff necessary to provide a more customer-oriented service, the review recommended a high and firm purchaser–provider split. The consultant thus proposed a root and branch reform that represented a radical departure from borough D's old structure and culture. The proposal was to set up an operations division and a commissioning division, both with client group subdivisions (children and families, mental health and adults/disability), and a support services division (see Figure 4.7). The support services division was established at the end of 1992 and included a contracts unit, which was needed to take on the task of dealing with nursing and residential home contracts from April 1993. This unit resembled the one in borough A more than the one in borough B. A new assistant director for support services was recruited in June 1993, but there was a delay of six months in recruiting a new assistant director for commissioning, possibly because it was decided that the appointee had to be prepared also to take on the work of the acting assistant director for children and families in the short term.

The slowness of this SSD to restructure is not easy to explain. The consultant's report stressed the importance of the culture of the department and, in this borough, culture was closely linked to the nature of the political administration. Before 1990 the borough had been controlled by a Labour administration firmly committed to direct service provision and opposed to contracting out. In 1990, a new Conservative administration proved as firmly committed to contracting out. There was a sense in which the SSD was understandably tempted to ride out the storm if possible. Other studies have found that political complexion has not generally determined whether an authority has been pro- or anti-enabling (Wistow *et al.* 1992). This was broadly true for our research authorities, except borough D. In the end members forced a review upon the department, but with the change of political complexion in 1994, the proposed changes were again subjected to scrutiny by members, who were not convinced of the need to increase the number of managers, and the implementation of the new structure slowed.

The third tier was put in place in the middle of 1994, but posts were ring-fenced for people at the appropriate level and others could not apply; as in borough C, there was no significant change of personnel. In addition, there was a dearth of strategic capacity in the department, due to both the lack of senior staff in post and the centralised nature of the department and of the authority in general; in the view of one senior manager, managers had historically not been encouraged to manage. The consultant recommended that a 'change management' team be set up to push through the structural changes, but such a team was not appointed because it was felt that staff were already too overloaded. Thus, while the structure of the SSD in borough D is one of the most radical on paper, encompassing as it does all parts of the department, in practice much remains to be done. The SSD approached the legislation by responding only as necessary: it produced a community care plan, introduced assessment, and bought nursing home beds, but it has not tackled the processual changes necessary for implementation.

Discussion

The pace of change has varied considerably in the different authorities. Given that all converged towards creating a functional division based on purchasing and providing, it might be suggested that those authorities who moved towards such a structure early – the county and borough A – hold the advantage. Certainly the director of borough C said late in 1994 that if he were starting again: 'I think I'd try and say "let's pull people off the job and give them specialist jobs and set tight time scales".' He feared that where the pace of change had been relatively slow in the first 18 months there would be even less incentive to speed up later. On the other hand, the authorities that were most successful in restructuring their departments are distinguished not so much by whether they began early or late, but by the extent to which they reached a clear understanding of what they hoped to achieve by purchasing or by care management. Both the county and borough B showed considerable evidence of thinking through the changes they wanted to make.

However, as a senior manager in borough B commented, the pace of change for many authorities has been 'fantastic . . . I have never known anything like it, the level of speed at which you have to get things done'. This has caused difficulties for all authorities in communicating the changes to staff. As the director in borough C pointed out:

A number of management concepts like devolution or joint commissioning I think become buzz words in a certain small coterie of organisations, and take a long, long time – longer than people actually understand sometimes – to become the natural currency with which the majority of people in those organisations do their business.

Understanding of the nature of the changes may be very different at senior management level than among front-line staff. Perceptions of how well change has been communicated certainly varied considerably between the different tiers in the organisational hierarchies of all the departments. In one authority a senior manager asked in a staff meeting early in 1994 whether staff did not agree that the department had done well in implementing the changes and was greeted by an eloquent silence.

However, the changes that have been demanded by the legislation have been so radical that they could be achieved only by the exercise of firm direction by senior managers. The importance of carrying staff along through the changes is demonstrated by the negative early experience of borough A. On the other hand, the experience of borough C shows that an overemphasis on achieving consensus and reluctance to dictate to lower-level staff can make the process of achieving structural change extremely lengthy. The strong management teams in the study tended also to set up departmental implementation groups to push through change. Yet, even in the county, these have shown a tendency to proliferate such that there is a considerable risk of duplication.

Local circumstances and cultures have been important in determining how the departments approached the issue of restructuring. In borough A, members' aspirations to make the authority a 'flagship' in turn meant that officers were under pressure to act quickly. In neither borough B nor C was there any political pressure on officers to make the department an 'enabler'. In borough B, staff became 'converted' to the idea in their own time and in borough C senior staff tended to stand back and wait for acceptance of the new concepts by the whole department. In the county, senior officers were also under pressure to 'externalise'. For them the introduction of a purchaser–provider split actually warded off the threat of externalisation to some sections of the SSD as well as representing a response to the legislation that they favoured. Officers in the county have also taken considerable trouble to educate members, for example by organising meetings outside the formal committee structure, something that has been less evident in the boroughs.

The move towards a functional division on the basis of purchasing and providing has been a leap in the dark for all authorities. In particular it has been hard to get the purchasing structure right, for while the thrust of the legislation is to move SSDs away from direct provision, in the initial phase of implementation providers underwent least change. Purchasers, while in the ascendant function, have had a steep learning curve and little history or experience to fall back on. In the county, where no significant reorganisation followed that of September 1991, changes were nonetheless made to the structure of the purchasing stream. In the London boroughs it proved hard to recruit to the new purchasing posts, probably because this was a new activity for SSDs, but this, together with high staff turnover, made stability hard to achieve. High turnover is not a new problem in SSDs, nor is it necessarily problematic during a time of rapid change, especially if new, well qualified people are brought in to fill newly created posts. However, in those authorities where a substantial vacuum was left for a considerable time by the absence of a director or by failure to recruit to new posts the consequences were more serious. The experience of borough C showed that without the 'right' structure, it was impossible to get other aspects of implementation 'right'.

Authorities have experienced difficulty in integrating work with children into the new purchasing and providing structures; thus a client split tended to exist alongside the functional purchasing and providing split. To this extent the old structural problems of SSDs in terms of juggling client and functional divisions persist. Similarly, in some authorities it was explicitly recognised that purchasing and providing perpetuated some of the elements of the old field work/residential care divide, and, insofar as field workers tended to become care managers and purchasers, some feared that the old status hierarchy would also persist. However, in many authorities the tendency to separate out work with children – together with the status of work with adults being effectively elevated within the new purchaser–provider split – has resulted in SSDs looking very different.

Everywhere reorganisation has been carried out in a climate of financial retrenchment, although this has been significantly worse in the London boroughs than the county. Thus posts tended to be lost. Borough A emerged from restructuring with a significantly flattened management hierarchy because of the abolition of the team leaders, although it was soon found necessary to put more tiers back in. In boroughs C and D the management hierarchy appears thin, if not flat. Large responsibilities for pushing forward changes have rested on a single second-tier manager. There has also been a significant lack of strategic capacity in many of the boroughs. One third-tier manager in borough A complained that 'there is no sense of where the department is going overall . . . everything is short-term current objectives'.

Work to develop new systems, quality standards, procedures and policies was undertaken only as and when time permitted. Only the county had a division separated from operational work that could do the thinking to produce certain tools that proved crucial to the implementation of the legislation, although the gap between strategic and operational work may at some point become problematic. One fourth-tier staff member in the strategy and quality assurance stream in the county said:

> I think that one of the problems that this department has in terms of having a separate planning/policy development team is making the leap from the development of policy into how that policy actually becomes translated into practice and implemented, and we are seen as a separate group of people and, particularly by staff under enormous pressures, we are seen as a fairly protected group of people.

One locality manager said more shortly that strategy and quality assurance 'might as well be the Treasury department'. Nevertheless having the right number of strategic thinkers in the right places has been important in both borough B and the county. Borough C's experiences with assessment and care management (see below) show that it is not enough to have people – in this case fourth-tier managers – who can think through the conceptual and operational requirements of service change. They must also be in the right place and be able to exert a strong influence on official departmental policy. Other third- and fourth-tier staff have tended to become bogged down in operational management; service managers in purchasing, for example, have had to check invoices. In its most recent reorganisation, borough A attempted to ensure that strategic and operational issues were not completely separated, but that managers involved in the latter nevertheless have time to think strategically. In the face of rapid and dramatic change, strategic capacity has been crucial to the process of implementation.

The need for strategists must be seen as part of the profound cultural change that has been part and parcel of structural reorganisation. It is hard to overemphasise the importance of strategic capacity to implementation. The Seebohm departments relied above all on professionalism, which provided an intuitive feel for the kind of services that were needed. Many of the new processes, for example assessment, were carried out but were not formalised in the same way. Rather, departments relied on professional discretion and much was carried around in social workers' heads rather than being made explicit. The new structures, based on purchasing and providing, and the new processes associated with them, have affected the culture of SSDs in two ways: (i) they have forced departments that have traditionally been 'doers' into becoming 'enablers', and (ii) they have required new systems to be put in place which in turn require managerial skills. Departments have thus been pushed into achieving a new balance between professionalism and mana-gerialism. The county was able to build on a pre-existing strategic capacity, but the London authorities were for the most part slow to realise the importance of investing in increased strategic capacity. For example, according to a June 1994 social services committee paper, borough A continued to take considerable pride in 'the lean nature of its organisation and department, preferring to place its resources in direct services where customers receive its services', even though at the same time it also requested £¼ million in systems and support staff. This contrasts with the county, where the creation of a new cadre of systems fixers is apparent.

It may be argued that social work has always been more subject to managerial control than has medicine, for example. Bamford (1990) argued that managerialism had eroded the autonomy of social workers. The bombardment of referrals after the setting up of the Seebohm departments made it impossible for social workers to carry out the psychosocial case work many of them had been trained in, and resulted in experiments with intake teams, team managers who monitored the flow of work, group allocation meetings and time-limited contracts with clients. However, the managerialism of the 1990s has been not so much a matter of changing social work practice but of changing the whole nature of the work of SSDs in order to introduce market principles. Senior staff, whether designated purchasers or providers, have had to learn new ways of thinking and behaving. The process of change has been rapid and they have for the most part been wholly caught up in the difficult process of trying to make it work. It is striking that posts in information and information technology, which are crucial to the operation of a functional division based on purchasing and providing, nowhere achieved the status that, it might be suggested, they both deserved and required.

The position of front-line staff, which has not been fully explored in this study, has been somewhat different. Because it has often proved difficult effectively to communicate the changes, there is some evidence that the attitudes and behaviour of front-line staff sometimes differ from those of senior managers. From the point of view of outcomes for users, which again was not the prime focus of this study, this may well prove significant, for as Lipsky (1980) observed many years ago, 'street level bureaucrats' still have considerable scope for determining the way in which departmental policy is actually implemented; subsequent chapters offer some examples of areas where there are gaps between policy and implementation. However, because of the evolution of the new structures towards high and firm purchaser–provider splits, it is fair to say that no part of the work of departments has been left untouched.

Some managers trained in social work have adapted happily to the new culture, others have not. In borough B one second-tier manager said: 'we all started life as community workers or social workers; once you become a manager you get interested in the management process, ... all my colleagues without exception are quite excited by the notion of running it as a business'. This respondent and another senior manager in the same borough seemed to embrace the changes because they offered the possibility of an enhanced 'bureau-shaping' role (Dunleavy 1991):

> People haven't so much been disrupted in the sense of great shifts of jobs, although there has been some of that, obviously; they have been disrupted by new ways of working that look quite alien to a lot of people in the public sector. Being expected to have a much more task-oriented, creative approach that in my subjective opinion has not been the hallmark of the public sector . . . I think in the new world of community care, particularly the bits like quality assurance, commissioning, planning, the last thing we need is the public sector mould . . .

On the other hand, there is no difficulty in finding people in any of the authorities who would describe themselves as 'reluctant' purchasers and providers. Irrespective of reactions to the changing culture, there can be no doubt about its depth. As one third-tier purchaser in the county commented on a 'vendor report' that the division produced at the end of 1993: 'I wouldn't have understood a word of this three years ago.'

Note

1 This is not just because of the profound structural changes to SSDs. Chapter 8 will show that the principles upon which the work of social services departments were based have also changed, particularly in terms of the shift from the aim of being universally accessible to more rigorous targeting.

5

Enabling authorities. I: The purchaser–provider split and market information

Unlike health authorities, SSDs have always been 'enablers'. The provision of social care has been more diverse than that of health care, involving voluntary and private agencies. However, the guidance following the 1990 legislation set out a more elaborate vision of enabling, involving three aspects:

- the establishment of a purchaser–provider split;
- an increase in the amount of independent provision;
- the regulation of providers by the use of contracts (Department of Health 1990a).

The idea was that SSDs should purchase *more* than they provided. This was seen as central to promoting user choice and services that were both high quality and cost-effective (Department of Health and Social Services Inspectorate 1991a). The separation of purchasing from providing was necessary to make sure that the 'respective interests of user and provider are separately represented' (Department of Health *et al.* 1991a: 15); we shall investigate this claim more thoroughly in Chapters 7 and 8, on care management.

The second dimension of enabling – increasing independent provision of social care – was designed to increase choice in the sense of enlarging the menu of services social services staff could choose from on behalf of the user, the idea being that independently provided services were more likely to be flexible and responsive to need as well as more efficient.

The third dimension, regulating providers via contracts, was intended to provide a surer check on quality and a more vigorous approach to management.

The meaning of enabling was thus clearly linked by the government's guidance to assessment and care management, and the more precise tailoring of services to need. It was not conceived of simply as 'contracting out' or privatisation, and the aim was not solely cost-effectiveness. However, there were significant and unacknowledged tensions in this approach.

First, government wished authorities to move from institutional to domiciliary care, but independent provision, which it also wished to promote, largely took the form of beds. The 85 per cent rule made it difficult to move to greater domiciliary care provision, as we saw in Chapter 3. In addition, a directive on choice (LA (92) 27) ruled that clients must be given choice of residential care.

Second, there were some tensions between the different aspects of the enabling policy. As Flynn and Hurley's (1993) research on 12 contracts showed, specialist providers tended to be monopolistic; this has certainly been the experience in the United States also (Propper 1993), where contracting has a much longer history. In addition, while block contracts often made sense for SSDs in terms of ease of administration and price, such arrangements did not necessarily promote choice. As Leat (1993) further pointed out, increasing the supply of providers was not necessarily the same as increasing the choice of providers of any given type of service, increasing the users' choice of a range of types of service (e.g. day care or sitting), or increasing the users' choice of providers within a particular type (e.g. male as opposed to female sitters). Thus, even at the macro-level the development of enabling was likely to be far from straightforward.

The main rationale for promoting the establishment of purchaser–provider splits and encouraging competition in supply lay in government's belief that: (i) their introduction would weaken the influence of providers' vested interests in the identification of needs and service specifications, thus making it more likely that services would reflect users' rather than providers' needs; and (ii) they would provide the framework within which competition could be introduced into the supply of services, thus also improving provider responsiveness to need. The Social Services Inspectorate's December 1993 *Interim Overview Report* on assessment and care management stated that a clear purchaser–provider split aided the process of moving from a service-led to a needs-led approach.

The assumption behind these beliefs is that providers are essentially self-interested. As Harrison and Pollitt (1994) have pointed out, this is only one of a number of possible models of professionalism. But it has become dominant in the rationale for introducing purchaser–provider splits. In fact, provider self-interest is as undifferentiated a concept as its rival: public ethos or duty. If providers are motivated wholly or partly by self-interest, then that of the hospital consultant is likely to manifest itself differently from that of the low-paid home care worker, as is that of senior provider managers from front-line staff. In addition, provider managers will have incentives to behave in ways their staff may dislike, for example in trying to introduce two-tier pay structures, or to worsen employment conditions in an effort to cut costs.

The emphasis on provider self-interest is derived from the influential public choice theory, which has portrayed public sector employees as budget maximisers. In the view of Pollitt (1990: 115) this idea of provider self-interest 'was a clockwork model that ran on targets and bonus pay, not a flesh-and-blood figure that needed public recognition and self-respect'. Dunleavy (1991) questioned the idea of public sector workers as budget maximisers, suggesting that the real interest of rational public officials lay in the pursuit of 'bureau-shaping strategies'. Self (1993: xii) argued that self-interest was a more dominant motivation than altruism, but 'the directions and degrees of self-interest depend very much upon the structure of opportunities within a given political system'. Dunleavy went on to suggest that the introduction of market mechanisms and the use of contracting might actually provide the new purchasers with additional opportunity for this. Hood (1991) also suggested that the new public management associated with the shift towards privatisation and quasi-privatisation assumed a culture of public honesty while at the same time removing the devices instituted to ensure it. The case for provider self-interest has thus been subject to considerable modification. If Dunleavy's view of the true nature of the self-interest of the public sector employee is correct, then it is not clear how public sector purchasers are going to prove immune to it.

Nevertheless, the case for moving towards market principles can be simply stated: more than 40 years of reliance on hierarchies has failed substantially to change the practices of providers. The new policy of community care assumes that provider-led services have been inherently anti-user and should be forced to change. Furthermore, only market principles can force such change.

Taken on its own terms, however, this view posed a central problem: how to use a self-interested bureaucratic hierarchy to create a market? Certainly the ethos and training of senior officers were not conducive to such a change. It took time even for authorities who had accepted enabling in the sense of market development to come to terms with its specific meaning in respect of social services. Some interpreted it as privatisation and took a while to understand commissioning as a process of deciding on and paying for services to meet assessed individual needs. Wistow et al.'s (1992) study of 24 local authorities revealed that only three were committed to enabling in the sense of market development. The rest remained committed to an idea of enabling as either community development or personal development (linked to ideas about 'normalisation'). Both Wistow et al.'s (1994b) subsequent research and the findings of this study show that the position changed substantially during 1993/4. The imposition of the 85 per cent rule was material in effecting this change; authorities realised that they were going to have to do more commissioning in the independent sector or hand back money to the government. Thus for senior staff budget maximising became congruent with bureau shaping and contracting out (Glennerster and Le Grand, 1995).

Government guidance was offered on contracting and on establishing a purchaser–provider split, but not on developing purchasing strategies (Flynn and Common, 1990; Department of Health and Social Services Inspectorate, 1991a). For example, the care management guidance stressed the importance of devolving budgets to care managers, but the problems of handling micro-purchasing (at the level of the individual) and strategic macro-purchasing were not addressed. The academic literature (see, for example, Le Grand and Bartlett 1993) concentrated on describing in the abstract the conditions necessary for the successful operation of quasi-markets, one being a large number of providers and purchasers, but even getting to the point where the market was properly mapped, let alone stimulating it, has proved a major task for authorities.

Negotiating new purchaser–provider relationships

The new relationship between purchasers and providers is determined more by managerial than professional considerations. After implementing a high and firm purchaser–provider split, it seems that a period of tension and mutual suspicion tends to follow before staff adjust to the changed relationship. A senior manager in borough A said in early 1994: 'as soon as you get the purchaser–provider split you put the fence up and you get the barbed wire . . . staff who before got on marvellously now say it's a them and us situation'.

In the county, the director made an explicit appeal to staff in an early memorandum, dated April 1992, 'to remember that we are three streams [purchasing, providing, and strategy and quality assurance] in *one* department and we need to work *together* to maximise resources for our clients'. Reference to the Marks & Spencer system of purchaser–provider alliances was made in this authority, but relations were nevertheless poor in the beginning. For example, home care providers distrusted care managers' capacity to assess and ration. At a home care managers' meeting an example was given of a care manager who had bowed to a carer's wish for support and had agreed to go in once a day 'to shake the duvet'. Home care providers in the county were proud of their assessment skills and resented passing assessment over to purchasers. Where relationships between these two groups were particularly bad, strict boundary lines were drawn, so that, for example, a home care worker would telephone the care manager to get her to call the water board on behalf of a client.

What seems to have happened in borough A and the county is that the firm purchaser–provider divide has been somewhat reconceptualised in the light of experience. Thus while a senior manager (purchasing) in borough A used a car maintenance analogy to justify a firm purchaser–provider split in mid-1993, saying that a car owner requested a service and the garage provided it, a not dissimilar analogy to domestic cleaning was used in mid-1994 to justify giving providers rather more scope: it would be usual to ask a cleaner to provide x hours of cleaning, but it would be wise to allow the cleaner to exercise initiative as to how best to go about the task. In the county, a senior purchasing manager also picked up and reworked the car maintenance analogy to suggest that the owner expected the mechanic to identify the fault, thus suggesting that there was room for provider input. A development consultant in the purchasing division of the county referred to the way in which providers were eventually involved in drawing up the specification for an enhanced home care tender: 'the [initial] exclusion was part of our animal behaviour in dealing with the reorganisation and the purchaser–provider split'. During 1993/4 providers in the county were also called in to visit potential suppliers and evaluate them. A senior purchaser welcomed this: 'the idea that you've got to be arm's length from these sorts of things is a load of old phooey'.

In the case of the authorities that moved more slowly towards establishing the purchaser–provider split, there is evidence of the same learning curve. The period of tension attendant on firm separation was beginning to diminish in borough B by the end of 1994, but was still evident in borough C, despite the insistence of senior managers on talking about a 'purchaser–provider relationship' rather than a split, even when introducing firm separation in mid-1993. In borough D the split was not fully implemented by the end of 1994.

The implementation of a purchaser–provider split caused considerable upheaval, particularly in the county, where it occurred at the same time as the creation of new purchasing localities, which were left to find their own way in the new order. In many respects, purchasers appeared as the 'golden people' of the new structures, but it has proved difficult to sort out their role.

In borough A morale among those in the purchasing division was initially extremely low because care management was perceived by senior managers as a way of 'taming' social work, and because while care managers had expected to be able to purchase needs-led care packages, failure to devolve budgets or to provide an extensive menu of services meant that they tended to be restricted to ordering set-list services, such as hours of domiciliary care.

In the county one fourth-tier purchaser admitted feeling that she had no idea whether she was doing the right thing. Purchasers were supposed to be able to tell providers what they wanted, but 'it feels more awkward somehow than if you were talking from assistant divisional director to another assistant divisional director'. In other words, purchasers have not necessarily known how to exert their authority and have experienced a loss of the fellow-feeling with provider colleagues that existed under the old system. However, it is not possible to generalise about the effect of the new structures on the morale of purchasers and providers. In the county, provider morale has on the whole remained high. A senior manager in the strategy and quality assurance division spoke of providers benefiting from the split:

> I think they have enjoyed themselves, their position has been clearer, and it has freed up this entrepreneurial spirit in a lot of them to go ahead and make a lot of changes in services that they might have wanted to do before . . . Up till now [mid-1993] they've made all the running . . .

The retreat of the threat of externalisation during the early 1990s and the commitment in 1993/4 to a 100 per cent block contract with in-house services must have helped to bolster morale in the county, although it is noteworthy that not all provider services took the opportunity to make changes. There is no immediately obvious explanation for the difference in provider response, although much can be attributed to personalities, as well as to contrasting perceptions of the likelihood of competition. Home care providers showed signs of the strongest corporate identity.

In contrast, a second-tier provider in borough C commented that the tendency was to assume that providers would just carry on, while a third-tier provider said at the end of 1993 that:

> the views of providers are not sought, the skills are not used as they should be, and it is almost as if overnight they have become redundant. I'm not suggesting it's intentional, but that is the feeling, the power is with the care managers, they make the assessments, the care plan, they decide whether they are going to come to you or elsewhere, but where does the provider come in?

Similarly, in borough B providers have felt marginalised as purchasers became strong in 1993/4. One senior officer felt that they were not 'getting much input into service development'. Another senior provider felt that providers were as liable to take direction from purchasers as from the director, which was something new. At the beginning the commissioning unit in this borough was rather bullish, talking about buying the best services and if that meant the end of in-house provision so be it. One provider observed that the unit comprised a new breed of male manager: 'Quite a lot has been written about commissioning units; they're male dominated and are a long step away from social care or social services.' This interviewee was obviously aware of the literature on gender and 'macho management' in the public sector (see, for example, Nixon 1993). In fact the head of the commissioning unit was determined to recruit people with both business skills and a commitment to ethical commissioning, and by late 1994 relations between commissioners and providers in this authority were showing considerable improvement.

The separation of purchasing from providing represents a major change in the thinking and culture of SSDs. The difficulties in adjusting to the new relationships involved are an important backdrop to understanding the problems that have been encountered in developing the purchasing function.

Developing the purchasing function

It was the purchasing function that was new for SSDs, and all authorities have found it difficult to develop. Difference in size has made the story for the county very different from that for the London boroughs, and we shall treat these separately.

The county

The purchasing stream experienced the most difficulties after reorganisation in September 1991. The most striking observation about purchasing in the county is the number of layers that exist in the purchasing structure. The London boroughs also have both micro- and macro-purchasers, but the picture is more complicated still in the county because of tensions between the centre and the localities. Purchasing in the county may take place at the behest of care managers, at the level of the individual locality or group of localities, or at the level of pan-county block agreements. It is also difficult to decide whether the numerous layers of purchasing are necessary because of the larger scale of the market, or whether they reflect tensions between the centre and the localities arising out of the particular structure that the county adopted.

The county is different from the boroughs in that the macro-purchasing function has been slower to develop than the micro, with the result that a purchasing strategy has been somewhat slow to develop, although this was also due to senior managers' caution in committing themselves to a particular vision of the social care market and uncertainty about what the optimum size of provider should be. This last point must be linked to difficulties in deciding at which level purchasing should take place. As one senior purchaser observed early in 1994: '[this county] has micro'd and then has had to pull back to get the macro. This is more difficult than doing the macro first and then going micro.' In part the pattern of development in the county may be explained in terms of the policy inheritance, which favoured maximum devolution and localisation. Budgets and decision making had already been substantially devolved to providers during the late 1980s.

During 1992/3, the pan-departmental senior management team and the community care implementation group took responsibility for setting the broad policy framework for purchasing. The purchasing division also tended to make use of external consultants for specific tasks, such as the preparation of contracts and service agreements, although their work was not without some duplication of effort owing to overload at senior management level.

Not until 1993 was a firmer cast given to macro-purchasing, because of two developments.

The first was the setting up of the purchasing management board, which included representatives from senior purchasers and members of the strategy and quality assurance division. The deliberations of the purchasing management board included all aspects of purchasing policy, from the way in which to allocate budgets between localities, to the pursuit of a block contract for enhanced domiciliary care, to the formulation of job descriptions.

The second development was the establishment, later in 1993, of a budgets and contracts section with a pan-county remit. Its purpose was to pull together budgetary and process work, for example the devising of a procedure for accrediting domiciliary care agencies, and to operationalise strategy, for example to organise a tendering process for a nursing home block contract for elderly and mentally infirm (EMI) clients. It was not possible to address some policy issues – such as the EMI tender – until the establishment of this unit. The unit also took the initiative in collating information on purchasing commitments to the main suppliers throughout the county and in negotiations about terms and conditions.

The contracts unit was given no budget and hence no direct purchasing power, but nor was it wholly reactive, as were similar units in boroughs A, C and D. On the other hand, it has not taken a leading role in deciding what to purchase, as happens in borough B. Macro-purchasing decisions and responsibilities rest with the senior assistant director of the division, the two assistant directors, and increasingly groups of localities. There was therefore no tension between it and the macro-purchasers, but there was some room for tension between it and the localities, who felt that it sometimes introduced procedures from above that were hard to implement locally.

A similar tension was sometimes experienced between the localities and sections of the strategy and quality assurance division, which played an important dual role in purchasing, for example in devising the principles for resource allocation and purchasing criteria. The strategy and quality assurance division was criticised by some localities for failing to appreciate local conditions and for making unreasonable requests. It has also been genuinely difficult to devolve appropriate activities while keeping others more central.

At the local level, care managers made individual placements for clients, or constructed care packages, effectively purchasing these with the authorisation of senior care managers using budgets held variously at locality level, group support level, or still within the providing division (see Figure 4.1). In the case of nursing home placements, the authorisation was granted by two central panels – one east, one west – comprising health and social services purchasers during 1993/4. After April 1994, nursing home budgets were held at locality level, and it was planned further to devolve these panels.

After reorganisation in 1991, it was assumed that locality managers would have a role in shaping the market by gleaning an understanding of local need and developing relations with voluntary organisations. Thus this assumption ran together the understanding of enabling as market stimulation with that of community development. A senior manager summed up the potential layers of purchasing within the SSD (there are also additional potential layers in respect of joint commissioning – see below) in this way:

> There's the little local deal which a care manager can actually set up with a volunteer, a neighbour, a small church group, quite easily. There is the slightly larger initiative which an individual locality manager could take, or a group of locality managers, if they had the wit, could get together and steal the ground from under the feet of people who sit above them . . . if 3 or 4 get together, then we are happy to have a block contract . . . Then there's the east/west layer, which is definitely big enough to have individual block purchases . . . and then there's [the senior assistant director] who tries to hold it together with his purchasing board.

Despite the county's commitment to devolution, it has not been immune to a tendency – common in the other authorities – for decisions to be taken at the centre. According to a senior purchaser in mid-1993:

> Very quickly you find decisions going back up the line because, things like – you've all individually made an agreement with the Spastics Society on the price of a residential place and you think 'we'd better get together and make sure that they're not charging us £30 per week more here than there'. There's also the issue of some localities being too small to generate at least some service developments, and they tend to push it up too.

In the view of some second- and third-tier purchasers, certain aspects of purchasing, like block contracting, were too time consuming to be undertaken regularly at locality level. This, together with the quest for consistency, which requires either a degree of centralisation or the use of centrally disseminated procedures, again signalled the tension between the centre and the localities. There have been real problems of communication between the purchasing layers.

The promise of budget disaggregation – a term used in the county to refer to both budget transfer (to purchasers) and devolution – was held out to the localities before restructuring as a way of persuading them of the benefits of the changes. However, as everywhere, budget disaggregation has proceeded slowly. Yet purchasing power amounts to more than a simple issue as to who has the money. Authority to spend is perhaps more crucial than budget holding *per se*, and in this respect purchasing power has been devolved to a significant extent.

During 1993/4, the county took the decision to transfer the budgets for domiciliary care, people with physical disabilities, and children's agency placements to purchasers. In addition STG moneys for domiciliary care were devolved to locality level, while the budget for nursing home care was devolved from east/west group level to locality level in 1994. Thus budget disaggregation has not been confined to the STG moneys. The county has been alone among the research authorities in taking the plunge and actually transferring budgets. A senior member of the strategy and quality assurance division said:

> I'm fully aware that when we transferred it [the physical disabilities budget] we hadn't thought it through . . . but I feel that we have to learn from doing; I think we'd still be here in 12 months' time thinking it through to be honest.

Certainly the authority experienced major problems in transferring moneys. Client turnover is much slower in social services than in health, which means that money is likely to be tied up in existing provision for many years to come. It also proved very difficult to get unit costings, because of uncertainty around attributing the costs of overheads and the full range of hourly rates that apply to different periods of the day, sickness and holiday leave, and so on. Indeed, in August 1993 unit costs for home care were recalculated and made retrospective, which rendered purchasers overspent. Home care had to enter all the data for their visits manually in order to convert them into the hours of care needed to arrive at unit costs.

Budget transfer has involved an enormous invoicing task, which has been administratively costly. Information technology systems were not in place and there have been problems of charging for care that has not been delivered, overcharging, and so on. Given that the county also undertook in 1993/4 to continue to make a 100 per cent block commitment to its in-house services, the leverage that purchasers were supposed to have from holding the purse strings was considerably diluted. The labour associated with budget transfer thus became more problematic, although it may, as senior purchasers have contended, permit more coherent thinking about purchasing for particular client groups and also enable purchasers to effect service alterations by requiring reductions in one area in order to secure expansions in another.

Devolution of the purchasing budget posed the problem of how to carve up resources between localities. The overriding principle adopted by the county was devolution on the basis of the risk/need status of localities' existing clients. There were some difficulties in doing this above and beyond the actual measuring of risk/need.

First, when devolving anything other than new moneys such as STG, it was necessary – and difficult – to calculate the proportion of the spend on in-house services attributable to each locality. Existing clients and services were not necessarily known to purchasers, and providers' information systems were not geared to giving such information.

Second, a locality with a relatively low level of existing provision, but a high score in terms of risk/need, might not have the local service infrastructure to spend a budget determined entirely by priority. Conversely, establishments in a well provided locality might require more funds than a straightforward analysis of priority scoring of its clients would warrant, in order to ensure the survival of provider units and the continued care of existing clients. Thus, in 1994, a departmental document on the subject explained that because each locality inherited a historic set of commitments, because allowance needed to be made for the uneven distribution of in-house services bought by purchasers, and because the practice of assessing individual risk and need was still being learnt in localities, 'it is necessary to ameliorate the pure risk/need allocation by other factors, largely population derived indicators'.

In the case of allocating moneys for children's services, a mix of risk/need and workload – measured by court work – was chosen initially. When locality staff pointed out that according to the Children Act a lot of court work may be an indicator of poor practice, the workload component was replaced by a measure derived by using the Bebbington and Miles deprivation index (Bebbington and Miles 1988). In the case of elderly people, it was decided to use the number of people aged over 85 in a locality as a basis for resource allocation.

A further question has been how to free up money once a user stops using a service: should it revert to a central pot for reallocation between localities, or stay within the locality in which the original user lived?

Nowhere have budgets been entirely devolved to care manager level, something the academic literature has considered to be crucial because a quasi-market relies on there being multiple, competing purchasers to ensure that supply is adequately stimulated and the pattern of service provision changed to meet the real needs of users (Challis 1992; Le Grand and Bartlett 1993). There are good reasons for this. First, given the difficulties of establishing a suitable formula for allocating resources between localities, the potential problems of allocating purchasing budgets between individual care managers in a way that reflects contrasting case loads are enormous. Second, it is far from clear that total purchasing responsibility should be completely devolved. It takes time for individual care managers to shop around. Multiple negotiations carried out at a local level can be costly, hence the tendency to push these decisions up to the centre, where a better price is likely to be obtained. Third, the contract monitoring function as distinct from that of client review is also costly for individual care managers to undertake when it might involve six of them all monitoring their individual contracts with a single home.

It is clear, then, that a distinction needs to be made between those budgetary responsibilities that are held by care managers, and those that are appropriately held at a higher level. What is appropriate will be closely linked both to the nature of what is required and to the state of the market. For these reasons, budget devolution to care manager level makes immediate sense only for the purchase of care that can be provided by informal providers. Yet it is not apparent in any of the research authorities that purchasing from the informal sector has taken off. In addition, all the authorities have been agreed in eschewing what a senior manager in borough B termed 'chequebook social work'. There is a widespread view that budgetary considerations will necessarily contaminate the relationship between care manager and user.

As a result of its experimental work, the Personal Social Sciences Research Unit (PSSRU) urged that budgets should be held by front-line managers. In the view of the PSSRU researchers, small spot budgets would not be sufficient to promote change in the pattern of service (Robbins 1993). However, what is interesting is that it is not clear whether the absence of budgets at front-line level actually matters. In the county, care managers making a decision to put an elderly client in a residential home have what is effectively their decision to purchase signed off by the senior care manager. The budget is notionally held at locality manager level, yet in practice care managers are empowered to use these budgets, while the authorisation to spend rests with senior care managers. What is less clear is whether the system permits adequate controls on spending. During 1994, pressure was exerted by senior purchasers on localities to keep within budget.

The London boroughs

The purchasing function in the London boroughs is considerably more straightforward than in the county. Because of the smaller geographical spread, it is possible to organise purchasing without several layers, adopting instead a more simple micro-/macro-division. It is also the case in the London boroughs that the purchasing function has tended to be confined to the use of the STG moneys, whereas in the county the STG has not been identified separately.

In borough B, there was a strong commitment to ensuring that the purchasing process was split between the care managers, who identified need, and the commissioning unit, which decided the best way to purchase care. In the first year of implementation, concern about the low level of STG transfer money led to considerable caution about overspending. The department established client-based panels chaired by third-tier managers from the community social services (purchasing) division to adjudicate cases where assessment had concluded that there was a need for either weekend/evening domiciliary care, or a residential placement. Initially the panel for older people comprised both purchasers and providers, but with the introduction of the purchaser–provider split, the provider from domiciliary care was replaced by an NHS purchaser. During the first year of implementation, if the panel agreed to the purchase of intensive domiciliary care, the social worker/care manager then negotiated with different agencies to purchase it. Where a residential placement was agreed, the commissioning unit searched for an appropriate placement.

In April 1994, this model was revised such that all community-based care packages were agreed by a fourth-tier team leader in discussion with the social worker (care manager). However, the care manager no longer had responsibility for negotiating the purchase of care; this function passed to the commissioning unit. Thus at the end of the research period, the SSD had a macro-/micro-purchasing function whereby care managers (in conjunction with their managers) decided on what care needed to be purchased and the commissioning unit carried out the market transactions. Thus, again, while the decision to purchase was devolved, it proved more desirable to hold the budget and make the purchasing transactions at a higher level in the SSD.

Commissioning in the borough has effectively straddled the community social services and QAP divisions and there have been some tensions around this. When the commissioning unit was first established it saw itself very much at the forefront of developing strategy. It was formed quickly and recruited people without a social work background (see Chapter 4). A member of the unit described its role in terms of strategic commissioning: 'ultimately what I hope we will have is a huge menu of services which we have commissioned that care managers can purchase'. Over time, however, it has become clearer that the macro-commissioning role of the unit is only one part of a truly needs-led commissioning process.

Borough A's commissioning strategy is also an essentially macro-/micro-model, but it is far less clear cut than that of borough B. Until July 1994, the department had a contracts unit located in the strategy and support division. Unlike the commissioning unit in borough B, this unit was established much earlier (at the beginning of 1992) and was identified primarily with the work of administering contracts for contracted-out services. Strategic thinking about purchasing was identified as the task of all senior managers. However, the care management division (as it was in 1993) had the responsibility for purchasing appropriate care with the STG moneys. The relationship between the head of the contracts unit and the care management division was poor. The joint commissioning officer rather than the contracts unit was given the job of market mapping and drawing up a contract for use with residential and nursing home proprietors in the lead-up to April 1993. In fact, the joint commissioning manager was virtually the only person available for carrying out this work, which indicates the lack of strategic capacity in borough A.

The care management division was to bypass the contracts unit again in April 1993, when it employed its own service-level agreements manager. As in borough B, care managers were expected to assess need, while the service-level agreements manager negotiated price and general purchasing arrangements. This model gave the care management division full control of the purchasing strategy. The role of the contracts unit was confined to the management of the existing block contracts for residential care, which arose from the earlier transfer of the management function of the in-house old people's homes.

At the beginning of the research period, some senior managers envisaged the strengthening of the central purchasing function, mirroring borough B. However, by the end of the research, the SSD had decided to devolve the contracts unit staff to the two purchasing divisions. Thus as borough A's purchasing model has evolved it has come rather closer to the user than that of borough B.

In borough C it was 1993 before the rather disparate elements of purchasing were brought together in one division. However, there have continued to be difficulties in communication between the various strands, which in this borough's case has included the joint commissioning machinery, in which it invested heavily. No clear purchasing strategy emerged for the borough over the period of the research, and roles have remained unclear, despite the emergence of a firm purchaser–provider split. For example, it was provider managers who wrote the first papers on shadow budgeting.

Budgets have not been transferred from providers to purchasers. However, authorisation of STG spend was from the outset a purchasing responsibility which remained at second- and third-tier level except in the case of elderly people, for whom small amounts of money were devolved to team leaders who could then authorise the purchase of independent domiciliary care. In the case of the most dependent clients, including those for whom nursing home care was recommended, decisions about the most appropriate care were made in multidisciplinary network meetings (similar to panels in the other authorities). Following these, the weekly meetings of purchasing team leaders decided on the priority of the case, for example in terms of how quickly the package could be purchased.

In May 1993, the borough established a commissioning support unit in its purchasing division. As is suggested both by its title and by its origins – it was created out of the previous voluntary support unit – it saw its role in terms of support rather than decision making.

In a sense, borough C has been reactive in developing its purchasing role. Senior managers did not favour importing people with purchasing experience, as has happened in borough B. In large measure practice has not changed substantially. The STG settlement for 1993/4 was very low, and the purchasing budget for the independent sector was correspondingly small. The only large-scale decision – to externalise a residential home – was forced by the imposition of the 85 per cent rule and was taken centrally by the senior management team. In all probability a micro-/macro-purchasing structure will emerge, but developments have been slow.

This is also true of borough D, where the purchasing division was still not fully functioning at the end of 1994. The contracts unit remained the only really functioning part of the purchasing structure in borough D at the end of 1994, but this was set up just before April 1993 to deal primarily with negotiations with residential and nursing homes, and its work has been administrative rather than strategic. Staff were transferred into it and did not possess commissioning skills. The borough used STG money only for residential and nursing home care, thus purchasers have not played the same role as their counterparts in other authorities (particularly the county and borough B) in respect of mapping and stimulating the market. Nevertheless, at the end of the research period, the borough had a proposal to devolve all budgets, not just STG moneys, to the third tier, on the basis of previous spends. But this is ambitious. In the view of one senior manager, they are trying to do 'about five years' work in five months' and in the absence of appropriate information systems.

None of the boroughs has succeeded in transferring budgets, although boroughs A and B have tried to operate a shadow budgeting system. The government's guidance acknowledged the difficulties of budget transfer (Department of Health et al. 1991a) and suggested that shadow budgets might be a useful way of engineering the transfer (Department of Health and Price Waterhouse 1992). Shadow budgeting has been dogged by problems of establishing accurate unit costs and it is unclear how far it has succeeded in effecting a shift in awareness and practice.

Thus in the boroughs, the purchasing tends to be attenuated as in the county, often involving care managers, panels, third- and fourth-tier budget holders and commissioning units. Nowhere are decisions made solely by budget holders. The 'menu system' of purchasing that seemed to be developing in some of the London boroughs has the virtue of clarity, but it does tip the balance in favour of the use of block contracts. In borough B, a third-tier manager agreed that care managers were more likely to draw off the menu because it was easier than dealing with a spot purchase. In borough A, too, the tendency was to draw off block contracts. Early enthusiasm expressed for creative purchasing by care managers, for example a pub meal rather than meals on wheels, had faded by mid-1994, not least because of the problems in monitoring the environmental health standards of occasional suppliers. Thus the tendency to continue to rely on 'off-the-shelf' services observed in two recent studies (Baldock and Ungerson 1994; Hoyes et al. 1994) is related to (albeit not fully explained by) the way in which the purchasing function has developed.

Market information

The new community care policy at first exhorted local authorities to stimulate the independent sector, and later, in 1992, forced authorities to seek independent suppliers via the operation of the 85 per cent rule. The task of SSDs was increasingly described in terms of 'shaping' and 'managing' the market (e.g. *Communicare*, September 1994: 5). This was no easy task. Not only was there more independent provision in the form of beds when the aim of the policy in part was to make more use of domiciliary than institutional care, but government also signalled its concern about possible market failure on the part of independent home owners and urged authorities to achieve change without 'noise'.

The kind of information necessary to manage the new social care market has been largely ignored in the academic literature[1] and yet its collection and analysis is a costly, time-consuming and difficult problem for SSDs. Arguably, it is also a key problem. The Audit Commission (1992a: 2) warned that: 'A lack of financial and managerial information is the rock on which community care will founder if devolved budgets and a split between commissioner and provider functions are implemented ahead of the necessary support systems.' In its report on progress with community care at the end of 1994, the Audit Commission again stressed the importance of the information task: 'strengthening and developing information systems of all types must be a priority if progress is to continue and this is a key message running throughout this bulletin' (Audit Commission 1994: 6). It is worth spelling out a little more clearly the dimensions of the new information task and its implications for authorities.

The 1991 Chartered Institute of Public Finance and Accountancy/ Association of Directors of Social Services (CIPFA/ADSS) Financial Management Partnership information strategy documents, which were prepared by Price Waterhouse and which cost £8500 to buy, provided an information strategy model that made clear the dimensions of the new task. The model detailed 22 activities for delivering community care set out in five main blocks: planning, setting the budget, managing the contracted service, care management, and monitoring and management of all activities. Each of the 22 activities was broken down into components or subactivities and the inputs and outputs for the activities and subactivities were then clustered around ten key information systems: care management, financial management, client records, in-house provider management, service profiles, contract management, inspection and registration, planning and forecasting, income assessment and collection, and complaints. These systems centred on care management and comprised the logical information systems architecture (LISA), which identified the interrelationships between the systems in terms of their information flows. From the ten information systems of the LISA, the document derived ten data flow diagrams, illustrating the files where data are permanently held, their interrelationships with other systems, and linking the previously listed inputs and outputs to several of the other nine systems and/or files.

Underpinning this information strategy model was the understanding of implementation as an interdependent set of activities. The complexity of the model shows how tangled the interrelationships are between the components of the new community care. It should also be noted that the model addresses only the information task that is internal to departments; however, SSDs also face information demands from central government: from the Social Services Inspectorate/regional health authority monitoring rounds, routine Department of Health returns and the Audit Commission Citizen's Charter indicators, and, in the case of counties in 1993/4, from the Local Government Review.

The kind of model represented by the LISA is daunting in the extreme and only one of the research authorities, the county, had come anywhere near having the information technology available to take it on board. As Wistow *et al.* (1994b) pointed out, SSDs received far less money for information technology (IT) from government than did health authorities in the wake of the 1990 legislation. In 1992 each local authority was given an indicative allocation of £93,348 (LAC (92) 3), and in 1994 £111,926 (LAC (94) 8).

It is possible to review the status of SSDs' information systems using a much simpler and more common-sense approach than that espoused in the LISA. We can suggest that three of the key elements to support enabling are: mapping the market, mapping client need and accurately tracking expenditure.

Mapping the market

The nature of the supply of beds and domiciliary provision varied dramatically between the research authorities and within a single authority. Thus in the county, for example, the eastern part had many domiciliary care providers, whereas the more rural west had few. The county as a whole had a large number of independent care homes, as did borough A. The remaining London boroughs had little independent provision of any sort at the start of the research period. But even the county experienced localised shortages, for example in respect of EMI beds. One of the key responses to the problem of shortage of supply among those authorities desiring to develop an active purchasing strategy was to move towards the security of block contracting. There was also evidence of considerable fluctuation in the market. For example, the county undertook a mapping exercise of domiciliary care provision in 1992, but a small-scale follow-up exercise the following year found that half of the 1992 suppliers had gone out of business. In borough A the number of beds supplied by independent home owners grew by 200 during 1993/4, despite the fact that a 1993 market mapping exercise revealed a substantial surplus of beds.

The county took purchasing seriously from an early date and the SQA division undertook an extensive exercise in 1992 to map the provision of beds in terms of their numbers, type, price and quality. Some 300 vacancies were revealed at this point, but in early 1993 it was discovered that neighbouring authorities were beginning to block-book beds in the county. The authority had already begun to draw up a list of accredited homes, essentially a 'preferred provider list', between autumn 1992 and spring 1993. Purchasers at the third and fourth tiers visited home owners, and homes that were identified as being of good enough standard were invited to confirm in writing that they had met the specification standards and wished to be on the list. This first round of accreditation was a time-consuming process and was somewhat undermined by the government's choice directive (LA (92) 27), which obliged authorities to respect the client's choice of a home. Early in 1994, senior purchasers decided not to repeat the accreditation exercise in its previous form, but rather to slide together accreditation and contract monitoring. Thus in future homes would remain on the list unless contract monitoring showed up poor quality.

Despite its thorough attempts to map the market, there remained substantial lacunae in the county's knowledge about its suppliers, which illustrates how difficult it is for authorities to manage the market. In 1993, the new contracts unit discovered that it did not know who the current main suppliers were in the county. The unit therefore asked each of the purchasing localities to supply a 'vendors' report' on their ten largest suppliers and the nature of the agreement. One of the purposes was to offer a county-wide view of localised purchasing so that, for example, if there were several local contracts, these might be rolled up into a larger, more cost-effective agreement.

Compared with the county, no London borough undertook as thorough a market mapping exercise. In borough A the joint commissioning project manager investigated all homes in the borough in 1993 to establish what they provided, client turnover, price, and where the residents came from. This information was used to estimate the number of beds needed, price and the potential for market failure among independent home owners. In estimating the number of residents who did not need to be in a home, the project manager used the figure of 14 per cent given by Price Waterhouse in their study of one-third of residents in Hampshire's residential homes (Department of Health *et al.* not dated but 1992), which was low compared with that arrived at by some academic commentators (e.g. Bradshaw and Gibbs 1988). On the basis of this information the borough estimated that of the 400 beds released during 1993/4, only 200 would be needed, which in turn raised concern about the possibility of home closures. As a result, the borough set its bed price at a relatively high level. As a senior purchaser explained: 'you have to look at the type of area this is; [x] is a bit like us and they are having to pay higher prices. We don't want places to go out of business; we don't want them to cut costs so the user is at risk . . .'. This borough decided that given the government's choice directive, there was no point in drawing up a list of approved providers. The borough also made an attempt to register domiciliary care agencies, but were disappointed by the lack of response.

In borough B market mapping was undertaken by the commissioning unit in mid-1993. There was very little by way of independent care homes in this borough and senior managers therefore felt that they needed to make the SSD attractive to independent suppliers. Part of that effort consisted of inviting proprietors to deal with just one group of people, the commissioning unit, rather than a multiplicity of care managers. Home owners were invited to join an approved list and were asked to demonstrate equal opportunities in employment and service development, whether they had a charter of rights for residents, what kind of activities they provided, and to supply inspection reports, as well as prices and numbers of residents. Thus the borough sought to translate its commitment to ethical commissioning into practice. In respect of domiciliary care, demand for this increased in the borough during 1993/4 and spot purchase from agencies was found to result in variable quality of care. Borough B sought to solve this problem and to secure supply by moving to block contracts for independent domiciliary care in 1994.

The remaining boroughs did very little by way of market mapping. Borough D did none and copied the practice of another authority. Borough C asked a former assistant director, acting as a consultant, to undertake what was a rather limited exercise early in 1993. He drew up a list of homes in neighbouring boroughs with a list of prices and vacancies, but the list was not comprehensive; the same was true of the borough's efforts to map domiciliary provision. On the other hand, to map comprehensively all out-of-borough provision would have been very expensive. In the case of independent domiciliary provision, while there were half a dozen independent agencies operating in the borough, the SSD was cautious, tending to use only those that were already known to it. The research period saw the expansion of the private market, including one agency set up by a former SSD provider manager. The hope in this borough was that the joint commissioning machinery would identify purchasing needs, but no clear directions were given to the relevant groups, which in any case operated under severe resource constraints.

Mapping client need

With respect to this second element of market information, the literature lists a huge range of potential sources of data and methods of collection and analysis (e.g. Department of Health and Price Waterhouse 1993; Hawtin *et al.* 1994), without attempting to suggest priorities or a phased or selective approach. In other words, authorities have received little guidance on how to make aggregate needs assessment manageable. For example, the official guidance listed local sources of demographic and epidemiological information available from client group registers, local surveys and research, and structured consultation, and stated that all have a role to play. The guidance gave a worked example of Greenshire, which used prevalence rates from the Office of Population Censuses and Surveys (OPCS) applied to demographic data in order to arrive at the numbers of elderly people with different types of disability and levels of dependency. This was supplemented with local information from the register of partially sighted people who approached the

SSD, a joint survey with the family health service authority (FHSA), and a consultation exercise with users and carers to determine preferred care packages. Additionally, the guidance made it clear that these macro-activities should be supplemented with information from the micro-level of individual assessment and care management. No guidance was given as to who should supervise, collect and collate the information. Perhaps it is not surprising that early monitoring revealed that:

> efforts to build up a picture of population needs still relied largely on basic demographic data. Links were required between 'top down' population level data and 'bottom up' data from a range of data sources including individual needs assessment and user and carer feedback.
>
> (Department of Health 1993b: 3)

For a range of reasons to do with data collection and interpretation, the integration of these different types of information was seldom achieved in a comprehensive way in any of the research authorities.

Over the period of the research, the county used both population-based data and risk/need information from existing clients in order to allocate budgets to localities, in addition to bottom-up locality planning and other discrete needs assessment exercises for particular client groups. In borough A, a senior purchaser described the collection of information on client need in terms of acting 'as a kind of spider picking up bits and pieces, because no matter how we try to log unmet need, it is a very imprecise science . . .'. Borough B attempted to collate and coordinate information from its joint commissioning groups, service review groups (formed on a client group basis during 1993), care managers, aggregate statistics and from users and carers, but it proved very difficult to pull the information together. Borough C relied on its joint commissioning structures alone, but the members of these were quickly overwhelmed, given that they were all engaged on other work that occupied the vast majority of their time. Bringing together 'top down' and 'bottom up' information on need is no easy task.

Tracking expenditure

With regard to the third element, what is required is more than having accurate accounting systems. Rather, information systems should ideally permit budget monitoring on a commitment basis, and provide management information related to individual care packages and overall spending categories. For example, the 1991 CIPFA/ADSS Financial Management Partnership material explained the interrelationship between the care management system and the financial management system thus: 'The updating of budgetary commitments feeds the care budgets financial data, which links with the financial management system through the two-way flow of budgetary adjustment information.' In practice this might mean, as it did in the county, aiming to interface a care packaging system with a client information system, in order to provide the capacity, for example, routinely to track spending against client characteristics, to compare average costs of residential care versus domiciliary packages for clients of the same or contrasting client group, and so on.

Insofar as the London boroughs have developed their capacity to track budgets, their efforts have been largely focused on the STG, not least because they have to prove that 85 per cent was spent in the independent sector. The broad budget strategies were discussed in Chapter 3. The extent to which regular monitoring took place at a more micro-level differed considerably. In borough A service managers got a weekly breakdown of expenditure on personal care, for example, together with a target figure. However, it was still possible for care managers to change the number of hours of care received by a client without this information routinely reaching those who arranged payment.

The county did not seek to keep its STG budget separate, and this, together with its early decision to effect gradual budget transfer and devolution, made monitoring of the purchasing budget an increasingly extensive exercise. In early 1993, work was being done to prepare a tender for a care packaging software system, which would interface with the client information system and produce the financial information required to support localised purchasing decisions. However, a tender was not finalised by the completion of the research. Meanwhile, the accounting system recorded only what had been spent – it did not track commitments. Instead, during 1993, a purchase order database was set up to record all units of service purchased. Insofar as this relied on all care managers routinely completing and coding purchase order forms, there were inevitable doubts about its accuracy.

Conclusions

Clearly, authorities have experienced difficulties in obtaining and interpreting information to address need, market shape and financial commitments as discrete exercises, but as the LISA made clear, there is the additional highly complex task of making sure that information systems feed one another. The majority of IT systems used by SSDs do not operate as part of an integrated environment. Most are stand-alone systems, with no sharing capacity. As a senior member of the strategy and quality assurance division in the county noted: 'nothing is ever compatible and despite whatever anybody ever says, it always has an impact on somebody else's system'. Borough C, which proceeded much more slowly with implementation and which was only at the stage of investing in an IT system at the end of the research period, opted for a single large system which will be able to interface with corporate financial systems. In respect of the IT component of the more general information task, there appear to be pay-offs for latecomers.

The complicated nature of the information task has had major implications for the work of SSDs. Departments have had to tackle this task alongside other major aspects of implementing the new community care policy. There have been substantial differences between the research authorities in the order in which they have undertaken the key activities. Government guidance stressed the linkages between all features of the community care changes, insisting that all the activities be modelled before devising the LISA, but SSDs have necessarily differed in the way in which they have approached implementation. Many had some information systems and IT in place before 1990, which immediately presented an integration/interface challenge. In addition, because of the time it takes to invest in and introduce IT systems, authorities could not necessarily afford to wait to refine their approach on all fronts. Hence, as a senior member of the strategy and quality assurance division in the county put it in late 1993:

> Well, yes, you get to a point where you have to say: 'we can develop a system, that's not a problem, but it's actually your business you've got to sort out first, the business requirements'. And I think in the past what's tended to happen is that the systems have come first, and we've not taken full enough account of the business. Partly because people didn't want to define the business. Yet when you're defining mega-systems like this, you've got to, it forces you to . . . When we started on care packaging we found out very quickly that we didn't have the definitions; what's an open case, what's a closed case, etc., etc., so we had to go back to basics . . .

This illustrates the interrelationship between process and IT software requirements. It also shows how procedures can become increasingly complex, and increasingly systems driven the further into the information task a department goes.

In terms of the information systems themselves, it seems that authorities must be prepared for 'second wave' problems that develop. In the county, which was a very early starter, there have been several examples of decisions being taken regarding the measurement and collection of certain kinds of data to feed a particular information system, and of staff accepting the changes in work practices that these entailed, but then challenging the information base and calling for refinements. For example, the staff in the county were persuaded to accept a new principle for resource allocation between localities in respect of children's services based on the measurement of risk and need, together with data on workload, but they then questioned the basis on which workload had been measured.

Authorities like the county which are advanced in their development of information systems find themselves awash with data. Various senior managers in the county made the point that they should focus on converting existing data into management information before calling for more data. For example:

I think we have got the information somewhere. We haven't got an integrated information set. Part of it is 'is it good enough information?' We've certainly got lots of information circling around about lots of different things . . . So I think there's probably enough information around . . . but it's not integrated and it's not linked to any objectives. So in other words, if you haven't got objectives, then information becomes data, and it's beginning to tie down what we're expecting . . .

This comment signals once more the problem that systems can all too easily begin to drive the process. It also begins to illustrate the voracious demands for information that can overtake departments. When the single post of head of information and communication was vacated in the county, the work was carved up into three: a full-time head of IT and a full-time head of information were recruited, while the public relations/communications aspect of the work was absorbed into the job of the senior assistant director of strategy and quality assurance. In borough C, which is only beginning to develop its information and IT systems, much of the information task flows into the remit of just two third-tier purchasers. Given that strategic capacity was found to be a problem in three of the boroughs, the development of information systems is bound to exert additional strain on staff resources. In addition, SSDs generally lack expertise in IT.

For the majority of social services staff the impact of the new information task on workload is experienced more simply in terms of systems that seem more bureaucratic. Thus in the county, a possible total of 14 forms – covering the assessment and purchasing process, as well as information for providers – must be filled in to access home care, although often the number is less. The *perception* of the requirements of information systems as overwhelming is widespread among front-line staff and observation in all the research authorities has revealed that front-line staff were often not filling in forms at the right time and sometimes not filling them in at all. There is, for example, a general lack of faith that recording unmet need will result in any change in the pattern of service, given the lack of resources. Yet this information is crucial to needs-based planning.

The firmer the purchaser–provider split and the more transactions there are between purchasers and providers, the greater is the need for information systems to manage the market and facilitate strategic planning. But at a time of profound resource constraint this poses considerable difficulties for local authorities.

Note

1 The special issue of *Public Administration*, vol. 72, no. 1 (1994) is an exception in this respect.

6

Enabling authorities. II: The market for social care

The independent market for social care

Local authorities have always operated in a mixed economy of social care. Wistow *et al.* (1994a) are probably right to argue that the new community care policy has produced a substantial shift towards more of a social care *market*. Indeed, the market in social care is changing rapidly in most local authorities. It is interesting to look at the degree of change over time, although discrepancies in the various data available and awareness of the difficulties authorities experience in collecting them at local level make us wary of drawing firm conclusions on the basis of it.

Table 6.1 shows that the number of residents in local authority homes for elderly and younger physically disabled people dropped precipitously in borough A between 1990 and 1991, when this borough transferred the management of its homes to private contractors, pushed as much by a commitment to contracting out in line with late 1980s policies as by the new community care policy. In the county and in boroughs C and D there has been a declining trend in local authority provision, but this began before 1990. In the county this decline has been matched by a rise in private sector provision. In borough B, where there is very little by way of independent sector provision, there has been no decrease.

The Department of Health data on the provision of home care, which are available only up to 1993, show extremely small levels of independent provision in the county (for 218 households with people aged over 65 compared with the 4288 served by the local authority) and for borough C, and nil returns for the other boroughs. However, the position changed during the last part of 1993 and 1994, particularly in borough B.

It is tempting to make a connection between the political complexion of the authority and the extent to which there has been a shift in favour of the independent sector. But this would be too simplistic. The shape of local

Table 6.1   Number of residents aged 65 and over in homes for elderly and younger physically disabled people, per 1000 population aged 65 and over by type of home as of 31 March

	County	Borough A	Borough B	Borough C	Borough D
Local authority					
1988	11.0	8.4	15.9	14.2	12.0
1989	10.1	8.3	17.1	13.9	11.5
1990	9.3	7.3	16.3	13.4	11.3
1991	9.1	0.9	15.9	13.0	11.4
1992	8.3	0.9	15.5	12.0	10.7
1993	8.2	1.0	17.2	9.4	8.1
Voluntary sector					
1988	5.2	10.6	4.4	4.2	6.4
1989	4.9	10.3	5.3	4.5	6.3
1990	5.4	10.6	5.3	4.5	6.8
1991	5.9	10.2	5.5	4.5	6.9
1992	5.5	10.0	5.2	4.4	6.5
1993	6.1	10.0	5.6	5.0	7.2
Private sector					
1988	11.0	5.9	0.7	0.2	6.3
1989	12.0	4.9	0.7	0.1	5.7
1990	12.6	5.0	0.7	0.1	6.6
1991	13.5	11.3	0.7	0.1	6.6
1992	14.0	11.6	0.7	0.2	6.5
1993	14.7	12.9	0.8	0.6	6.7
Total					
1988	27.2	24.9	21.0	18.6	24.7
1989	27.0	23.5	23.1	18.5	23.4
1990	27.2	22.9	22.3	18.0	24.7
1991	28.5	22.3	22.1	17.6	24.9
1992	27.8	22.5	21.5	15.1	23.7
1993	29.0	23.9	23.6	15.1	22.0

Source: Department of Health (1994c)

markets is also important; for example, Conservative borough A agreed that it would purchase domiciliary care for vulnerable people only from agencies registered under the London Domiciliary Care Initiative (a scheme developed by the London boroughs in the absence of statutory regulation). However, when the borough advertised during 1994 for agencies to register, the response was very poor. Labour borough B on the other hand received a considerable response to its invitation to tender for a block domiciliary care contract. Government regulation has also played a part; thus while the

Conservative council in the county during the late 1980s threatened externalisation of in-house services, it was in fact Labour borough C that externalised a care home in order to meet the 85 per cent rule.

The county

Purchasers in the county calculated that the first year's STG money would not be enough to buy the same number of beds for elderly people in 1993/4 as had been provided the previous year. The shortfall was estimated as being equivalent to 300 beds. The county therefore decided to spend all its STG moneys on beds in the independent sector. There was a plentiful supply of beds in the county, but the authority nevertheless set its purchasing prices high because, given the budgetary shortfall that it predicted, it feared market instability. This was not dissimilar to the position in borough A. During the first year of the new community care regime, the county also committed itself to maintaining all its in-house provision, which amounted to a 100 per cent block contract, but with the intention of reducing this commitment in future years.

In fact, as in the vast majority of authorities, placements in residential and nursing homes during the first quarter of 1993/4 were very much lower than predicted (Kenny and Edwards 1994), there having been a rush to place people before the implementation date of April 1993 and caution sub-sequently as people adjusted to the new procedures. However, placements increased in both the second and fourth quarters. There was at the same time a growing tendency to create domiciliary care packages. As a result, the county vired £750,000 from the residential and nursing homes budget to home care.

During 1994, the county held down bed prices and, with the change in political administration, the commitment to the 100 per cent in-house block contract continued. However, the SSD had to put the externalisation of part of its home care service back on the agenda because of the difficulty it anticipated in meeting the 85 per cent rule, and because of difficulties in stimulating independent provision of domiciliary care. As one senior purchaser remarked: 'to expend approximately £2 million on an immature market presents huge challenges'. By the end of 1994 the county was contracting with some 31 independent home care agencies, but on the whole its own in-house providers offered a more flexible service; for example, independent agencies offered one-hour units of care, while in-house pro-viders were prepared to offer 30-minute units. The county's position in respect of the 85 per cent rule would have been worse if it had not had to vire £219,000 from the budget for elderly people to that for people with learning difficulties, most of which was spent on placements in the independent sector.

As a result of its experience during the first year of implementation, the county decided to initiate a block contract to generate more EMI nursing home beds, and to seek independent provision for enhanced domiciliary care. With regard to EMI beds, the contract in the west of the county was awarded to a dual-registered private home, but in the east the tender failed to produce a satisfactory supplier, with the result that discussions with in-house providers were put in train. In respect of enhanced domiciliary care, two known suppliers were chosen, a health authority trust in the west of the county and a voluntary organisation in the east. As one senior purchaser remarked, this was the one major area of success in stimulating independent domiciliary provision in the county, but it had required a considerable amount of money in the form of a substantial contract.

Borough A

This borough also had a plentiful supply of independent care homes and yet agreed a bed purchase price above the DSS rates to avoid market failure, and also to save clients having to 'top up' the amount paid by social services. Since April 1993, 200 new beds have become available in the independent sector, mainly in large units. There is therefore the possibility that smaller, less cost-effective homes will be forced out of business and that provision will become dominated by a few large suppliers. During 1993, a domiciliary review group consisting of purchasers and providers was set up in the borough and it agreed to purchase a new intensive home care service, for which it produced the service specification. However, the social services committee decided that such a service for highly dependent clients should be provided in-house and funded by the STG, which meant that the borough faced problems in meeting the 85 per cent rule.

This was an interesting decision, which contrasts with that taken by borough B, where it was decided to contract out 'the heavy end' of domiciliary care work, keeping the lighter work in-house. The explanation for borough A's decision has to be sought in both its historical experience of contracting and the scandals that attached to late 1980s practices in this respect, and the perception on the part of members that lighter work was more likely to attract the private sector. Borough B on the other hand had a relatively inflexible, strongly unionised in-house home care service, which made it difficult to meet the needs of highly dependent clients in-house.

Borough B

The shortage of independent care homes in borough B meant that it experienced considerable difficulty in finding placements. It was therefore prepared to pay more than neighbouring borough D (although, as we have seen, good supply does not necessarily result in lower purchasing prices). In fact beds in the borough's own homes cost considerably more than the purchasing price set by the SSD, something that was also true in the county, where the difference was effectively written off through the 100 per cent block contract. There was no level playing field for providers in the county or borough B. While the limited number of local authority homes in borough B have been in high demand because clients wish to stay in the borough, during 1994/5 the SSD moved partially to a block contract for beds in the independent sector to ensure a degree of choice.

Like the county, this borough switched to purchasing domiciliary care packages to a greater extent than was anticipated in the first year of implementation. It also experienced considerable difficulty in negotiating spot contracts with independent domiciliary care agencies, which were unwilling to provide less than two hours' care at a time, even though the client may have needed one hour in the morning and one hour in the evening. The authority thus decided to move towards a block contract in this area of provision as well, setting aside 20 per cent of its STG moneys (£500,000) for the purchase of out-house domiciliary care. While this is a substantial sum, it should be noted that the SSD still spent some £5 million on its in-house domiciliary care service. But a senior purchaser said that this should be reduced:

> I think whether it is three, five or ten years, until they [in-house providers] are put into a competitive mode they won't believe the world has changed . . . in three years I would like to see a percentage top-sliced so that, say, we have £3 million for Monday–Friday 9–5 [in-house services], but the £2 million is chopped up to meet whatever need emerges and it goes out and they can compete and good luck if they get it.

Stimulating the independent sector as a means of promoting change in in-house services was also a strong motivating force in the county.

Boroughs C and D

Compared with the other authorities there has been little real change in the pattern of purchasing and service provision between 1993 and 1994 in these boroughs, which reflects their lack of development of a purchasing strategy. Borough C was alone in not having set a formal purchasing price for residential and nursing home beds. Decisions taken in these boroughs have been in the main reactive, for example borough C's decision to externalise a residential home in order to meet the requirements of the 85 per cent rule. In respect of domiciliary care, borough C contracted with three agencies known to the SSD in 1993 and eight in 1994, but the tendency has been to see independent provision as a stopgap until in-house services can pick up the work. One senior officer said in the autumn of 1994 that he had had a telephone call from an independent domiciliary supplier but had not been sure how to handle it, which indicated the degree to which this authority had failed to establish a clear purchasing strategy.

Borough D, which had more independent care homes than many London boroughs, especially in respect of nursing home beds, committed all of its STG moneys to the purchase of beds in 1993/4. A similar decision was taken by the county, but, unlike the county, borough D did not review its decision. Only £16,000 of STG money was spent on domiciliary care in the first year of implementation; neither the balance between institutional and domiciliary provision, nor the pattern of purchasing and provision changed. Again, independent provision of domiciliary care has tended to be used as a stopgap, particularly during holiday periods.

Discussion

According to the Audit Commission (1993: para. 38): 'It is very important that the flexibility and value of this effect [of the new STG moneys] is used to the full in the early years to set up a wide range of alternatives before the money becomes fully committed and the flexibility is reduced.' Authorities have experienced varying degrees of success in stimulating the independent sector. Nowhere has it been easy, particularly in relation to domiciliary care, the importance of which has increased in many authorities as care packaging has become more significant. It has been difficult to get new entrants to the domiciliary care market in some areas and in respect of some kinds of care; in the county it required a large injection of cash to secure acceptable responses to the invitation to tender for enhanced domiciliary care. The response of independent domiciliary agencies was also disappointing in borough A. However, some authorities, for example borough C, have not taken the initiative to work out how they might use independent suppliers or to stimulate supply.

Two authorities, the county and borough A, anticipated market failure in the independent homes sector, but this did not materialise during the first year of implementation, either in these authorities or more generally (Henwood 1994). Thus there has been little by way of exit from the market in respect of residential care, although indications from the market mapping carried out by the county indicate that the domiciliary care market is more volatile. In part the lack of exit was due to authorities acting cautiously, in setting purchasing prices for example, and working to avoid the closure of homes. In the case of a home that tried to negotiate high prices by threatening closure, the county chose to work with another county that also had residents in the home to reach some agreement. Neither authority wanted to see disruption to its clients. Senior purchasers in the county voiced suspicions that some home owners were surviving on a combination of reserves and reduced profit margins, which raises the issue of what might happen when the STG comes to an end.

Some homes in the county also hoped that the SSD would underwrite their attempts to diversify, but here the authority drew the line. Indeed, very little diversification has taken place. One small home owner in borough A argued that it was too difficult to diversify into domiciliary provision. Respite care posed a greater risk of vacancies, and day care raised the issue of how to mix day care clients and residents: it was bad enough if a resident sat in the wrong chair, let alone a day care client. Diversification also raised the problem of staff cover, which would inevitably prove difficult for a small-scale operation.

It was the aim of the new community care policy to increase independent provision, thereby giving more choice in terms of the range of provision and more cost-effective, high-quality care. In the first place, not all authorities had a firm concept of commissioning as a means of increasing choice. In borough D, for example, the primary concern was to secure provision in order to avoid blocking beds in hospitals. Authorities must keep a watch on such matters, but where the response to the Act was entirely reactive there was little hope of securing real improvement in what was offered to clients.

In authorities where choice was taken seriously it is hard to reach firm conclusions. In borough A, the department felt that client choice had been enhanced in relation to residential care, although there was concern that the new larger residential homes that had just opened might squeeze out small providers. In borough B, it was felt that the first year of implementation had resulted in increased choice regarding residential care and the ability to stay in one's own home, but initial optimism about purchasing more appropriate residential care for people from ethnic minorities had not happened as quickly as the department would have liked. Such hopes were in line with the Audit Commission's injunction to use the STG moneys to innovate. But in borough B, the key to achieving more responsive services for minority groups might well be the expansion of in-house provision.

Finally, both in borough B and the county in 1992 and 1993, senior purchasers were optimistic about competition in the domiciliary care field producing a change in the practices of in-house providers. There was no sign of this having happened in borough B by the end of 1994. In the county, in-house home care providers are exceedingly flexible: in part as a result of changes made in response to recommendations from the Social Services Inspectorate in 1988, which advocated moving away from home help services and towards home care (that is, as a result of external pressure, but from a regulatory body rather than competition); in part as a result of good management on the part of the providers of this service; and in part as a result of the threat posed by externalisation in the late 1980s and the early 1990s. It was arguably the threat of competition, more than competition itself, which affected the behaviour of this particular set of in-house service providers, but other in-house providers in the county were not equally affected.

Table 6.2   Assessments resulting in service from one or more agencies, 1993/4

	County	Borough A	Borough B	Borough C	Borough D
No. of assessments leading to service from one agency	19,291	4599	12,669	6453	4004
No. of assessments leading to service from more than one agency	215	902	11,493	1282	608

Source: Audit Commission (1995)

The emphasis in all authorities has been rather more on the need to develop a social care market with a division between purchasing and providing than on developing a mixed economy involving the voluntary, informal, private and statutory sectors. Only in borough B has there been significant mixing of service provision by agency (Table 6.2). Most senior managers expressed no particular preference for the voluntary sector, although contracts with voluntary agencies had certainly been developed. One locality manager in the county said that she preferred to contract with the private sector because it was more straightforward. Negotiations with voluntary organisations could mean setting aside an afternoon because volunteers might be involved and had given up their time. There was possibly a latent preference for doing business with the voluntary sector in borough C, but here the purchasing strategy was not developed.

Nor was there much sign anywhere of developing informal networks. Early in 1993, a senior purchaser in borough A was enthusiastic about stimulating informal provision, but by the middle of 1994 was much more cautious about the problems of monitoring this:

how do you address things like security, health and safety, probity . . . if a neighbour lifts someone into bed do we have an obligation to provide training; if they injure their backs are we liable? . . . What do we do if their standards aren't up to much, if we think their attitude is patronising?

Authorities were also aware of the ethical debate around paying neighbours along the lines of the PSSRU's care management project in Kent (see Leat and Ungerson 1993), and on the whole expressed disquiet about following the PSSRU lead. Thus while in the late 1980s there was considerable attention being paid to the role of informal care in the form of neighbours and networks, the developments in the first year of implementation in the research authorities have been very much more in the form of private provision.

Contracts

Independent providers

The official guidance suggested that SSDs should develop different forms of contract to reflect the different kinds of relationships (e.g. more or less trust) with different kinds of suppliers (Common and Flynn 1992). However, there is no sign of this having happened in the research authorities. Rather, variations on the theme of simple letters, service agreements and contracts were used, depending on the size of the sum involved. The main focus of attention for authorities has been contracting with the private sector, and in particular the difficult issue of the appropriate balance between spot and block contracts. Decisions regarding this balance depend on the nature of the market, the history of the authority and the structure of purchasing. Grants to the voluntary sector are in the process of being turned into contracts or service agreements (the distinction is usually unclear) using the same model as that employed in negotiations with private suppliers, which has caused problems for small voluntary organisations. More generally, voluntary agencies have faced a profound change in the nature of the voluntary/ statutory relationship, which may in turn have implications for the nature of voluntary activity.

All the research authorities began with a tendency to use spot rather than block contracts, leaving aside the heavy commitment to in-house services (which amounted to a block contract) and borough A's large block contract with its privatised homes. All the authorities except borough C developed a standard contract to use with independent home owners after April 1993. Care managers used this contract together with the authority's guide prices (effectively ceiling prices) for beds to purchase care.

In the case of the county, this contract went through nine drafts before it was acceptable to home owners. In dispute were such issues as the authority's effort to get home owners to collect any payments due from the client (borough A successfully inserted a clause to this effect in its contract, even though the client has the legal right to ask the local authority to collect the money); its attempt closely to specify matters to do with the 'quality of life' of residents, for example the requirement that homes specify a key worker; and, similarly, the attempt closely to specify admissions procedures.

In borough A, there were some moves towards involving providers more in the contract during 1993/4; for example, it was agreed that home owners would be responsible for the care plan. One home owner explained in April 1994:

> We have got them to agree that you just have 24-hour nursing care and that the care plan will come from the home, because there is no point in an unqualified care manager devising a care plan until they are admitted to the home and the assessment is made by the home itself . . . you can't devise a care plan in ten seconds, it takes two or three weeks to devise.

Borough D also had problems in getting independent home owners to accept its standard contract. Early drafts were extremely rigid. For example, on quality criteria, it specified 'adherence to the menu plan, food presentation and portion sizes', compared with borough B's more open food (and activities) quality standard, which said that there should be: 'opportunities to influence the daily routine, menus and social activities through residents' meetings, direct consultation with users and their families'.

During 1994 there was a tendency to move towards block contracting in many authorities. This was to ensure supply, for example in the case of EMI beds in the county, and both nursing home beds and domiciliary care in borough B; to ensure choice – scarcity of institutional provision meant that borough B had to block-book beds; and to ensure quality – again in borough B doubts over the quality obtained by spot purchasing domiciliary care was in part responsible for the decision to move to block purchasing. From the providers' point of view, block contracts were often preferable because they were less costly to administer than spot contracts. Block purchasing became easier as trends became clearer, at least in those authorities where there was sufficient information to make these known. In general, when suppliers are being asked to innovate or take risks, purchasers will opt for block contracts as the only way of bringing about change.

In part, the move to block purchase is another aspect of the tendency which we have already observed for decision making to pass back up, or to stay at, the centre. In the county, the contracts unit made a deliberate effort to map purchases in order to work out who were the authority's largest suppliers. One of the purposes was to offer a county-wide view of localised purchasing so that, for example, if there were several local contracts it might be worth rolling these up into a larger, more cost-effective, agreement. As one senior purchaser put it:

> The reasoning for using a block contract is that if you have a supplier who is accredited and people are happy to be using them, the unit costs of a block contract are considerably less than using a spot. For one there is less administration, and, secondly, we can use it as a negotiating tool. Because we can guarantee someone's cash flow, they

can bring their unit costs down so that they are not trying to recover everything through one-off spot contracts.

The contracts unit in the county had managed to negotiate a five per cent reduction on a block contract by offering to pay in advance. As the layers of purchasing have developed in the county, block contracting has become more likely; for example, two or three localities may get together to contract with a supplier.

However, block contracts also have disadvantages. Negotiating a contract may be very time consuming. A long contract freezes the shape of provision and makes change impossible. This has been the case in respect of borough A's decision to transfer the ownership of its homes. It has also meant that this borough continued to pay relatively high prices at a time when prices were falling. When block contracts merely replace one (local authority) supplier by another (independent) supplier the 'set list' syndrome is perpetuated and choice is not enhanced.

This was not the case in respect of borough B's domiciliary care contract, which sought to fill a gap – in terms of evening and weekend provision – in the local authority's service. However, it proved difficult to secure flexibility on the part of the providers, even though the authority focused on quality issues when negotiating the contract. A small independent supplier with limited staff had difficulty in putting a high proportion of clients to bed at the time they chose. Borough B used a competitive tender for this block contract, which attracted interest from 19 companies. The county also used a competitive tender for the EMI beds and enhanced home care contracts.

Monitoring contracts is a crucial part of the process and has been shown to be the most flawed in the United States (see for example, Gutch 1992). In the early months of implementation it was acknowledged at all levels in the county that there was no clear procedure for monitoring contracts. In 1994, a policy of 'contract ownership' was introduced, whereby the owner had to be a budget holder. This meant that the contracts unit could not monitor contracts. The policy was intended to sharpen local purchasers' sense of responsibility regarding contracts, but some have remained sceptical of their capacity to undertake monitoring, especially of domiciliary care. As one locality manager said: 'I always sit with my tongue in my cheek when they talk about monitoring domiciliary care.' Another felt that he had trusting relationships with his suppliers and was uneasy about formal monitoring. Borough A, in line with its history of block contracting as 'contracting out' rather than enabling, has monitored its block contracts using a penalty points system, though this may change as purchasing becomes more client focused.

The position of the voluntary sector in respect of contracting has arguably been particularly problematic. Most authorities gave consideration to the implications for voluntary organisations of moving from grants to contracts during 1992 and 1993. In the county, a 1992 report, *Empowering the*

Voluntary Sector, called for working models to be established for funding arrangements and for these to be considered by a joint voluntary-sector consultative committee. This document followed the Griffiths report (Department of Health and Social Security 1988) in acknowledging that mixed funding for voluntary organisations might be appropriate. However, its recommendations seemed to get lost in the move towards bringing in service agreements. In 1994, lengthy new procedures were introduced governing local arrangements with voluntary organisations. These were still bedding down at the end of the research.

Borough A also prepared a document on funding voluntary agencies in the middle of 1992, which emphasised the need to make such arrangements more businesslike, but which counselled against competitive tendering. However, when a contract for day care was renegotiated with a local voluntary organisation competitive tendering was used. Otherwise, the shift to service-level agreements has essentially involved the formalisation of existing arrangements. In borough B, a late 1992 report of a working group on funding strategies with the voluntary sector stressed the importance of a partnership approach, but, with the setting up of the commissioning unit, the authority moved relatively quickly towards developing service agreements without consulting the working group, although it did organise meetings with voluntary organisations to help in the preparation of their submissions.

All these authorities have moved to introduce formal contracts for voluntary organisations in receipt of local government moneys. In borough D, too, grants to voluntary organisations were given to the contracts unit to administer and organisations have been asked to justify their funding in terms of quite complicated performance indicators, notwithstanding the borough's tardiness in developing a purchasing strategy. As one senior manager acknowledged:

> They are asked questions which I doubt if many of the people in the local authority could answer, let alone some person who is running a small organisation based totally on volunteers. They are asking questions about what performance measurement they are using, how do they measure and control and the effectiveness of their service delivery, how do they quantify customer satisfaction, and the people sit there and think, what the hell are these people talking about?

Only in borough C have service agreements not been introduced, although a decision was taken to do so in 1993. Voluntary organisations in this borough have played a much more central role in the implementation of the new community care policy through their participation in the joint commissioning machinery, and there is a sense in which the idea of partnership, if not entirely equal, means more in terms of participation than in the other authorities. Elsewhere, voluntary organisations have increasingly been treated as alternative providers; thus their role as decision makers within joint commissioning forums, while always fragile, has been further diminished.

The introduction of service-level agreements has effectively formalised the relationship between local authorities as funders and voluntary agencies. A 1993 survey of 500 organisations found 37 per cent to be running contracts, of which 40 per cent considered that they represented an improvement and only 10 per cent said they were worse off (Davis Smith and Hedley 1993). In their more detailed study of 12 contracts, Common and Flynn (1992) emphasised the degree of trust characterising contracts with the voluntary sector. While relationships between voluntary agencies and statutory authorities became more formal during the period of negotiation, they tended to relax afterwards, although there was variation in the degree of formality with which the contract was managed. The 1993 survey shows that contracts have not swept the board, although the local authority funding survey by the National Council for Voluntary Organisations (1993) showed that voluntary organisations lost £12 million in grants during 1992/3, while contract fees increased by £78.4 million (134 per cent). However, it does seem that voluntary agencies are facing the erosion of 'grant aid culture' at the same time that there is a trend in many towards cuts in the money given to the voluntary sector.

The transition to service-level agreements has involved voluntary organisations in new ways of working. While Davis Smith and Hedley's (1993) survey indicated a relatively high degree of satisfaction with contracts, the evidence from voluntary organisations in the research authorities was mixed. In the first place, voluntary agencies have experienced difficulties in dealing with the new structures in SSDs. They have usually had to deal with the new contracts units rather than with a 'grants liaison officer'. In borough B, while grants moved to the commissioning unit, the old liaison officer moved into the strategic planning section of the purchasing division, and representatives of voluntary agencies expressed confusion as to whom they should consult in the authority.

The negotiations over new service agreements have often been protracted. The experiences of the directors of different branches of the same national voluntary organisation in the county and in borough A were similar. In the county it was reported that:

> We have been in negotiations with them for months. The agency agreement has to become a service-level agreement. The money stays the same and the service and everything else stays the same, but we have to re-word everything. We have agonised and it has cost us a lot of money.

In borough A, contract negotiations took nine months in 1991 and both sides called in legal representation towards the end. Initially, the contract was managed through the active involvement of staff from the local authority (analogous to Common and Flynn's (1992) 'partnership' management model), but with the creation of a contracts unit and the bringing in of a contracts manager from industry, the model for managing the contract shifted to Common and Flynn's 'contract manager' model. Active officer involvement was replaced by more detailed specification and monitoring. On the face of it, the management of the contract was less intrusive and hands on, and review was less testing, but it was also less supportive and developmental. Thus, the relationship between the signatories to the contract may be hard to predict over time.

On the basis of intensive observation of the operation of a national voluntary organisation's contract to supply day care for elderly people in borough A over the period 1992–4, and two sets of interviews with representatives from the same national voluntary agency in the county and borough B in 1993 and 1994, it seems that formalisation of grant aid has had three particularly significant effects: it has forced greater professionalisation on the voluntary agency; it has had an impact on governance and accountability; and it has had an impact on the goals of the organisation.

The staff of the voluntary organisation in borough A said that they were forced closely to define the scope of the service they were prepared to offer; the contract stopped particular areas of work being taken for granted. But running the contract did require more and different skills from managing a grant. The director of the organisation estimated that as much as 75 per cent of her time was absorbed by running the contract. None of the voluntary organisations had the requisite skills at the beginning to produce accurate and detailed costings; the problem of costing volunteer labour has proved particularly difficult. The voluntary treasurer of the county organisation did not like the nature of the new task. The director of the agency in borough A found herself working at a wide range of levels and the heavy degree of responsibility tended to open up the divide between her and both the other paid and volunteer staff. When the voluntary agency in borough A began running the day care contract, half the managers of the day care centres were volunteers; however, they found the formalisation of procedures demanded by the contract oppressive and resented in particular the time required to fill in the performance indicator returns, which they felt diminished the time they could spend with clients. One of these volunteers resigned and was replaced by a paid manager. The management of volunteers also became more challenging as more attention was paid to developing uniform practices. For example, managers had to face the issue of how to 'retire' a volunteer who could no longer be trusted to carry out tasks satisfactorily. The contract imposed professional standards of assessment, management and evaluation, which met with resistance from some, but not all, voluntary staff.

In terms of governance, the pace of change has bewildered many executive members of voluntary agencies. Commenting on American non-profit organisations, Powell and Friedkin (1987) have noted that as technical complexity increases, broad-based governance declines. Taylor (1990) also remarked that the unpaid management committee is one of the key defining factors of the voluntary sector, but that its future in a system that requires more sophistication and expertise must be called into question. In the contracts culture, accountability is increasingly to the purchaser in the first instance, which leaves the position of the trustees ambiguous. It is noteworthy that the executive committee for the organisation providing day care in borough A had no clear grasp of the community care changes and seemingly little appreciation for the changed ways of working of the organisation's staff. Lines of accountability also became confused. Day care managers found themselves responding to the director of the organisation, but also to the chairmen of their local groups. Common and Flynn (1992) emphasised the problem of divided accountability between voluntary agencies and local authorities for contracted out services, but the lines of accountability within the voluntary organisation may also be blurred.

Finally, in respect of goals, the most strongly contested issue was the dependency of the clients to be served. In the county, the director of the agency spoke of the problem of the local authority choosing to send a number of highly dependent, possibly incontinent, elderly people to the agency's day care centre and the effects of this on the agency's traditional client group, the socially isolated. During its contract negotiations, borough A fought to maintain a place for the socially isolated in its day care centres. The contract specified that all clients would be assessed by the SSD, with 60 per cent being required to meet social services' criteria for admission. As local authorities target the more highly dependent, this issue will become more difficult for the voluntary agencies.

More broadly, voluntary organisations expressed the fear that in being invited to contract for services, their advocacy, campaigning and information services would suffer. In borough B, the national voluntary agency's desire to provide a welfare rights service was not recognised as a priority by the SSD. These sorts of services are often dependent on core funding, which both the Griffiths report (Department of Health and Social Security 1988) and the Home Office *Efficiency Scrutiny* (1990) sought to protect, but in this, as in all else, local authority practices are likely to vary.

Contracts tend to assume that the contractor inhabits the same form of organisation as the purchaser and do not make allowance for different forms of management. In line with Harden's (1993) reflections on the significance of a shift towards a 'contract state', Self (1993: 123) argued that:

> the massive use of contracting introduces a new type of relationship between governments and private organisations, which changes the behaviour of both parties, increases their interdependency and blurs the traditional distinctions between them.

Taylor and Hoggett (1993) have considered the potential for remaking contractors in the image of the purchaser, and Billis (1993) has warned of the dangers of an instrumental use of the voluntary sector that emphasises only those attributes that are of direct use to government. The process of contracting, which carries with it the idea of formalising arrangements between the parties and/or producing a uniform, high-quality service, highlights both the tensions inherent in the relationship between the statutory and voluntary sectors and the ambiguities inherent in the nature of voluntary organisations.

Billis (1989) has argued that while voluntary organisations are primarily associational, they overlap both the personal and bureaucratic worlds. The management of ambiguity requires an understanding of the ground rules of both the associational and bureaucratic worlds, an appreciation of both membership, missions, informality and democracy on the one hand and managerial authority and accountability, levels of decision making, career progression, staff development, conditions of service and explicit policy making on the other.

Voluntary organisations balance the demands of bureaucracy and associ-ation. It may be suggested that contracting will tend to shift the balance towards the former. Certainly Knight's (1993) report for the Home Office on voluntary action, in which he pushed enabling to its logical conclusion and advocated dividing voluntary organisations into autonomous campaigners on the one hand and a 'third sector' of contracting service providers on the other, rode roughshod over the participatory and associational nature of voluntary agencies. The nature of the new partnership between the voluntary and statutory sector in the future is far from certain.

The internal market

In-house provision has remained very important in all the research authori-ties, although borough A has gone furthest in externalising virtually all its residential care provision. Commitment to in-house provision has also been an issue in the county, where early in 1993 it was believed that the 100 per cent block contract with in-house providers would be gradually diminished and in borough B, where senior purchasers would like to change the balance between in-house and independent provision of domiciliary care. However, in the county in 1994, after a change in political administration, the commitment to the 100 per cent block contract was renewed for an indefinite period, and in borough B the proportion of money devoted to independent as opposed to in-house care remains small. In boroughs C and D, there has been less overt questioning of commitment to in-house services, notwithstanding the externalisation of a home in borough C, and there are very few signs of any development of a formal internal market.

Given that budgets have not been transferred to purchasers anywhere other than in the county, it is difficult for the internal service-level agreements that have been developed in three of the authorities to have much real impact. Even in the county, where budgets have been transferred, one provider said 'they are just documents, aren't they?' Thus threat of external competition has probably been a more important factor in bringing about change in the practices of in-house providers than internal service agreements. However, some provider managers were at pains to view positively the scope for change, even with the 100 per cent block contract. Thus where managers were committed to making them meaningful, such agreements may be useful.

Notwithstanding their 100 per cent block contract, in-house providers in the county have expressed the view that they are less favoured suppliers because of the 85 per cent rule, and because, in the case of care homes, the authority can recoup more income support money from clients entering independent homes. However, the decision to pay a higher price for in-house beds was taken in order to compensate for this. But all the STG money spent on residential care has gone to the independent sector; and there has been no new money to improve in-house residential services. Yet, insofar as domiciliary provision has increased, it has been largely in-house providers who have picked up this work, although because of the 85 per cent rule only independent sector providers were permitted to tender for the contract for enhanced domiciliary care. Indeed, there has been a substantial overspend on in-house home care in the county, which may be due in part to inaccurate unit costings, but is probably also due to purchasers buying more (expensive) weekend and out-of-hours care from in-house providers. Purchasers have thus shown no inclination consistently to favour providers from one sector over another.

In all the authorities where a firm purchaser–provider split has been created, there has been a period of tension between purchasers and providers, which was bound to carry over into discussions over service-level agreements. In the county immediately after reorganisation, providers were excluded from anything to do with service specifications, but they were involved in drawing up the tender for enhanced domiciliary care, which signalled a 'thaw' in relations between the two and the achievement of a new equilibrium. But providers in the county and to some extent elsewhere were still liable to feel that purchasers do not really know what they want.

The county has been ahead of the other authorities in developing service-level agreements between in-house providers and purchasers. By July 1993, it had some 18 of these drawn up by locality and group managers. These followed a common format: introduction, care specification and service statement. The service statements are a comprehensive inventory of all the service units, detailing what they provide. The care specifications apply equally to in-house and independent providers and include sections on values (for example, privacy and choice), the purpose of the service, staffing, employment policy, involvement of users and carers, the care plan, record keeping and quality assurance. The introduction is important for the statement it makes about agreed marginal changes to be made in the service for the year and agreed long-term purchasing intentions, together with agreed review arrangements. The marginal changes are understood to be those changes that can be made within current budgets, whereas the long-term purchasing intentions are a statement of agreed requirements that require an injection of funds. Agreements are revised annually, with the marginal changes that were not met and long-term purchasing intentions carried over into the new agreements. Monitoring the agreements was acknowledged to be difficult. Purchasers tended to feel that providers had a pretty free hand. One senior manager felt that the agreements were in any case more useful for solving disputes than as working documents.

The process of arriving at agreements in the county was not universally easy, as three examples illustrate. In the case of domiciliary care, the home care providers made the running; as the purchaser involved in negotiating the agreement acknowledged, 'it was often hard to keep up'. But purchasers supported what providers wished to do. Second, purchasers had some doubts about home care providers taking decisions about capital expenditure without feeding them through the purchasers, believing this practice to be a result of the leverage exerted by providers through the 100 per cent block contract. However, this is illustrative of a lack of clarity about what is a 'legitimate' degree of purchaser influence, for it is not clear that providers in the private sector would have to go back to purchasers before deciding to refurbish buildings. In the case of residential and day care for elderly people, the providers felt that the purchasers were not clear enough in stating their requirements. As one senior provider put it:

> When you asked 'what do you want from us?' you would get the same sort of answers: 'we want more respite care, more care for EMI'. But when you actually get into, 'well what actually do you want from it? And how much? When? . . .' they had difficulty.

The 1994/5 agreements indicated some changes achieved in line with the 1993/4 desired marginal changes, but at a slower pace, with negotiations and further discussions outstanding. In the third case, of children's services, purchasers complained that providers would not make the changes they wanted to see. Here, purchaser–provider relations were the most strained, because of a combination of factors: (i) the continuation of tensions that existed for this client group before restructuring; (ii) particular difficulties experienced by purchasers in effecting a change to care management and introducing purchasing criteria, which, some felt, could not be easily harmonised with the requirements of the Children Act; and (iii) poor communication within the providing stream for this client group.

Borough A also set up a service-level agreement between the care management (purchasing) division and the community social services (providing) division in 1993, but this did not involve service specifications, and had more to do with identifying the costs of hours of home care. The commissioning unit in borough B introduced a service-level agreement for the care managers providing HIV services in mid-1993, which effectively treated the micro-purchasers – care managers – as providers. The focus of the agreement was on productive hours of work, with no allowance for the time taken to train new workers, and it demanded unit costs in terms of hours rather than in terms of the number of posts. This agreement involved minimal consultation and resulted in considerable tension. However, between 1993 and 1994 the macro-commissioners realised some of the complications involved for the providers, and trust was in large measure re-established.

All authorities have encountered problems in trying to establish unit costs for services, which is a necessary preliminary to setting up meaningful service-level agreements. In borough C, a senior manager said in mid-1993:

> I don't believe our accounts are significantly behind other LA accounts, but they are not in shape to facilitate an internal market. We are several years' development away from that and it is not the priority for the council to run an internal market.

Providers in this borough and elsewhere have shown some suspicion of unit costs because they believe that they will show in-house services to be more expensive (because staff tend to be better qualified and to enjoy better pay and conditions, and because of the huge layer of support services that has to be apportioned between services), and thus provide a rationale for shifting the balance more decisively in favour of the independent sector on cost grounds.

Almost all authorities have made some changes in the conditions of work for in-house employees. The county created two tiers of home care staff, those carrying out more intensive personal care and those in the more traditional home help/home care tasks. Certain anomalies have also been tidied up; for example, staff can no longer be paid double if they fall sick on a Sunday. In borough A in 1993, as the home care service became more flexible, with greater weekend and evening working, staff were put on what are essentially call-off contracts, so that they know they will be employed, but not for how many hours. Borough C has reduced annual leave for staff by one or two days a year and made car mileage allowances a fixed sum, but the borough is still uncompetitive with the private sector in terms of its holiday and maternity leave entitlements. Borough B, where the trade union is particularly strong, has done less in this regard. Staff in home care still work mainly either full time or part time between 9 a.m. and 5 p.m. Purchasers in this authority, as in some others, acknowledge 'the genuine concerns about the terms and conditions of independent sector agencies . . . and it is awful the idea of anyone losing their jobs, their terms and conditions which trade unions have fought years and years for'. The 1993 NUPE/UNISON home care survey showed that, of 1200 home helps and home carers, two-thirds lacked sick pay and pension provisions.

Conclusion: choice and responsiveness

It is difficult to come to firm conclusions as to whether the market in social care is 'working'. Measured in terms of an increase in the number of suppliers from the independent sector, particularly in domiciliary care, where there were historically few, then progress has been variable between and within authorities. Measured in terms of the cultural shift required on the part of SSD staff in becoming enablers, the change has been much more profound in many places. Staff are, on the whole, conscious of a new way of thinking and this might be expected to produce more change in ways of working in the future. But at present the upheaval in terms of implementing the purchaser–provider split, together with its information requirements, seems large relative to the outcomes achieved. The main aim of introducing market principles into community care was to increase choice for users and to ensure the provision of more flexible, appropriate care. Authorities are a long way from delivering tailor-made packages to meet assessed need. There has in some places been an increase in choice and responsiveness of particular services, but services have nevertheless remained a 'set list' and are likely to be so for the foreseeable future.

To take a very familiar problem – the client who wishes to be put to bed at 10 p.m., but who instead gets put to bed by the staff from a social services department at 5 p.m. – it is worth asking whether such an apparently simple issue has now been resolved in favour of the user. The position in the research authorities may be briefly summarised as follows.

In borough D there was no evidence of any change in the pattern of provision. In March 1994, the director of a local voluntary organisation told the story of a client who was trying to get more help for her highly dependent husband:

> all she wants – they are trying to force her husband to go into nursing home care, she doesn't want him to go into nursing home care – all she wants is someone to get her husband up in the morning and put him to bed in the evening . . . what they offered was that a home carer could go in at 12.30 and if she wanted him put to bed he would have to go to bed at 5.30.

This is exactly the kind of pattern of service provision that it was anticipated the introduction of market principles would change. This borough could as an example of a largely unreformed authority in that so far it has mplemented only an assessment system. It was only beginning the s of reviewing its domiciliary care provision and addressing the issue of evening and weekend care by in-house providers and by purchase via the STG moneys at the end of 1994.

In borough A, it was possible, but not certain, that the user's wishes would be met. The borough had little independent home care provision, but it did have relatively flexible in-house providers, whose contractual conditions of employment had been substantially modified.

In borough B, the client had a reasonable chance of success. There was some independent home care provision, but in-house providers remained relatively inflexible. In all probability the client would have had to have been new and highly dependent, and therefore eligible for care management and the expenditure of transferred moneys on purchasing closely specified independent sector care.

In borough C, there was little flexibility in-house, not much STG money (in the first year of implementation) with which to purchase care, little monitoring of the quality of independent care, and little by way of a coherent purchasing strategy. A client would have had little chance of success in the short term. However, the home care service was under review.

In the county, it was almost certain that a client would be put to bed when wished by a member of the flexible, in-house home care workforce.

Thus it is clear that it is not possible to generalise about a client's chances of success. Furthermore, in the authorities where the client was most likely to have such wishes met, the relationship between the achievement of a flexible service and the introduction of market principles was not clear cut either. In the county, the service was flexible because of the changes that had been made by in-house providers at the end of the 1980s in response to the threat of externalisation, the push to reorganisation of the service by the Social Services Inspectorate, and the high quality of provider managers managing their own budgets. In borough A the in-house service was also relatively flexible, but in this instance because of innovation as a result of a 1993 review by a joint purchaser/provider group on domiciliary care. In borough B, where new, highly dependent clients stood a good chance of having their wishes met, this was in large measure due to the availability of private sector care, although some problems have developed regarding the company's ability to put clients to bed when they wish. Only in this borough had actual provision by independent suppliers proved important in meeting clients' wishes.

The formalisation of the internal market between purchasers and providers through service-level agreements was intended, as with the promotion of external competition, to produce greater responsiveness and flexibility, this time on the part of in-house suppliers. In fact, other pressures on providers to force change may be more potent: actual or threatened competition, which we have seen has had a significant effect on some services in some authorities; and the link between the care management approach (which is explored in the next chapter) and enabling. It was the idea of purchasing as a response to the assessment of individual need that converted senior managers to enabling in borough B.

What is actually needed in order to operate a social care market of this kind is still under discussion in all the authorities. Whether money actually needs to change hands between purchasers and providers is another matter. Such transactions undoubtedly add to the paper chase. Some purchasers believed that both the transfer of budgets and formal service-level agreements were necessary to force providers to change their practices, and that agreements in the absence of transferring budgets had little chance of success. Many providers doubted the capacity of purchasers to translate their sense of the changes needed into precise requirements. It may be argued that purchasers will acquire these skills, but formulating a service agreement with in-house purchasers is but one part of a purchaser's job, whereas it is central to the provider's existence. It is therefore likely that the providers' input will be valuable.

Finally, the commitment of providers to their service should not be underestimated, as the assumptions behind the new legislation are wont to do. In the county, the biggest changes in practice have taken place in home care, where providers are most energetic and skilled. And those changes began to take place in the late 1980s, prompted by a push from a regulatory authority and the introduction of devolved provider budgets.

Some aspects of the new policy of enabling actually discourage change on the part of providers. The 85 per cent rule means that in-house providers are not permitted to try to sell as much of their service as they can. Even if an in-house service is of proven quality and in high demand it cannot attract more by way of new money via the STG. Thus in borough C, for example, home care managers would like to introduce a night sitting service, but the 85 per cent rule means that it is difficult to give money to an in-house service.

It seems that the implementation of enabling has involved a number of different things: the establishing of a firm purchaser–provider split, steps towards increased commissioning from the independent sector, and the formalisation of the internal market. Our research indicates that external provision may increase an SSD's capacity to respond flexibly (although, as we saw in the case of borough B's domiciliary care contract, there may still be problems in this regard) and that the threat of competition can, but does not always, promote a change in the practice of in-house providers. However, the requirement to spend 85 per cent of new moneys in the independent sector has tended to maintain spending on institutional rather than domiciliary care and has tended to thwart change on the part of in-house providers.

Evidence regarding the purchaser–provider split is more equivocal. If its main purpose was to achieve an increase in independent provision, then the 85 per cent rule made it unnecessary. At the end of 1994, it seemed that the Audit Commission was prepared to recognise the limitations of the purchaser–provider split, commenting that it does 'not guarantee either greater flexibility or more responsive service. If handled clumsily, it can introduce barriers and rigidity. Conversely, flexibility and devolved budgets can be introduced without a firm split' (Audit Commission 1994: 42). However, the idea of trying to make social workers purchasers and thereby to think as surrogate clients and to articulate need more clearly (which is what proved attractive to local authorities) is a powerful one, although there are major problems in actually separating the assessment of need from the provision of service, as Chapter 8 shows. It remains the case that the elaboration of the purchasing function has proved extremely difficult and the information requirements, together with the formalisation of service agreements, have resulted in a vast increase in bureaucracy.

7

Care management. I: The idea of care management

In Chapter 2 we suggested that care management was not a 'normative core' policy, but it was presented as central in the political rhetoric. It was an important element in selling the overall policy. The 1989 White Paper on community care referred to assessment and care management as 'the cornerstone' of high-quality care (Cm. 849 1989: para. 1.11). The 1991 practice guidance put care management 'at the heart' of the new approach (Department of Health *et al.* 1991a: para. 9.2), while the CIPFA/ADSS Financial Management Partnership (1991) documents made care management the central information system, as did the Audit Commission (1992b). In its illustration of the 'cascade of change', the Audit Commission (1992b: 38) placed 'putting users' and carers' needs first', at the top of the cascade. From this all other changes would flow. The influential official guidance on assessment and care management stated clearly that the empowerment of users and carers was the rationale for reorganising community care (Department of Health *et al.* 1991b: para. 9.6). However, as Stevenson and Parsloe (1993) pointed out, the term 'empowerment' was not used in the rest of the copious guidance issued after 1990. Other official guidance saw care management as one of the key changes that would promote the more efficient use of resources, make services needs-led, and offer users greater choice.

Experiments in care management were well established before the passing of the 1990 legislation. The projects directed by the PSSRU at the University of Kent were particularly influential. Care management has had a much longer history in the United States, where it spread rapidly in the absence of other radical restructuring, in part to save money and in part to aid the coordination of care (Davies 1992). The North American literature and practice also makes more of the brokerage and advocacy roles open to the care manager, which have not been a feature of British innovations in the field. The British experiments have put most emphasis on care management as a mechanism for linking and coordinating services (Challis 1994c: 3).

The PSSRU listed the core tasks of care management as case finding and screening, assessment, care planning, and monitoring, and it differentiated care managers from key workers by their long-term involvement with clients and by their work with multiple rather than single teams and services (Challis and Davies 1986; Challis 1992, 1994a, b). The 1990 guidance stated additionally that care managers, unlike key workers, would not be involved in the direct provision of services (Department of Health 1990a). The PSSRU projects of the 1980s were of course designed in the absence of a purchaser–provider split. In the PSSRU's formulation, the goals of care management were improved client use of support and services, developed capacity of social networks and services to promote client well-being, and the promotion of service effectiveness and efficiency.

Davies and his PSSRU colleagues observed that particular social services were expected to achieve policy goals for quite different clienteles. Home helps, for example, had traditionally been used to monitor those believed to be at risk and to encourage, motivate and act as confidantes, as well as to perform tasks for frail elderly people. Thus their services had been offered to a general population of elderly people not at risk, to people at high risk of institutional care, to people who had suffered a health accident or who needed short-term help, and to informal carers bearing large burdens. The PSSRU has recently emphasised that as community care develops, targeting must be based on need rather than on risk of entering institutional care (Davies *et al.* 1990; Challis *et al.* 1995). Between 1980 and 1985, there was a slight increase in home care provision, but the service was spread more widely rather than targeting those most in need (Bebbington and Davies 1993). The PSSRU researchers commented on the apparent lack of sophisticated targeting of services, on the lack of criteria for stopping service, and on the lack of data as to outputs.

The PSSRU's pilot projects involved targeting in order to substitute domiciliary for institutional care. The target population was therefore on the verge of institutional care. The researchers stressed the importance of both careful initial screening and review of clients (Davies *et al.* 1990; Challis 1994c; Davies and Knapp 1994). The aim of the work was not necessarily to cut costs, although all the projects were cost-effective. In Gateshead and Kent, care managers spent up to two-thirds of the cost of a residential bed in constructing a domiciliary care package. In Darlington alone, significant cost savings were achieved because the project was explicitly designed to provide an alternative to long-stay hospital care. Care managers were also given budgets. The success of the projects depended on them not just topping up domiciliary care services, but radically rethinking the nature of provision. The power to commission services, whether from the independent or the informal sector, was therefore crucial.

All the pilot projects were small in scale and case loads per care manager were kept low (at 25–30 clients). The work also focused on a single client group, elderly people. It has been suggested that problematic clients may have been filtered out (Means and Smith 1994), but targeting was in any case central to the projects. As Challis (1992) explained, if care management was applied to clients with lower levels of need, where the opportunity for substitution of institutional by community care was less, then there would be a possibility of rising costs. The PSSRU did not claim that there was an automatic link between structures and outcomes, or say that there would be improvement in the quality of life for users and carers if care managers with lower budgets and higher caseloads targeted high-priority cases (Davies 1992).

There were two crucial elements in the findings of the PSSRU, which fitted with the preoccupations of government: that gains in the quality of life for users and carers could be made at no greater cost, and that there was the possibility of engineering a shift from institutional to domiciliary care. Over 60 per cent of those receiving care management in the PSSRU pilot projects were enabled to stay at home, many more than in the control group. The first objective listed in the 1989 white paper was to encourage the targeting of home-based services on those people whose need for them is greatest.

However, generalising the kind of work carried out by the PSSRU to large populations of different kinds of clients posed new challenges, especially when SSDs were also being expected to implement purchaser–provider splits. The meaning of care management and the model to be adopted was by no means clear in many authorities in the early 1990s. In addition, there were also major tensions inherent in the role of the care manager, who was expected to make his or her practice needs-led, but who also had to be aware of resource constraints. Nor did government guidance give any indication as to where SSDs were expected to find large numbers of care managers with skills that were to range from the interpersonal to the capacity to handle a budget. Finally, there were tensions regarding the position of clients. The official guidance stressed the idea of a new kind of partnership between users, carers and care managers, but users were also being invited to exercise choice and act as consumers, which held out the possibility of more adversarial, rights-based behaviour, while the needs and interests of carers were quite likely to be different from those of users.

This chapter explores first what the research authorities made of the idea of care management and then goes on to look at the impact of care management on social work. The following chapter examines what have become the core elements of care management: assessment, in terms of the way in which this has been carried out and whether it in fact amounts to needs-led assessment, and the imposition of eligibility criteria for service.

Models of care management

The 1989 white paper implied that care management should be extended to all clients; however, the PSSRU projects had used a very particular form of intensive care management with clients on the brink of institutional care. The white paper and the guidance that followed talked about care management as a process, involving the publishing of information, determining the level of assessment, assessing needs, drawing up care plans, implementing care plans, monitoring and review. By the early 1990s, PSSRU researchers were making a distinction between intensive care management and a more general 'care management approach', meaning better procedures for assessment, individual care plans and regular reviews (Challis 1992; Challis 1994c; Davies and Knapp 1994). There was, though, no common understanding as to what care management meant and who should be care managed. Some authorities implemented 'universalist' models of care management, while some confined it to highly dependent clients; some sought to care manage all client groups in a similar manner, while others introduced a degree of client specialisation. As Davies (1994) has observed, local authorities have a tendency to rename rather than fundamentally to change, and in the early 1990s it was all too easy to conceptualise care management as a job rather than a process, and appoint 'care managers' with the idea that they should assess, and put together and coordinate a basket of services.

In the context of purchaser–provider splits, there was also a tendency to make care managers purchasers. The official guidance referred to the undesirability of past practice whereby assessment had been 'undertaken by a person with a vested interest in supplying that service' (Department of Health *et al.* 1991b: 17). If the pattern of service was to respond to need it was argued that assessment would have to be separated from service provision. However, making care managers purchasers was not necessarily straightforward. As Challis (1994a; see also Challis *et al.* 1995) has pointed out, the purchaser–provider split can be deceptively simple; while at the micro-level the care manager may be a purchaser, it is possible at the macro-level for care management to be commissioned as a service. As we have already seen, during the first year of implementation this characterised the position of care management in respect of people with HIV in borough B.

In addition, we have seen that SSDs proved resistant to devolving budgets to care managers, both because of reluctance to give up the economies of scale and the control that attach to centralised purchasing, and because of the long-standing British reluctance to mix social work with money. Indeed, Challis (1994a, b) warned that a too-rigid purchaser–provider split might give rise to an overly 'administrative' model of care management, whereby traditional social work skills were labelled as the prerogative of providers and squeezed out. He pointed out that 'the essence of the assessment process involves engaging a person, forming a relationship, giving advice, and therefore at an early stage, a range of human relationship skills including counselling' (Challis 1992: 19). In fact, none of the research authorities have ended up with a narrowly administrative care management model, although there were signs of such a model developing in borough A in the early 1990s.

The county

The county introduced care management with 'a bang' in September 1991, at the same time as it established the purchaser–provider split. Borough A followed the same pattern, but, unlike borough A, the county had from the beginning a clear concept of care management. What is difficult to account for in the case of the county is the slow development of principles into procedures. Care management procedures and guidelines were not finally clarified until the middle of 1993.

The SSD set up five care management pilot projects, which ran between July 1990 and September 1991. These explored a range of options; indeed, in the view of one respondent they represented various people's 'pet projects'. As was the common experience (Department of Health and Social Services Inspectorate 1991b), the overall evaluation of the pilots was not completed until after the introduction of care management and thus there was no time for all the lessons learned to inform the model of care management that was adopted. One prescient part of the general evaluation was the recognition that the importance of common assessment lay in the acceptance of one professional's assessment by another, rather than in the use of a single common assessment form. The evaluation also warned that monitoring and review would prove problematic, but no steps were taken to address these aspects of care management between 1991 and 1993. The value of pilot projects is in any case hard to assess. As one fourth-tier manager said in mid-1993:

> In pilot projects when things began to get a bit rough, they still had colleagues working in the old way to fall back on in terms of coping with overload. But once the department was completely different, everybody felt adrift and there was nothing of the old to hang on to.

The main function of the pilots in the county was probably to encourage staff to think in different ways, rather than systematically to map out new ways of working.

The care management system that was introduced in September 1991 involved the appointment of 480 care managers (out of a total staff of 3800), who were recruited from the department's social workers, occupational therapists and home care organisers, the common link being the skills these people were deemed to have in assessment. From the beginning, care management in the county was seen not just as, or even primarily as, care packaging and coordination, but rather as requiring relationship skills. As a second-tier manager put it:

> We are locating social work within care management, which means there is a continuing professional counselling, support, and reviewing role. And I think that's fundamental to our system, because it means that the expertise is on the purchasing side, which is where it should be. Assessment is not a mechanical operation, it's a skilled process that requires skilled practitioners, and it doesn't stop when you've done the assessment, you have to continue with your engagement. . . .

As we have seen, implementation of the purchaser–provider split in the county was undertaken in part out of a commitment to save social work services from externalisation.

The county opted for a 'universal' care management model in the sense that every person who has an 'enquiry interview' (which may or may not result in an assessment) comes into contact with a care manager. However, the imposition of eligibility criteria limits the number of clients receiving services. Thus the care packaging, monitoring and review tasks of care managers involve only those with the most complex needs. The skills of professional specialisms are still used and recognised within the model of a universal, single care manager. Teams within localities comprised workers specialising in children and families on the one hand and disability (including the elderly client group) on the other. A smaller number of multidisciplinary teams for people with learning difficulties and mental health problems coexisted with locality teams and worked on broadly the same principles. If a social worker (care manager) found that a client needed an occupational therapy assessment for a major adaptation, he or she made an internal referral to an occupational therapist on the team who would conduct that part of the assessment; thus the original care manager continued to coordinate the assessment, while calling on others to take part.

The county conceived its universalist model *in conjunction* with the move towards enabling. Senior managers rejected the idea of restricting the use of care managers to relatively few clients, embracing instead the idea of 'care management and commissioning'. This seemed to hold out the possibility of generating real change in the pattern of service provision for all clients: care management would be aligned with financial devolution and better-developed abilities on the part of care managers to capture needs, and to articulate and aggregate them. The close link between the SSD's thinking on care management and on purchasing was demonstrated during 1994, when the possibility of linking client review with contract ownership and accreditation was discussed.

The purchaser–provider split has nevertheless not been wholly unproblematic in respect of implementing care management. For example, in the view of some, though not all, social services managers, certain difficulties experienced by the community mental health and mental handicap teams, which comprised both health and social services workers, arose because the SSD members were deemed to be 'purchasers', while the health members were 'providers'. As elsewhere, the multiagency aspects of care management posed a number of challenges. In one half of the county a system was successfully devised whereby assessments carried out by all community psychiatric nurses (CPNs) who had been trained in the SSD assessment procedures were respected as a means of triggering SSD resources. In a few cases, general practitioners (GPs) tried to access SSD resources via non-trained CPNs, but this loophole was closed in November 1993. A more far-reaching problem was the conflicting pulls operating on the CPNs working within the joint teams. While GPs wanted them to work with non-acute clients, the SSD eligibility criteria were such that only clients with acute problems could be prioritised. However, in many respects the joint teams continued to work well and there was less reference in the county than elsewhere to difficulties arising from a conflict between care management and the care programme approach, introduced in 1991 for patients with mental illness being discharged from hospital.

Children and families teams have also experienced difficulties, in part because the design of care management processes has tended to be focused on adults, and in part because the goals of the new community care differ significantly from those of the Children Act. Whereas the former is about targeting and determining eligibility, and reducing the role of the SSD as a provider, work with children continues to be focused strongly on child protection and prevention, and the Act requires SSDs to work in partnership with families to support children.

The care management procedures and guidelines that were introduced by the county in 1991 were rather vague in many respects; for example, how to carry out an assessment was not spelled out, nor was it made clear which forms were to be used. As a result, care management procedures took different forms in the different localities. One locality manager said that he allowed care management procedures to evolve between 1991 and 1993 because of the stress experienced by care managers as a result of restructuring, and in the knowledge that procedures were going to be revised. When the new procedures were finally issued in mid-1993 he took personal responsibility for implementing these and carried out the training in his locality himself.

The long delay in reviewing care management procedures may be explained by: the trauma of restructuring; the fact that no single individual or group was given lead responsibility; the fact that the individuals who were given responsibility did not, or were unable to, make progress; and the lack of coordination and accountability within the purchasing division because of its 16 localities and east/west structure. While some major procedures, such as the use of the risk/needs matrix to determine eligibility for service, were accepted by all localities by the end of 1993, other practices continued to vary considerably. There was also the important problem of what amounted to an increasing awareness of the interdependence of procedures on the one hand and the requirements of information systems on the other. For example, the attempt to develop a care packaging system forced the department to refine its definition of an open and a closed case.

Thus the difficulties in implementing care management in the county provide an interesting example of the problem of implementing so many of the community care arrangements simultaneously. The sentence: 'Everything connects with/touches everything else' was frequently heard in meetings in the authority. In contrast, in borough C, aspects of care management proved hard to define because of the postponement of various aspects of the changes, in particular those relating to resourcing and purchasing. It is hard to see that there was any ideal way of timing the changes.

After the issuing of the new care management guidelines, practice across the county became more uniform. However, there were still some major gaps in the new guidelines; for example, clear monitoring procedures were not developed, although a start was made on these towards the end of the research period.

Borough A

Like the county, borough A introduced a system of care management at the same time that it established the purchaser–provider split in January 1992. Care managers were located in the purchasing division. However, just as it took borough A a while to develop a more sophisticated understanding of enabling with regard to social services, as opposed to the simple contracting-out model the borough had employed for non-human services, so there is evidence to suggest that care management was initially conceived of as a job rather than a process.

Some respondents in the borough believed strongly that there had been an antipathy towards social work on the part of some senior managers in the early 1990s. Even if that view was exaggerated, there was certainly a move to redefine the task of social work. According to one senior manager:

> it was also something to do with how social work was being perceived
> by the authority and the fact that as a social worker I could see that
> probably we had got ourselves into a situation where the role was so
> unclear, where we had become people that dabbled in all sorts of things
> rather than having our own professional expertise . . . so you can see
> that care management was also a reflection of the fact that we were
> trying to determine what skills were needed and whether they were

particularly in the social work profession, or whether there were other professions that could do it as well . . .

The way in which care managers were appointed differed profoundly from that in the county: very little regard was shown for assessment skills when care managers were appointed. All social workers were invited to apply for the specialist social work jobs that would remain in the field work division. Those who were unsuccessful were automatically offered a position as a care manager. Thus at the outset care managers tended to feel themselves second-class citizens. According to one third-tier manager:

> I think the fundamental mistake in [borough A] was that there was an assumption . . . that care management would be about rushing out and putting together a package of care in the most simplistic way; I think they thought all care management clients would be simple 'home care' clients – they just needed a few hours of personal care, you put that together and you can close that within weeks.

Another third-tier manager reiterated the view that, initially, borough A had seen care management primarily as an 'administrative/financial task . . . something you could obtain via a checklist'. Yet another said: 'I think they thought that it would turn the whole process of dealing with elderly and disabled people into an administrative process and that people would go out and do an assessment according to a formula . . .'. This was an extreme version of the PSSRU's model of 'administrative' care management and something that was much feared in the social work profession (e.g. Smale and Tuson 1993; Smale et al. 1994). There had been no care management pilot work in borough A. However, a pilot testing the purchaser–provider split within home care separated assessment from provision and pointed towards an administrative model of care management whereby care managers assessed for services.

In addition, the model of care management implemented in 1992 was universalist in the sense that all clients requesting assessment came into contact with a care manager and that the same model of care management was implemented across client groups. This meant that overnight the borough went from fairly specialist intake teams to a situation in which care managers with a home care background might end up interviewing the parents of a disturbed 14-year-old. The idea seems to have been that such a client would be passed rapidly on to the specialised social workers in the field work division, in other words, that social work was to be a service provided as a result of care management rather than as part of a care management assessment. However, concern about inappropriate initial assessments led to the field work division setting up its own duty desk in 1992. This caused considerable conflict because care managers felt that the field work teams could be highly selective.

Almost as soon as it was implemented, the care management system was subjected to review. By September 1992, the importance of skilled, specialist assessment was being recognised. A senior purchaser said:

> There are a significant number of clients now being dealt with by staff in care management teams, who have complex long-term problems and it is felt that those clients would receive a better service if dealt with by an experienced worker with specialist knowledge and skills.

The same senior purchaser spoke early in 1993 of the need 'to blur' the purchaser–provider split in such a way that care managers could practise their counselling skills. By the middle of 1994, there was widespread conviction in the department about the need for a shift towards more specialised practice. According to the same informant:

> I don't think the idea of generic care management is tenable over a long period . . . I think we have realised that community care is something a little more sophisticated than that and does involve some kind of varied sensitive interaction between the assessor and the user, but what increasingly we are aware of is the person doing the assessment does need to have a body of knowledge and expertise to build up an understanding about the particular sets of needs with which they are confronted . . .

The conflict between the field work and care management divisions was also solved at the end of 1993 by effectively making field work a children and families division, with the staff retaining the title social worker, while care management was renamed community care and continued to employ care managers.

Thus in borough A there has been a move away from seeing care management in rather mechanistic terms, which has in turn been accompanied by a move towards greater specialisation and a recognition of social work's traditional assessment skills. This important shift has been paralleled by a reconceptualisation of enabling, although it still tends to be true that the bulk of a care manager's time in borough A is taken up by assessment for off-the-shelf services. The borough's model of care management has been largely confined to assessment and care packaging. The increased burden of assessment made it likely at the end of 1994 that the SSD would opt for a distinct category of workers to carry out reviews.

Borough B

Borough B began its thinking about the new policy of community care by focusing on care management; the borough did not move decisively towards developing its purchasing function until the second half of 1992. As a senior manager put it in mid-1993:

it started really from the view that the reforms won't mean anything if we put in place structures that you don't feel good about – they will only affect change if the person's experience is different. We started from an approach with care management which would try to make the experience different.

Like borough C, borough B participated in a King's Fund workshop on care management and assessment in mid–1992 and came away strengthened in its commitment to user-centredness.

From the beginning, this borough rejected the idea of care management as an administrative process. A senior purchaser said firmly that in no way was care management envisaged as:

> a tick box, mechanistic sort of process . . . I mean somewhere along the line, there was an idea that care management was like going into Sainsbury's where you picked the package of services, and put them together in a little basket, but it is a much more complex process than that, in terms of really working out what needs are, it is a very skilled task.

As in the county, senior managers in this borough saw care management drawing on traditional social work skills, especially in the realm of assessment:

> I am certainly convinced that the initial assessment and the initial negotiation of the care package is a social work task. Maybe other workers can do it, but I think social work is the best profession suited to do that work.

The county recruited care managers from the ranks of those who were considered to have developed specialist assessment skills, for example home care organisers, but in borough B care managers are social workers. Indeed, social workers in this borough had substantial input into the formulation of the care management model.

Borough B's model of care management was not universal, as it was in the county and borough A. Not every client came into contact with a care manager. The borough set up a wide range of pilot projects between 1992 and 1993, although there was no time to evaluate these before the care management system was implemented in April 1993. It seems that the pilots served the purpose of, as one senior manager put it, 'getting people into the thinking, into gear', or, as another said, they were a way of carrying staff along with the changes.

The HIV pilot was particularly influential, although aspects of other pilot work, such as the brokerage scheme used in an independent living pilot, have also been developed, even though such models did not provide the organising framework for care management. Assessment was separated from purchasing in respect of HIV clients in 1991, when an HIV commissioning unit was set up. In part this was because the HIV client group was new and social workers quickly found that established ways of working with these clients would not do (for example, an offer of meals on wheels was not usually welcomed), and in part because money was not tied to existing services, as it was for other client groups. This pilot confirmed that social workers were best placed to carry out the care management tasks of assessment and care packaging; it developed a common assessment form; and it demonstrated that not all clients needed to be care managed. Thus, care management was being defined in the sense of 'intensive' work on the lines of the PSSRU definition. The same principles were believed to underpin care management practice for all client groups. However, the borough introduced specialist social work in 1991 and has maintained specialist contact under the care management system.

Care management in borough B was therefore understood as something that would be confined to highly dependent people, drawing on the 'new' STG moneys. This is a model that the county consciously rejected because it believed that care management had to be linked to commissioning for all clients in order to change the pattern of service across the board. In this view, the danger of borough B's model is that changes in the pattern of service provision will be achieved for only a minority of clients.

The borough's initial work on needs-led budgeting for the financial year 1993/4 showed that it could afford to purchase residential/nursing home care (or care packages in the community at a similar cost) for only 65 clients, and it was therefore agreed that eligibility criteria for care management should seek to include only highly dependent clients. The number of complex assessments carried out was much higher than predicted during the first year of implementation, although the number of residential and nursing home placements made was close to the estimates, reflecting the tight eligibility criteria. At the end of the research period, borough B was intending to review more stable clients, such as those in residential care, separately, using social work assistants.

Because not all clients came in contact with a care manager, there was more chance of care management becoming a service that was available only after assessment. Thus while care managers were designated as purchasers, as the borough developed its purchasing function in 1993, care management for clients with HIV became a service that the commissioning unit purchased via a service-level agreement.

Senior managers have also discussed the possibility of commissioning care management for particular ethnic groups. Given that care managers hold only a small spot purchasing budget, because of the strong conviction that 'the assessing role doesn't quite fit with rationing', and because of the emergence of a model of commissioning in which the commissioning unit aims to set up a 'menu' of services from which care managers may draw (see Chapter 5), the purchasing and providing roles of care managers were somewhat blurred.

Borough C

Borough C implemented new assessment procedures in April 1993, as it was obliged to do by the legislation, but implementation of care management has taken much longer, with a system still under discussion at the close of the research period. Borough C's incrementalist approach has posed problems; in particular it has proved difficult to graft care management on to the assessment system that was developed in 1992/3. In large part this was because the assessment system entailed the adoption of 'care coordination', which had the potential to deliver much of the care management process as defined by the government guidance, but which was in many ways closer to a key worker system.

Borough C began the process of implementing the new policy of community care with a firm commitment to the user and to meeting users' needs via changes in assessment and organisation, rather than via the commitment to both care management and the diversification of supply through enabling, which characterised the county from the beginning and which came also to be the hallmark of borough B. The new process of assessment and care coordination was developed in borough C during a period when the purchaser–provider split was confined to a single division. Senior managers in the borough had little taste for the PSSRU experiments, which they strongly associated with making social workers into gatekeepers and budget holders. As a team leader said in mid-1993:

> Care management to me means money. A care coordinator does exactly what a care manager does without the money. If you've got a care manager with a budget, making an assessment, putting together a care plan and monitoring an assessment etc., there's a conflict, because that person controls the budget yet makes an assessment that is weighed down with responsibilities of managing the finances for which he or she is responsible.

Care coordination was linked firmly to joint working; it was intended that a worker from any agency should be able to become the care coordinator for a client – the only criterion was closeness to the client. However, it proved difficult to realise this multiagency ideal and a model using mainly SSD social work staff became increasingly the *de facto* reality for the most complex cases. Thus in February 1994, it was agreed that SSD staff would undertake all comprehensive assessments, although this decision was later modified out of a lingering respect for the multiagency model to allow staff from other agencies to undertake such assessments if they made a special arrangement with the SSD to do so. As the SSD also moved towards consolidating a high and firm purchaser–provider split, further questions were raised about the position of care coordinators. In 1993/4, the borough moved away from its original conception of care coordination towards a form of assessment and care management located within purchasing that had more in common with other authorities.

The borough thoroughly piloted and evaluated its scheme for assessment and care coordination between May and November 1992 and indeed continued to carry out thorough evaluations following the introduction of the system in April 1993. In this it was unique among the research authorities. The thinking on care coordination may in fact be traced back to the late 1980s, when reference was made to the intention 'to obviate the need for a plethora of different people dropping in to see the older person, all seeking answers to similar questions'.

The pilot was largely devised and run by fourth-tier staff and proved extremely influential, because, according to one of those involved, there was nothing else on offer. The pilot was focused on the needs of older people. It tested the idea of three levels of assessment and developed the notion of the care coordinator as the primary contact point for the user, liaising across agencies, furthering information flow and instigating review. A client approaching the department was assessed by a care coordinator, who might come from any agency and any part of the SSD. The care coordinator then organised a 'network meeting', which was compared to a case conference, at which another care coordinator might be appointed. The model envisaged several possible changes in the person of care coordinator, according to changes in the circumstances of the client, the overriding principle always being proximity to the user. This pilot formed the basis of what was introduced in April 1993.

The assessment and care coordination system received considerable support from front-line workers in the SSD and from voluntary agencies, but it proved difficult to implement. An exploration of the system of assessment and coordination for people with mental health problems undertaken in late 1993 found that while the system was supposed to be applicable to all client groups, with assessors using a common assessment form, mental health social workers preferred to follow the care programme approach. (As Schneider (1993) has pointed out, care programming is led by health authorities, while care management is led by local authorities.) Specialist social workers in the mental health field argued that: the population in need of care was known to them and required continuous reassessment, rather than the assessment (often at a time of crisis) and care plan approach of care management; accountability for the client rested with the consultant psychiatrist for those detained compulsorily under the Mental Health Act; key workers often came from the health service; and the forms for the care programme approach overlapped with the form relating to general assessment of need, designed for use by care coordinators. Thus even though borough C was explicitly committed to joint working, it did not prove easy to implement a common system across client groups. Other specialist workers also objected to a universalist approach, but were happier to use the common assessment form once it was established that it was not intended to replace specialist assessment altogether.

Practical difficulties also dogged the multiagency care coordination model. For example, district nurses had limited access to the photocopiers necessary for inter-agency working and were in addition reluctant to spend the time carrying out comprehensive assessments in cases where they were unlikely to end up providing the majority of the care. Voluntary organisations also found that they were unable to bear the costs of carrying out assessments and acting as care coordinators. Because the SSD had made no progress in transferring budgets, there was no immediate way of solving these resource issues. In 1993/4 it seems that senior managers devoted their attention to developing a new care management system rather than solving the problems of care coordination. In mid-1993 one described the value of the multiagency, customer-focused assessment process in terms of 'teaching each other to trust each other, . . . it must be the ambition in three years' time to downsize some of this investment'. Possibly the care coordination model was perceived as being too ambitious.

Care management began to be discussed in 1992, but there was considerable confusion in the papers on the subject as to its meaning and in particular as to whether care managers could be providers as well as purchasers. This continued well into 1993, when a senior manager expressed the view that long-term care managers would almost certainly be providers. During 1993 and 1994, a care management system was discussed largely outside the realm of the formal joint planning machinery, in which the department had invested so heavily and which was designed to take forward the process of implementation. In part, this was because care management was designated by central government as a social services responsibility, and in part it was a reflection of the difficulty of achieving decisions via the complicated joint planning machinery established in the borough.

A 'planning and review' model of care management was designed by purchasers and piloted in the borough in late 1993 and early 1994. The authority's 1994/5 community care plan referred to care management as 'the process which takes place after services have been agreed'. This model of care management was thus designed to be grafted on to the existing assessment and care coordination system. It envisaged providers monitoring the needs of those receiving comprehensive assessments and members of a planning and review team carrying out reviews. The idea was not to effect a radical transformation of social work practice, but rather to promote good practice within the existing system. Despite the substantial amount of time and effort invested in piloting this system of care management, it was not implemented, and towards the end of the research period other possibilities were being discussed. One idea was that social services' purchasing staff would carry out comprehensive assessments and would also be responsible for review, except in the case of out-of-borough placements, where providers would undertake reviews.

It seems, then, that the separation of different parts of the care management process was felt not to be desirable in most cases, besides which, questions of cost and feasibility came increasingly to influence the perceptions of which model should be adopted.

Thus, while borough C clearly understood care management as a process, implementation was rather slow and rather messy. The borough adopted an incremental, 'learning by doing' approach. This was determined in part by central government's imposed timetable, which meant that the borough had to adopt an assessment system only by April 1993 and could postpone the implementation of care management; in part by the lack of clear direction from senior management in respect of developing a system before the summer of 1993, when the purchaser–provider split became firmer and the responsibility for developing care management changed (it is notable that the 1992 pilot was devised and run by fourth-tier staff); and in part by the lack of progress regarding other aspects of the changes required by the new system. In particular, the lack of development of purchasing made it difficult to make decisions about the location and operation of care management. Thus, whereas the county and borough A implemented complete care management systems and then faced second-order problems, borough C experienced a continually evolving system. Front-line staff in the borough seemed to have little faith that the latest variant in care management would be the last, and practice has therefore been variable.

Borough D

At the end of 1994, borough D had not implemented a care management system nor had any care managers been appointed, even though two external consultants had been employed to look at assessment and care management systems, as they had been to help establish the purchaser–provider split. The borough conducted pilot projects on assessment and implemented an assessment system, as it was required to do, in April 1993, but in the absence of any other progress in implementing the changes this proved problematic, as senior staff acknowledged:

> I think we recognised very soon after April [1993] that implementing just an assessment system caused us many problems. We had one set of assessment systems in the areas, financial assessment that happened centrally, and budget holders on the provider side, and I think there have been no end of problems with that.

A report from external consultants in mid-1993 revealed support for a universal model of care management, covering all client groups and involving specialist social work, but there was disagreement about whether care managers should hold budgets. Disagreement on how a care management system should relate to the purchaser–provider split (which was established at the end of 1992, although restructuring was still not complete at the end of 1994) was revealed at meetings with the consultants at the end of 1993. In particular, different views were expressed on whether assessment should be separate from purchasing and on whether social work should be a providing function.

The existence of a model for establishing a purchaser–provider split effectively constrained the choice of a model of care management. The consultants proposed five possible models:

(i) designated care managers within either a specialist or a generic team, and either centrally or area based, and probably located in purchasing;

(ii) a model whereby workers from a variety of disciplines could be appointed to work as care managers;

(iii) a care management team that would be located in purchasing and carry out all complex assessments;

(iv) a service brokerage model in which a single worker or agency acts on behalf of the client;

(v) service users acting as their own advocates or care managers.

Given the commitment to a high and firm purchaser–provider split, only (i) and (iii) were feasible, although adopting one of these as the structural model would not necessarily have ruled out the additional use of brokerage, for example, as the case of borough B has shown. The borough decided to adopt model (i) and at the end of 1994 was planning to replace the teams of social workers headed by a social work team leader by teams of care managers headed by a commissioning manager with responsibility for a particular client group.

Thus as with purchasing, change in borough D had not proceeded past the planning stage by the end of the research period. In contrast to all the other authorities, there was very little understanding of the meaning of care management; respondents often found it difficult to articulate their views on needs-led assessment, for example. A director of a voluntary organisation remarked: 'It is the ethos and culture ... you can piddle about with the structures until kingdom come; it is about changing the ethos. The thing about [borough D] is that there is not a climate of change ...'. A senior manager in the SSD also recognised this fundamental problem:

I suppose in a sense it feels like nothing has happened and the real shift we have to make is not about which model but a cultural one, the way social workers perceive their role in the future and their relationship with money; until we shift that culture, it doesn't matter what model you've got.

These views underline the importance of senior managers having a clear vision of the changes and what they hoped to achieve, together with the ability to communicate them.

Discussion

There has been a tendency in all authorities for a single-worker, single-agency model to evolve. The county and borough A employed occupational therapists and home care organisers as care managers, but in the county their numbers were relatively small and in borough A there has been some talk of the possibility of making a social work qualification a requirement for newly appointed care managers. Borough C was particularly committed to a multiagency, multidisciplinary model, but this proved difficult to sustain in the case of comprehensive assessments for a number of reasons: voluntary organisations and health workers lacked resources to do the work; the care coordination model was linked firmly to assessment, but not to other parts of the care management process; and the SSD had to rethink the model in the light of the consolidation of a purchaser–provider split and the cost implications of care management.

All authorities experienced difficulties in developing a model of care management, but it seems that where all aspects of the process were considered together from the first, as in the county, there was at least a firmer sense of direction. However, all authorities have lagged behind in implementing the tasks of monitoring and review. Historically, review has tended to be neglected in SSDs, and they face large resource problems in instituting systematic review.

Only one authority, borough A, began by conceptualising care management in administrative terms, but this borough quickly changed its approach. However, the nature of social work practice has changed as a result of the shift to care management, because of the increased burden of assessment that it brings, and because of the increasing emphasis on work with highly dependent people.

There has also been a shift towards more specialisation on the basis of client group. In borough C, procedures used in work with children proved influential in developing aspects of care coordination. However, in the other authorities and in the work of the PSSRU, the development of care management procedures was driven by work with elderly people, and difficulties have been encountered in generalising them to other client groups, for example to people with mental illness, for whom the care programme approach was already in existence, and to children. The Department of Health (1993a, 1994b) has commented on the lack of integration between care management and the care programme approach and has noted that little guidance was given to authorities on how to operate both.

In respect of children, having generalised care management to all client groups, borough A established a separate children and families division at the end of 1993. The emphasis on prevention in work with children has proved particularly difficult to reconcile with the much lower priority accorded to prevention in work with elderly people.

Care management was implemented in the context of moving towards enabling, and there was nothing in the PSSRU experiments to guide authorities in this respect. In the county, care management and commissioning were linked *conceptually* from the outset, even though this did not prevent procedural difficulties from arising. In borough D, where the meanings of both care management and enabling were less well understood, the prior existence of a purchasing–providing structure effectively determined the choice of a structure for care management. There is an irony about this, in that nowhere have budgets been devolved to care managers, despite their designation as purchasers. Care managers have taken responsibility for authorising expenditure, but it has been the commissioning structure as a whole that has been central to the effort to change the pattern of service for users. In the county, the logic of this situation was interpreted to mean that all clients had to be in touch with a care manager, although only some would be intensively care managed after assessment. In borough B, the changes have been deliberately more limited; only new, highly dependent clients come into contact with care managers, who use the new STG moneys to provide packages of care.

A large part of the reason why care management has developed relatively slowly, despite being a part of the changes that most authorities felt some affinity towards, is the problem of linking it to other parts of the new community care policy. The pilots run by authorities, usually on a particular aspect of care management, had little relevance when it came to generalising procedures across departments and across client groups, and relating them to purchasing systems.

The job of care manager

The 1989 white paper seemed to suggest a care manager who combined management, financial and interpersonal skills, who was, in other words, above even the trained social worker. But in fact government thinking on the role of care managers was very woolly. After all, the 1988 Griffiths report had seemed to suggest that very few skills were required to coordinate care for older people. Social workers certainly feared that the job of care manager would effectively deskill them. As one third-tier manager in borough B said:

> If we have a robotic interpretation of care management it is deskilling, and I think in the very early stages I was worried that social workers would go with the form in their left hand and knocking on the door with

the right, saying I have an hour, I have this form to complete, what is your name, date of birth? Now anybody can do that, it doesn't require social work skills . . . I think they are more comfortable now that what they must do is exercise the skills they have had in terms of interviewing technique, not leading people, but the whole exchange bit about getting people to articulate what their problems are.

As we have already seen, ideas about care management as a purely mechanistic process easy to generalise to all client groups were relatively rare, despite the fears of social work professionals, and disappeared quite rapidly. Nevertheless, care management has involved substantial changes in ways of working for front-line workers and these have particularly affected social workers.

The workload of care managers is very hard to assess. In borough C, for example, cross-agency work makes it hard to measure the workload of care coordinators. Generally, care managers tended to have large numbers of cases, but not more than 25–30 needing intensive work. In the county, for example, a case remained 'active' until the care package was put in place and the first six-week review carried out. If the services provided were agreed to be satisfactory, the case was then classified as 'open but inactive' and became the responsibility of the team rather than a named care manager. However, the nature of the work required of the care manager is significantly different from the kind of work traditionally prized by social workers.

Two changes are of particular importance: (i) that an increasing proportion of care managers' time is taken up with clients who are heavily dependent; and (ii) that there seems to be less time available for care managers to counsel clients. More time is devoted to the more practical tasks that were arguably always done by social workers, but that were accorded less prestige. These changes are of course linked. Among several pieces of research analysing the work of care managers in the county during 1993 and 1994, one study revealed that they spent 80 per cent of their time on clients falling into the top three priority categories. Social work assistants tended to work with clients in the lowest priority groups. Only one-fifth of the care manager's time was spent on direct work with clients, yet, as Wilson (1993) has shown, it is this kind of work that staff report as giving the highest levels of job satisfaction.

Care packages for clients with high levels of dependency can be very complicated. For example, a disabled client in the county was receiving home care twice a day and visits from the night warden scheme twice at night. She visited three different day centres during the week, two voluntary organisations provided the transport, and a laundry and a delivery service provided incontinence pads. If one of these elements broke down, the care manager had to find an alternative quickly or the whole package was endangered.

The administrative work necessary for collecting information on clients for assessments and planning and coordinating packages of care loom much larger in care management than in social work. A locality manager in the county cited the example of a client who had suffered a stroke and who needed a substantial care package to illustrate the difficulty the care manager had in doing anything more than assessment and care packaging. As a result of the assessment process, the care manager involved in this case felt that the client and his wife/carer needed help in coming to terms with the changes that the illness had brought about, especially in view of the fact that the illness had revealed difficulties in the relationship between the client and his wife. The care manager felt that counselling was essential if the caring relationship was not to break down with the result that the client would require more services from the local authority. However, the demand for assessments for equally high-priority clients was such that the counselling did not take place, to the frustration of the care manager. Concern about both the loss of work in respect of emotional needs and the pressure to complete assessments in line with the agreements signed with health authorities on arrangements for hospital discharge was also expressed by social workers in borough B.

Thus while there has been a general recognition of the importance of traditional social work skills to the work of care management, particularly in relation to assessment, the balance of work has nonetheless swung firmly away from counselling. The burden of increasing administrative work has been especially resented. In borough A, a third-tier manager said:

> I think people have felt weighed down with the extra paperwork . . . and they feel the department wants to turn them into administrators and financial processors. All the emphasis is on filling out forms, and a lot of staff are saying 'That isn't what I was trained to do . . .'.

Similar concern at the increase in bureaucracy was expressed by staff across the research authorities. This disquiet may be a component of what Pahl (1994) described as a growing cynicism among front-line staff about the community care changes. Our interviewing was done in the main with senior managers, but limited observation of front-line workers on duty desks in the research authorities revealed less enthusiasm for the reforms among them than among senior managers, something that has also been commented upon by Nixon (1993).

The status of care management *vis-à-vis* social work remains an issue. In the county, social workers and occupational therapists fought to retain their professional identities in their job titles: social worker (care manager) and occupational therapist (care manager). Interestingly, home care organisers are known simply as care managers, reflecting difference in their perceived status at the outset. Similar examples can be found in the other authorities. In borough C, a director of a voluntary organisation reported that when social workers were asked if they were a care coordinator, they would reply: 'No, I am a social worker.' In borough A, care managers initially felt themselves to be second-class citizens and additionally found themselves without a career hierarchy; team leaders were removed in the reorganisation of January 1992. Gradually more supervisory grades have been reintroduced, so that the number of tiers in the care management division have expanded from a very flattened four to seven (see Chapter 4). After the reorganisation of late 1993, which once again separated work with adults from that with children, the social workers in the community care division were told that they must retain the title care manager, but those in the children and families division continued to use the title of social worker.

Resistance to care management was grounded in the fear that it would erode much valued aspects of social work practice. The wider aspects of the community care changes have been driven by managerial rather than by professional processes (James 1994). Traditionally, SSDs ran their finance and administration divisions with a managerial approach and their operations divisions with a professional one. The introduction of the purchaser–provider split and the location of care management in purchasing has meant that this is no longer so. The work of the care manager is part of a developing purchasing function and, even if care managers do not hold budgets, they must provide information for purchasers and often authorise expenditure. Some of the biggest changes in the county were experienced by staff who used to concentrate on the work of professional supervision. To their jobs the financial work associated with authorising expenditure was added to that of professional supervision, while they were also engaged in seeking new providers in the independent sector. The Department of Health's (1994b) monitoring report on care management commented on the way in which the work of team leaders was beginning to focus more on budgets.

The nature of the career ladder open to care managers has thus changed significantly. Nevertheless, a third-tier manager in borough A felt that care management might prove 'the saviour' of the social work profession,

> because for many people in the country social workers are synonymous with ineptness, or with people who really aren't able to think clearly about what should be done or how things should be handled . . . care management in one sense is a kind of social work with a financial responsibility added on to it . . . [we shall] actually move away from sort of doing the 1950s/1960s therapy.

In this interpretation, the greater emphasis on practical work within the context of a purchasing discipline is positive for the professional image of social work.

Conclusion

As with the development of purchasing structures and strategies, a coherent conceptual framework together with commitment and leadership on the part of senior managers has been crucial to the development of care management systems. We found wide variation between the models of care management in the research authorities. Understandings of care management differed widely in the early 1990s, and the government's requirement that an assessment system be put in place by April 1993 meant that many authorities concentrated on developing this without giving sufficient thought to the whole process of care management. Even in authorities that did take the larger view, the resource problems of implementing all aspects of the care management process, particularly systematic review, have yet to be solved.

The Department of Health's (1994b) investigation of care management also found widespread variation, which they explained as follows:

> The message of the practice guidance that a differentiated strategy was a logistical necessity, reinforced by the PSSRU research finding that the intensive model was only likely to be cost effective for the minority of users with the most complex needs, did not appear to have impacted upon initial strategic thinking about the implementation of care management.
>
> (para. 5.6)

This is not quite fair. The PSSRU certainly began to hammer home its message about targeting the highly dependent from the late 1980s. But the 1989 white paper read as if care management should be generalised to all client groups. Nor was it ever clear where the people with the requisite care management skills were to come from or how they were to be trained. The 1991 practice guidance described many different models, but was not prescriptive (Department of Health *et al.* 1991b). Care management was described as the cornerstone of the changes, but government guidance was most confused on this aspect of the reforms. After 1991, the central government became much more preoccupied with how to manage the social care market.

Besides which, authorities faced the problem of implementing care management *together* with purchaser–provider splits on their own. No element of the guidance addressed the problems of implementing different aspects of the changes together. It seems in fact that whether care management and enabling were implemented simultaneously, or whether sequentially and in piecemeal fashion, there have been problems. The process of becoming an enabling authority has had a major effect on care management. In borough C it influenced the shift away from the care coordination model as it was originally conceived, and in borough D it effectively dictated the choice of care management model. Only the county linked the two aspects of the changes conceptually, which was a major strength, even though the authority faced major challenges in actually making the links between the two operational. Borough A has ended up with a not dissimilar model, but the development of the purchasing function was much slower, particularly in relation to the stimulation of the provision of independent domiciliary care, which means that care managers have much less room for manoeuvre when it comes to care packaging. Borough B has been less ambitious, seeking only to implement care management for the highly dependent. It is not clear that there has been much change for less dependent clients.

Care management changed the way in which social workers function. This has not been so much a matter of a move towards mechanistic practice, as was feared, but rather a change in the balance of activity towards the administrative tasks involved in assessment and care packaging. There is evidence that increasing bureaucracy, due to both care management and purchasing, has created a gap between front-line workers and senior managers, with the latter expressing more enthusiasm for and belief in the changes than the former during the research period. It is also the case that there has been a fundamental shift away from the dominance of the professional culture. The team leader is now less a professional supervisor and more a manager with financial responsibility, which has implications for how social workers at the start of their career see their job developing and hence for social work training.

8

Care management. II: Assessing need and deciding eligibility for service

The nature of assessment

The official guidance on assessment and care management made it clear that the process of assessment was crucial to securing needs-led services (Department of Health, Social Services Inspectorate and Scottish Office Social Work Services Group 1991a, b). SSDs were told to assess needs and only then to think about the best way of meeting them. It was believed that in the old system providers of services had inevitably fitted need into the pattern of existing services. The new approach would mean that purchasers would go out and find services that would actually meet need. One of the central questions begged by this new approach thus became whether assessors would be able to divorce the assessment of needs from what they knew was or was not available by way of service.

All authorities were obliged to have an assessment system in place by April 1993 and, as we have seen, many of the care management pilot projects carried out by the research authorities were dominated by assessment. Despite this, assessment systems have proved difficult to establish, and despite the early realisation that needs-based assessment could not be a mechanistic exercise, the development of an appropriate assessment system has tended to be dominated by the search for the right set of levels for assessment and the right set of forms.

Levels of assessment

The 1991 guidance referred to the possibility of six levels of assessment (Department of Health, Social Services Inspectorate and Scottish Office Social Work Services Group 1991a). It is therefore not surprising that most authorities began with the idea of establishing at least three or four levels of assessment. However, the trend in all cases has been towards simplification. In addition, the PSSRU research in particular emphasised the importance of screening to establish which level of assessment a client needed. However, in universal models of care management there has tended to be a commitment to open-access assessment.

The county was alone in not differentiating between levels of assessment from the beginning. Staff did not wish to judge the level of assessment needed before becoming familiar with the circumstances of the client. There were a number of forms in the county comprising a full assessment portfolio. The idea was that the assessment 'builds', with the possibility of more information being collected by various professionals as the need for further investigation unfolds. One senior manager estimated during 1993 that of those approaching the SSD, half were offered information and half progressed to further assessment. Inevitably, there has to be some prioritisation for assessment and in some localities care managers allocated a score on the risk/needs matrix (see below) after first meeting the client and used that to prioritise for assessment, revising the score at the end of the assessment process. One locality manager expressed horror at the idea of different levels of assessment: 'It sounds appalling . . . How can you tell?'

Clear differentiation between levels of assessment has indeed proved problematic elsewhere. In April 1993, borough A had an essentially two-stage assessment process. The first stage consisted of a common assessment form that could be completed by any agency or by the user him/herself. The idea was that where a predominantly health need was revealed, the client would be referred to the NHS and where the need was predominantly social, to the SSD. The common assessment form for the first stage was abandoned in 1994 because the level of information collected was perceived as being too detailed for the duty desk and not detailed enough for other professionals. It was also felt that the form was confusing for users. During 1994, the department replaced the form with a leaflet explaining the assessment process. For people requiring a simple service, such as a bus pass, appropriate documentation was enough to trigger service. Where the referral appeared to be more complicated, a one-sheet referral form was completed and a further, more detailed form was used as more complex needs were assessed.

The second stage of assessment used a form that was supposed to be a prompt, rather than dictating the nature of assessment. Eligibility for assessment was decided on the basis of urgency: category 1 included those where there was substantial risk to life, or risk of major injury or admission to long-term care caused by, for example, carer loss or breakdown; category 2 included those whose carers were showing severe stress, or who were experiencing acute physical or mental deterioration; category 3 was low priority and could apply to clients who were previously in the first two categories and who required regular support, or to clients whose safety was at some risk; category 4 had no priority and referred to clients for whom intervention was desirable to improve or enhance the quality of life.

There were problems in borough A in distinguishing exactly when an assessment became comprehensive. A third-tier manager said:

I have a problem about this notion about simple and complex; people move backwards and forwards. It seems to me that I may today have a simple need, but tomorrow a more complex need, the following day more simple again, so what do I do? Do I get passed backwards and forwards within the organisation? I hope not . . . I think my preference would be that the people who deal with the complex needs also deal with the simple needs, however you define that . . .

Similar problems have arisen in borough B in terms of distinguishing what happens in the middle ground between simple and comprehensive assessment. The latter was carried out by a care manager and the need for it was defined by the client being highly dependent. This was something of a tautology, in that access to comprehensive assessment was based on meeting the need for care management. Borough B operated three levels of assessment. Simple was similar to that in borough A; it involved the request for a simple service and was granted or denied by the duty teams. Core or service assessments involved assessment for two services, both provided by the local authority. Unlike in borough A, these assessments might be done by providers; for example, home care would assess for that service. Information on referral was often insufficient to decide whether there was a case for comprehensive assessment, so the duty worker would visit to collect more information. One fourth-tier manager said in July 1994 that she had never firmly distinguished between the three levels of assessment.

Borough C began by distinguishing four levels of assessment in one of its pilot projects: simple, limited, specialist, and comprehensive. The pilot found that very few clients needed specialist assessment; those requiring a single specialist service in fact usually needed simple assessment, for an occupational therapy aid, for example. It was also found that 'limited' did not adequately describe the kind of assessment that happened between the simple and comprehensive levels. As a result, borough C's intermediate level of assessment was called 'multiple'. Multiple assessments were supposed to be for those with a range of needs and where one or more agencies might be involved, but where there was no threat to independent living.

The criteria for comprehensive assessment were situations in which there was a threat to independent living, where it was likely that a number of agencies would be involved in providing care, or where a user had asked to move into residential care. While the criteria for multiple and comprehensive assessments were couched in terms of levels of dependency, further explanation of the criteria was given in terms of likely level of service response, albeit with no prescription as to the type of service. The same form for general assessment of needs was used for both multiple and comprehensive assessments, but staff from any agency (purchaser or provider) could undertake multiple (and simple) assessments.

There was a lack of consistency in operationalising multiple assessment and the distinction between it and both simple and comprehensive assessment was blurred. For example, if a person needed a major occupational therapy adaptation then this might or might not be classified as a multiple assessment. The older persons team experimented with a schema that set priorities for assessment against levels of assessment. This showed that it was possible for a user to be categorised as high priority and yet get a simple assessment, or be medium priority and be eligible for a comprehensive assessment. A combination of factors determined the level of assessment, one of them being the capacity of the carer to care.

Borough D also introduced three levels of assessment in April 1993, with a different form for each. Initial assessment was designed for those requesting a single service; in practice, these assessments often constituted the first part of a further assessment. Limited assessments were carried out by trained and untrained staff from a variety of disciplines, but were in turn hard to distinguish from comprehensive assessments, which were carried out by social workers. At a training day in March 1993, it was found that the outcomes of limited and comprehensive assessments were very similar. At the end of 1993 the poor quality of assessments was acknowledged at a meeting of the Community Care Umbrella Group and a new, open-ended assessment form was proposed for use with all users other than those seeking a simple service. Thus borough D has moved towards a two-stage system of assessment similar to that of borough A.

Authorities that followed the official guidance and tried to establish levels of assessment have experienced severe difficulties, which begs the question as to why it was considered necessary to distinguish between levels. The Department of Health *et al.*'s (1991a) *Managers' Guide* on assessment and care management stressed the importance of allocating the right grade of staff to undertake a particular kind of assessment (paras 2, 13–14). Given the increased burden of assessment falling on authorities as a result of the new system, this is an important consideration, but the problem has been resolved in the county by conceptualising assessment as a continuum and drawing staff into the process as and when it is deemed appropriate. This seems to have clear advantages, especially for authorities operating a universal care management model. Not only are staff drawn in as they are needed, but the authority obviates the need to set eligibility criteria for assessment and does not have to worry about what happens to people who turn out to need a different form of assessment from the one they requested or were allocated. In the case of borough B, which does not operate a universal care management system, the position is a little different. Here it was inevitable that there would be something of a link between the level of service anticipated and the level of assessment; the criteria for comprehensive assessment were allied to the need for intensive care management.

The PSSRU model of care management stressed that clients should be screened, in the sense of allocated to the right level of assessment or filtered

Table 8.1   Number of assessments 1993/4

	County	Borough A	Borough B	Borough C	Borough D
Number of adults referred for assessment	20,208	6247	40,967	8754	9689

Source: Audit Commission (1995)

out, so that services could be effectively targeted. But the concept of filtering out is somewhat at odds with the idea of needs-based assessment. Borough C denied that its levels of assessment amounted to a filtering process because assessment was universally available. Something that may have amounted to screening (in the sense of filtering out) was observed on the duty desk in borough A, where people requesting home care were told of the long waiting list and were referred to a list of private suppliers. In borough B access teams explicitly screened clients, making a decision whether to pass them on for assessment. In the county, the concept of assessment as a continuum made decisions about screening irrelevant.

It is difficult to see why there should be levels of assessment with particular eligibility criteria attached to them other than for the purpose of keeping a check on the numbers of complex assessments in relation to financial resources, which again signals a tension between separating the assessment of need from the resources available for meeting it. However, statistics on the different kinds of assessments carried out differ hugely, and there is some doubt as to their reliability (Table 8.1). The Department of Health's (1994b) monitoring report on care management in seven local authorities also noted that the proportion of referrals receiving comprehensive assessment ranged between 10 and 60 per cent. Even in the county there was, in 1993, some fear that enquiries were being counted as assessments and allocated a priority score because the allocation of money between localities depended in part on the number of assessments carried out. These suspicions were substantially allayed once consistent care management procedures were introduced and practices audited, although differences remained in terms of when the assessment scores were allocated.

Assessment forms

In borough D, a considerable amount of staff time was spent on designing and revising the assessment form. The level of assessment has tended to be referred to as the 'level of form', indicating the extent to which the process of assessment has become dominated by the search for the right form.

The county developed different forms for different stages of information collection in respect of its single level of assessment. The design of these forms was driven by the demands of the IT system and the understanding of these demands was mixed among front-line staff. The formalisation of the process of assessment has put a new premium on standardised practice, but there have been difficulties in securing this. When two localities were merged, it was found that there was wide variation between the two in terms of allocation and recording. The new care management guidelines issued in mid-1993 were intended to make practice more consistent, but because these were diffused locally, many locality managers remained concerned about variations in carrying out and recording assessments, even though the scores of clients at the same level of dependency and risk were shown to be consistent between localities.

Factual information about the client in the county was recorded on the assessment information form, which was entered on to the main computer system. This took about 45 minutes. The form consisted of a comprehensive set of boxes designed to describe clients and their circumstances. Further information was entered on a separate assessment record form, which was in effect a blank sheet, completed over a series of sessions with the client, all of which were recorded and dated. It was designed to be used in conjunction with the check list of headings supplied in the assessment guidelines (Department of Health and Price Waterhouse 1993). All the information entered on these two forms was summarised on the assessment summary and care plan, which had to be discussed with and preferably signed by the client, whose views, together with those of the carer, were also recorded. A financial assessment form was completed last. It was revealed at meetings that not all forms were always filled in. In addition to the forms associated with the process of assessment, the care managers had to complete a large number relating to the purchase and provision of service. There has been widespread dissatisfaction on the part of care managers with both the amount of form filling and the fact that at the end of it all the main computer system was not necessarily able to provide the information that the care manager needs. Thus localities were in addition running their own manual systems, with a concomitant increase in workload.

Borough A produced five drafts of its first-stage assessment form between January 1992 and April 1993, but was nonetheless forced to abandon it in 1994. The original form was biased towards ticking boxes, something the department has sought to move away from. In addition, a simple administrative error in March 1993 resulted in major problems. The initial detailed assessment form was designed as a rainbow pack, with the intention that staff would complete sections of it as necessary. However, administrative staff stapled the packs together, which resulted in social workers thinking that it was necessary to complete the whole thing. It was observed on the duty desk that before the second-stage form was revised, it was sometimes completed only when the case was about to be adjudicated; in other words, the assessment form was turned into an application form. This kind of practice is more understandable if it is remembered that social workers have always assessed, but have tended to carry the information in their heads. The need for formalisation is not always apparent to front-line workers, especially when the constraints on resources and inadequacies of supply mean that needs cannot be fully met.

Borough B used the same form at all levels of assessment, but only comprehensive assessments carried out by social workers were intended to be needs led. The form was not very popular with staff, who had difficulty completing the social work assessment, which they regarded as confidential, when the client had access to the form. By the end of 1994, it had been agreed that the form should be revised.

Borough D abandoned its three separate forms for each of three levels of assessment in favour of a single form for all assessments beyond simple assessment, but this form had yet to be used at the end of the research period.

Borough C endeavoured to develop a general assessment of needs (GAN) form that could be used by workers from a variety of disciplines and agencies. This was extremely ambitious and there is some evidence to suggest that not everyone appreciated the significance of what they were trying to do. For example, it was not understood that the use of such a form would involve changes in the forms that already existed to control access to a service such as occupational therapy. In line with its care management model, borough C's forms were user rather than systems led, but as IT systems developed, so there had to be changes to the GAN form.

The GAN form consisted of some 30 pages. The first part was less detailed than the equivalent information forms used in the county, but the last part, designed to elicit the client's needs, was more detailed. Staff were encouraged to see the form as something to be filled in over a series of visits to the client, and not as a questionnaire. The length of the form was one of the main reasons given for not using it. Community nurses had to complete their own set of forms in addition to the GAN, which they termed 'the yellow peril'. Nor would community nurses complete the financial assessment forms. Inevitably, nurses did not give the GAN form priority, which helps to explain why the process of assessment increasingly became one for SSD social workers.

Borough C is the only authority to have tried to use a joint assessment form as its chief tool for mainstream assessments. An attempt to do so was abandoned in the county, although discussions on the subject continued. It proved very difficult to get enough specialist content on to the GAN form to please all disciplines, and attempts to revise the form during the first year of implementation failed to shorten it for this reason. Health professionals were somewhat suspicious of the emphasis placed on recording the users' perceptions.

There are a number of beliefs that justify moving towards common assessment:

(i)   that the user benefits from a seamless service (this was borough C's starting place in implementing community care and constituted a commitment that pre-dated the 1990 Act);

(ii)   that a seamless service is best achieved when there is good inter-agency working;

(iii)   that good inter-agency working is best achieved by agreeing and working on a common task;

(iv)   that devising a common assessment process is a worthwhile common task;

(v)   that a common assessment form is a good starting place.

Any one of (ii) to (v) may become ends in themselves. Nor is the causal relationship between these beliefs necessarily clear. In borough C's pilot on assessment, the common task/form was used in some measure to promote interagency trust, that is, (v) was used to achieve (ii). This stands in contrast to the county, where a common assessment pilot in 1992 may have actually worsened relations between certain participants, in which case step (ii) was in no way linked to (v). Thus, it is by no means clear that a common assessment form will result in good inter-agency working and progress towards seamless care.

Thinking about the *purpose* of common assessment is also rather muddled. Is it about getting one professional group to accept the judgements of another and thereby save the client from being subjected to a whole series of professional assessments? This certainly has merit, but in borough A health professionals refused to accept social services' assessments. However, it remains still to specify the level of judgement that will be accepted. If it is a matter of common information about the client, this may not amount to an assessment, but may rather be a referral. If the aim is to get an assessment made by one professional accepted by another, then it may be easier to agree to accept one another's forms, rather than to attempt the difficult task of developing a common form.

The forms demanded by the assessment process (which are only part of the total number of forms that require completion in the new context of enabling) take a considerable amount of time to complete and enter on computer systems. The Department of Health's (1994b) monitoring report on care management found that a comprehensive assessment took anything between 3 and 60 hours to complete. There is evidence that front-line staff have been reluctant to fill in many of the forms because they do not think that they will benefit users. A certain distaste on the part of many social workers for the work of financial assessment might be expected, especially when, as in borough A, it has involved increasing amounts of verification to establish the precise nature of a client's housing tenure. But the promise of changing the pattern of service rests on the identification of the gap between assessed need and the services that can be provided. As we saw in the previous chapter, it is certainly possible to find examples of clients for whom imaginative packages of care have been put together. But, on balance, it seems to front-line workers that to date the weight of bureaucracy has outweighed the advantages. The words of a member of staff in the county, who had been involved in discussions about the possibility of a common assessment form, seemed to capture the mood about forms in general: 'at the end of the day it's just a form. I keep saying this, it's just a form. If you don't want to fill it in, you won't fill that one in any more than you fill anything else in.'

Needs-led assessment?

While there has been widespread support among staff for a needs-led approach to assessment, it has nevertheless proved difficult for many staff to implement this aspect of the changes. This is in part because of the cultural shift required to think first about needs and then openly about the services that might be offered, rather than in terms of services that were known to exist. The formalisation of assessment has made social workers' thinking on assessment public for the first time and every authority had some examples of poor-quality assessments. As a senior manager in borough C explained, many of those working with elderly people were untrained social workers and found the shift particularly hard to make: 'they still think of a resource, for example "I've seen Mrs X and I think residential care"'. In borough A, it was observed in the summer of 1993 that two care management teams working in the same office produced very different assessments: one tended to apply only for residential care, while the other was putting forward quite innovative care packages. As the Department of Health *et al.*'s (1993a) report on assessment commented, many assessments show staff describing, but not analysing, need, because as yet they do not have 'the language' to do so. However, as Braye and Preston Shoot (1995) have pointed out, the Department's guidance has been somewhat muddled, asking for care managers both to determine need and yet also to step back from their 'expert' role and become a resource that clients may use as they choose.

But there is the larger issue as to whether it is in fact possible or even desirable entirely to divorce the assessment of needs from the knowledge of what services are in fact available. Richards (1994) has neatly summarised the problem thus:

> Separating the assessment of needs from a subsequent decision about eligibility depends in fact on the concept of need being operationalised independently of the agency policy and guidelines that are to determine what is to count as need, and that is where the difficulty lies.

Cheetham (1993) has similarly insisted that 'assessment must remain rooted in the appreciation of the realities of service provision', and that 'it is not sensible to separate rigidly "needs talk" from "service talk". The assessment of older people with complex needs is a continuing process, impossible to disentangle from negotiation and service provision.' The Department of Health's (1990a) *Policy Guidance* warned that assessment should not take place in a vacuum, but separating assessment and care management from service provision nevertheless appears to attempt to do just that (Smale *et al.* 1994). It may not be possible. Challis's (1992) description of care managers balancing need and resources, scarcity and choice, seems to be a more realistic model.

As we have seen, the criteria for eligibility for assessment are often related to service provision. Borough C's 1994/5 Community Care Plan made the link explicit. It defined assessment as 'the process by which the care needs of an individual and their [*sic*] carer are worked out with them, so as to discover which services they are eligible to receive [and] are suitable to meet needs'. It may seem pointless to a care manager to assess a client as being in need of 'help with food', rather than being in need of meals on wheels, if she knows that the latter is effectively all that is available. As Chapter 6 showed, for the most part care managers were still choosing from 'set list' services.

The 1990 Act made it clear that local authorities and not users were to identify needs. Nevertheless, authorities were expected to involve users and carers in the process of assessment and to pay attention to their perceptions of their needs, although the Department of Health found itself in some difficulty on this point. On the one hand, it was anxious to dissuade SSDs from doing too many comprehensive assessments in order to seek out need; meeting presenting need was likely to prove enough of a struggle (Department of Health and Social Services Inspectorate 1991b: 45). On the other hand the Department was also anxious that local authorities should not adopt a wants-led approach to assessment (Social Services Inspectorate 1993: para. 5.2). An authority like borough B, which allowed clients to ask the SSD for an assessment for home care, might be considered more user centred than the county, for example, which channelled all clients through assessments carried out by care managers even if they came in with a specific service request. But borough B is not necessarily more needs led.

Authorities have made strenuous efforts to report the views of users and carers on the assessment forms. All had separate spaces for recording the circumstances of carers. However, it is more difficult to assess how far users and carers have been actively involved in the assessment process. The Social Services Inspectorate (1993) was sanguine about the involvement of users and carers in its inspection of assessment procedures, but the study on 'informing users and carers' commissioned by the Department of Health from Peat Marwick (1994) found that users knew little about the process and many did not even know they had been care managed. These findings were echoed in Baldock and Ungerson's (1994) study of stroke patients, which found that virtually no one realised that they had had an assessment or could name their care manager. Similarly, Hoyes *et al.* (1994) remarked on the failure to involve carers and users in assessment. Yet the idea of empowering users and carers was seized upon eagerly by many authorities and for the most part the assessment forms developed in the authorities look progressive on this count.

Our research did not involve monitoring interactions between users and carers and professionals, but we would caution against accepting procedures and even good intentions as measures of success in this regard. It is very difficult for users and carers to be equal partners in the process of assessment. Not only is it often difficult for them to articulate need, but the very circumstances of assessment may militate against user and carer participation. For example, few authorities could be more explicitly committed to user centredness in their implementation policies than borough C. Network meetings, referred to by one senior manager as 'the final flourish of assessment', where the service response to needs was discussed, were supposed fully to involve users and carers. However, observation at one of these taking place in a hospital early in 1994 revealed that the user did not actually attend because he was insufficiently stable; in other words, the network meeting was taking place early in order to accommodate the hospital's need for the bed. A second network meeting, observed two months later, also took place at a hospital. It was held in the ward kitchen, was rather rushed, and the user did not have any pyjama bottoms. It is unlikely that users and carers will be able fully to participate under such conditions. As Ellis (1993: 5) has commented: 'assessment is as much about the differential power participants have to influence the outcome as competing definitions of need'.

Finally, it is possible to consider whether there has been any change in the pattern of service that might provide evidence for a move to needs-led assessment. Several officers in the authorities questioned the reliability of the Chartered Institute of Public Finance and Accountancy data, and the figures are difficult to interpret, but it looks as though expenditure on residential care increased between 1988 and 1990 and then fell (Table 8.2). The fall in the years immediately preceding the implementation of the 1990 Act (in April 1993) is particularly striking, especially in the county. All authorities except boroughs A and B showed an increase in expenditure on home help services during the same period (Table 8.3), although in the case of borough D this merely served to recapture the share of expenditure devoted to this service at the beginning of the period. In general, after implementation in 1993, expenditure on both residential and home care rose (Tables 8.4 and 8.5). Authorities were having to purchase residential care for a new cohort of clients, but there is some evidence that the underlying trend was nevertheless away from institutional care and towards domiciliary provision. The county vired money from its residential and nursing home budget to home care, and borough B spent substantial amounts of the new STG moneys on home care.

Table 8.2 Percentage breakdown of gross current expenditure on services to elderly and physically handicapped people – residential care, 1988–93

	County	Borough A	Borough B	Borough C	Borough D
1988/9	52	36	51	54	50
1989/90	51	42	51	N/A	50
1990/1	52	42	52	55	51
1991/2	50	39	50	49	43
1992/3	40	36	50	49	41

Source: Department of Health (1990c, 1993c)

Table 8.3 Percentage breakdown of gross current expenditure on services to elderly and physically handicapped people – home help, 1988–93

	County	Borough A	Borough B	Borough C	Borough D
1988/9	27	34	24	18	31
1989/90	29	34	23	N/A	27
1990/1	29	33	33	20	30
1991/2	28	35	31	22	31
1992/3	34	33	30	25	32

Source: Department of Health (1990c, 1993c)

Table 8.4 Net expenditure (£1000s) on residential care for elderly people, 1992/3 and 1993/4

	County	Borough A	Borough B	Borough C	Borough D
1992/3	6456	2623	5224	4000	3943
1993/4	12,387	4995	6332	4842	5911

Source: CIPFA (1994, 1995)

Table 8.5 Net expenditure (£1000s) on home care for elderly people, 1992/3 and 1993/4

	County	Borough A	Borough B	Borough C	Borough D
1992/3	6826	3820	4466	6639	4042
1993/4	9269	4008	4781	2916	4035

Source: CIPFA (1994, 1995)

Laing and Buisson (1995) recorded that the number of elderly people and those with disabilities in homes and long-stay hospitals fell in 1993/4 for the first time since statistics began. Furthermore this happened in the face of increasing levels of dependency. The evidence for increasing dependency remains largely anecdotal but is pervasive; for example, most authorities could cite an increased demand for holiday, out-of-hours and weekend cover among their home care clients. However, it would be a mistake to assume that greater provision of home care necessarily means that needs are being met. Baldock and Ungerson's (1994) study contains extremely damaging evidence regarding the provision of expensive packages of set list services that clients did not actually need. The extent to which home care staff and those authorising the service monitored the appropriateness of the care provided varied in the research authorities.

Eligibility and the provision of services

The purpose of the PSSRU projects was to target services more effectively. To this end, the PSSRU researchers emphasised the importance of screening clients properly. However, in authorities where all clients come into contact with a care manager and where all are entitled to an assessment, other ways of reconciling needs and resources must be found. At the end of 1993, the Audit Commission warned authorities of the importance of establishing firm eligibility criteria for service such that they allowed 'just enough people with needs to exactly use up their budget (or be prepared to adjust their budgets)' (para. 15). The Audit Commission made it clear that authorities had only a limited number of ways to contain expenditure: they could refuse to provide service, they could set firm eligibility criteria, or they could charge for services. The Audit Commission focused on the second of these, as did most authorities in the first year of implementation.

Towards the end of 1994 policies in respect of charging were beginning to assume a much higher profile in the light of two major issues. (i) Problems were raised by the fact that, subject to means testing, clients must pay for residential care, whereas if they receive a package of domiciliary services (the cost of which may in some authorities actually be higher than that of a bed), they may pay relatively little or nothing. The fact that the county had contracted with the health authority to provide a service for which it was intending to charge further illustrates the difficulty of the 'charging border' between health and social services. (ii) The problems that were raised by the need to impose or increase charges for domiciliary services. The October 1994 report by the Association of Metropolitan Authorities concluded that in those authorities where charges had increased, the take-up of services had dropped noticeably. Davies *et al.* (1990) noted that charges would surely become a bigger issue in a social care market, and while none of the research authorities had substantially changed their charging policies, the issue was beginning to be debated. At the end of 1994, the county was conducting pilot work to explore how to charge for packages of care rather than for individual services.

In respect of eligibility criteria for service, authorities are obliged to publish them in their community care plans. The Audit Commission (1993, 1994) reported that while only two-thirds had done so by the end of 1993, all had complied by the end of 1994, although only half had listed their priorities. The research authorities varied considerably in the extent to which they operated according to clearly set out criteria. In 1992, the District Audit Service described a system for constructing needs-led budgets, which provided SSDs with the means of allowing through only so much need, to paraphrase the Audit Commission's injunction. Authorities were invited to define high, medium and low levels of need and the components of care for each of these levels. They were then to agree and cost the standard service level for each component of care and to estimate the numbers of clients falling within each level. From these figures, they would be able to work out how many clients they could afford to make provision for within each level of need.

Borough B adopted this model, largely because of a predicted shortfall in the STG moneys. The eligibility criteria for intensive care management were defined as cases where the client was in hospital, where the client was in the community but at risk of entering residential care, and cases where the carer was at risk of breaking down. These criteria were expanded in 1994 to include people exhibiting challenging behaviour where there was a risk to the person or to others. A care management review in mid-1994 revealed that in one area, of 119 open cases 111 were being care managed; in other words, it was being decided that most old people met the criteria. In contrast, the authority managed to keep within its estimates for residential and nursing home beds because the eligibility criteria for beds were tightened considerably. As a senior manager admitted:

> I think the people who are losing out are those people who would have become isolated, the family had moved away, they are beginning to get anxious about falling, old age, and feel it is time to move into a residential home. It was basically like moving house into a more supportive environment. I think those people will lose out.

Eligibility for care management was set at different levels for different client groups, reflecting the amount of money available; for example, the budget for HIV came mainly from the Department of Health and was sufficient to meet a much wider range of need.

Where eligibility criteria are drawn tightly, there is an incentive for assessors to classify a client's level of dependency such that she or he will be sure to receive service; this may explain the large numbers of elderly people classified as 'high need' in borough B. Eligibility for all services drawing on

STG moneys – beds and intensive care packages – was decided by a panel in borough B, consisting of health and social services staff. Initially, the panel performed an important task here and in some other London boroughs in terms of checking the quality of assessments. In a sense, the care manager appeared as an advocate for the client before the panel, although a senior purchaser expressed some unease with this:

> I think social workers come [to the panel] trying to think about how they can provide the maximum for their client. Fine, that's a traditional social work way of doing it, but I think what this process is about is looking at what the real needs are in the context of a limited budget; it is not to change the need, but to look at what the needs are . . .

It is possible to see in this statement the struggle that necessarily takes place at the meetings of the panel to reconcile needs and resources. After April 1994, the panel looked only at cases involving residential care because of the existence of the block contract for domiciliary care, which was divided into hours of care and devolved to team managers. At the end of the research period the plan was to dismantle the panel entirely.

The county explicitly rejected the idea of establishing indicative spends for levels of need because senior managers felt that such a system was overly mechanistic and allowed little room for professional discretion, and because they believed that clients at the same level of dependency might nevertheless be in very different circumstances (particularly in respect of their access to informal care) and therefore have very different needs for service. The county thus developed its own method of determining eligibility for services: the risk/needs matrix. The matrix originated in an attempt to find a way of allocating resources to the geographical divisions before restructuring in 1991. The vertical axis of the matrix identified the area of problem and the horizontal axis the degree of risk in relation to the dependency of the client, or the extent to which external intervention was required. It was possible for a client to score between 1 (high) and 8 (low) and there were different matrices for each client group. Thus the physical disability matrix gave a score of 1 for a situation in which the client had 'progressive terminal illness or severe disability requiring continuous care by others who are unable or unwilling to continue'. A client in the same vertical need group (that is, physical health and development/functional ability) about whom there was 'some concern about demands placed on carers by illness or disability of individual' scored 5. Each client group matrix took into account physical and mental dependency, statutory requirements and the availability of informal care, and determined priorities for service. It measured more than just dependency and identified those whom the authority could not ignore.

The matrix worked at the individual level to determine eligibility, but it also served to set eligibility criteria at the macro-level. A locality audit in 1992 revealed that 84 per cent of the SSD's expenditure was going to those clients categorised as priority 1–3. This *de facto* situation was then translated into a policy statement, which guaranteed that the authority would purchase service on behalf of clients falling in the top three categories of priority. If the budget settlement were to become less favourable, it would be possible for the authority to alter its criteria *vis-à-vis* the matrix such that it provided service for only the top two categories. The county did not set eligibility criteria in relation to particular services because access to all services was via care managers, although in fact home care organisers complained that some clients who would have been turned down in the past obtained home care from care managers. The passing of assessment from providers to purchasers has been a source of tension.

The risk/needs matrix was accepted by care managers, despite the fact that it called for a considerable degree of standardisation in its use. In part this was because it served to protect care managers from having to bear the whole responsibility for denying service. There have, however, been problems in making its use consistent across client groups and across localities. It was felt, for example, that care managers might seek to inflate matrix scores to secure service for clients and that locality managers might encourage this to secure more resources. But the information was recorded and published and, in fact, when a late 1993 audit examined 307 cases – four clients at priority 3 from each team – it showed a high degree of consistency in the use of the matrix. It is also the case that the matrix worked better for some client groups than others. The Chronically Sick and Disabled Act made it clear what people with disabilities can expect, so the matrix is also clear. But the matrix for people with learning difficulties was much more vague and some social workers have suggested that it does not allow for a measure of personal development. Nor did it take on board prevention in the case of children. The matrix for children was modified in 1994 to give more emphasis to child development. Finally, it proved difficult to determine when to allocate the matrix score. The 1993 care management guidelines issued by the SSD said that it should be awarded at the end of the assessment process, but increasingly the matrix became part of the process of assessment, with a score being awarded early on to help to determine priority for assessment, and then revised at the end of the process.

The other research authorities have not formalised eligibility criteria to anything like the extent of borough B or the county. Borough A had no clear criteria and responded to risk and urgency. Care managers decided a client's eligibility and priority for service and their assessments were checked by a panel of health and social services staff. Clients could be put on a waiting list; there was a one-year waiting list for home care and no effective means of prioritising those on it. However, senior managers have been moving towards the idea of introducing needs-led budgeting. In mid-1993 a senior manager was sceptical about this: 'I think it's an area of greyness for us . . . we are running as we always did in that we will listen to anybody; rather than respond to eligibility we tend to respond to urgency.' But by early 1994 the SSD had met with members to discuss the idea of needs-led budgeting. Members were cautious. According to the same senior manager the idea represented a major change for the borough; members liked

> to spread their jam thinly across everybody, and if you are going to reduce a service you nipped a quarter of an hour from everyone; well, they have now accepted that you can't do that. If we are up against it then the resources must go to those with the greatest dependency.

The borough decided to use measures of high, medium and low dependency to decide priority for its new intensive home care service.

Borough C published preliminary eligibility criteria in the autumn of 1993 and firmer criteria for particular services in early 1994. It guaranteed to purchase service on behalf of those deemed to be high priority. Medium-priority cases could be placed on a waiting list. Assessment of both eligibility and priority was deemed to be a matter of professional judgement. Eligibility criteria comprised a mixture of risk, statutory responsibility and dependency.[1] These criteria were used by the network meeting to determine eligibility and providers then conducted service assessments.

During the first year of implementation, borough D operated a modified version of its old system and a lot continued to depend on the judgements of providers assessing for service. The borough developed eligibility criteria for assessment and services in its first community care plan, but in the second year of implementation the department began working on a client scoring system, by which points allocated according to levels of dependency and risk triggered different levels of expenditure. However, this system required more developed purchasing systems than the borough possessed at the end of 1994.

Local authorities must effectively decide what is 'eligible need' when it comes to service provision. Table 8.6 shows the number of assessments that led to no service being received. In practice, eligible need is usually related to levels of risk and dependency, the same variables that tend to determine the priority for assessment. Davies et al. (1990) were critical of reliance on risk because it is difficult to estimate and evaluate. They pointed out that the home help service has traditionally been poorly targeted in respect of actual dependency levels because local authorities have sought to use it to monitor risk among vulnerable people. However, authorities saw such provision as serving the aim of prevention, which is of course also hard to measure and justify. It is feared that the introduction of both charges and eligibility criteria will have an adverse effect on preventive work. Insofar as charges affect the less dependent, they also raise questions about prevention in the sense of sustaining people at home. The House of Commons Health Committee (1993) raised the possibility of less dependent people having to enter institutions if their relatively more simple, but nevertheless vital, needs for

Table 8.6   Number of assessments not leading to receipt of service 1993/4

	County	Borough A	Borough B	Borough C	Borough D
Number of assessments	702	746	16,805	1019	3860
% of all assessments	3.5	11.9	41	11.6	40

Source: Audit Commission (1995)

service are not met. The danger is that people with simple needs – for example, for shopping – will not receive service.

Having encouraged authorities to adopt strict eligibility criteria, the Department of Health's (1994a: 8) monitoring report on the primary health care services and community care appears to acknowledge the danger that losing services poses to those at lower levels of dependency:

> DHAs, FHSAs and LAs should encourage and develop links between SSDs, GPs and PHCTs in order to encourage early and positive interventions which aim to prevent the apparent need to experience a crisis before statutory services are mobilised. This needs to take place at a local level, facilitated by senior managers, *as this can run contrary to the financial pressures of responding to those in greatest need in accordance with eligibility criteria.*
>
> (Our italics)

Concern about prevention was reiterated in the monitoring report on community care from the NHS Management Executive and Social Services Inspectorate (1995).

Borough C stopped providing a shopping-only service in 1993 and in borough B senior managers have expressed concern about weighting service so heavily in favour of the highly dependent:

> I think what the new system has done is create more consistency. I think there was much more room for individual judgement/discretion as to who got what. At least now it is within one system; there is less room for that very broad discretion . . . I think people with complex needs are getting a service, it is people down the other end of the scale . . . it will be someone who needs cleaning, issues about whether that would be preventing something happening – the preventive role will come up.

In the county, during 1992, members expressed interest in the devising of a prevention matrix to mirror the risk/needs matrix. This would have formalised the allocation of 16 per cent of expenditure that was already going to those clients scoring below 3. However, given the difficulties in categorising, let alone measuring, work around prevention, the prevention matrix was abandoned. This did not mean that commitment to prevention was dropped, for in May 1993 members insisted that a further £450,000 be put aside for a preventive strategy.

The introduction of eligibility criteria has made the system more transparent and decisions more consistent, but need has come to mean high dependency and high risk. As dependency levels in the community increase, this trend can be expected to strengthen.

The imposition of eligibility criteria has also raised in a more explicit fashion the question of unmet need. One of the main aims of needs-based assessments was to detach the meeting of need from established services and to encourage care managers to look for new suppliers from whom to purchase services that would more precisely meet need. If there was no supply to meet a particular need this would be recorded and the information would inform future purchasing strategy. Thus the recording of unmet need was crucial to changing the pattern of service provision. However, the tension between needs and resources caused the Department of Health to introduce a note of caution at the end of 1992, when guidance from the Social Services Inspectorate warned local authorities that once they had admitted a need for service they would be under a legal obligation to provide it (see Chapter 2) (CI (92)34, para. 13).

The county chose to ignore the advice, and continued to record information in client notes under the category 'needs still to be met'. In addition, it collected information about service deficit and its cause: budget insufficiency, market failure (the service was not available), non-priority (the client scored too low on the risk/needs matrix), client refusal, or a shortfall on the part of another agency. However, care managers have tended to fail to fill in the service deficit forms. As one locality manager explained:

> the message they are getting continually is cuts, privatise, more cuts, privatise, so that filling in service deficit forms in that climate seems a waste of time. There are no goodies that are going to be presented to care managers if they fill the forms in.

Borough B split its assessment form in two as a result of the Social Services Inspectorate's letter, so that need was identified on one form and whether the client met the eligibility criteria for service on another. Service review groups were set up to look at trends in unmet need for particular client groups.

Borough A took its waiting lists as an indicator of service deficit, but then had no means of knowing whether there were things that people wanted that were not available.

Borough C chose to take the issue to members in the autumn of 1993, before which time no systematic records of unmet need were kept, while in borough D there was also something of a hiatus after the receipt of the SSI's letter. The decision was then taken to record both the nature of the unmet need and the reasons for the service shortfall. However, it was not until summer 1994 that a form was piloted, with a planned launch alongside new procedures late in 1994. As in the county, the forms have not been routinely filled in.

The recording of unmet need was originally conceived of as a crucial stage in ensuring that services became more needs led. However, the tension between needs and resources has caused both the Department of Health and local authorities to back off from identifying unmet need.

Conclusion

The introduction of care management has been driven as much by the aim of targeting services as assessing need. However, deciding on eligibility for assessment and service has posed major problems. In a universal care management system, which makes sense in the context of the development of commissioning, assessment on a continuum without specific eligibility criteria (as practised by the county) seems to be the best option. Priority for assessment tends everywhere to be by urgency and risk, which may be inevitable when care management is applied to the totality of social services populations. Services themselves have always been rationed; with the introduction of eligibility criteria the process has become explicit and there are merits in this. However, the long-term outcomes of defining need in terms of high dependency and targeting resources on the heavily dependent are unknown. In many ways it is a high-risk strategy. The conclusion of Allen *et al.* (1992: 308) at the end of their study of the views of elderly people in the community and in institutional care is worth stating:

> It is possible that there has been too much concentration on intensive packages of care and that the real point of community care has been missed. Targeting those 'most in need' and providing services for them may, in fact, be easier than caring for those who are less obviously in need. The lessons from this research suggest that more preventative services for more people may perhaps be of greater overall value in keeping elderly people out of residential care than concentrating services on a very few.

The problem is that we do not know. Nevertheless, the decision has been made to resolve the fundamental tension between needs and resources by targeting the highly dependent. Increasing levels of dependency among people in the community have exacerbated this trend.

Finally, the aim of meeting the needs of highly dependent people in a more creative way, such that they are permitted to continue to live in the community, may be admirable, but, as we have seen, it is remarkably difficult to separate the assessment of need from the services that are known to be available. There may also be another issue to be faced as the numbers of highly dependent people in the community increase. As a senior manager in one of the London boroughs said: 'if you are going for needs led it must be much more flexible, but if you are going to be flexible it is bloody expensive and that was why you bunged people in large institutions'. Genuinely individualised needs-led care packaging that does not use off-the-shelf services – a trip to the opera instead of day care, a pub meal instead of meals on wheels – will be expensive. It is by no means clear that all aspects of care packages are being properly costed in all the authorities, or that the costs of really creative care packaging can compete with those of residential care.

Note

1 Eligibility for residential care was defined in terms of there being danger to life, limb, physical or emotional health; or that existing care arrangements are breaking down; and that the person requires constant supervision, or more regular care and attention than can be provided in the community, or rehabilitation from illness, or independence training that can be given only on a residential basis. It was added that the person would normally require help with three or more of the following: eating and/or drinking, getting to the lavatory or commode and changing incontinence pads, washing, dressing, taking medication, and aggressive behaviour. There were similarly detailed criteria for nursing home and domiciliary care.

9

Collaboration in community care

Collaboration between health and social services has been a key plank in the new policy of community care. The ambition is hardly new, but the emphasis in the 1990s on making services more responsive to users' needs has resulted in a new push for collaboration. The 1990 *Policy Guidance* referred to the aim of 'seamless care' (Department of Health 1990a: para. 1.9), meaning that the user should not be aware of any divisions between health and social services. However, given the very different nature of the organisation of health and social services in terms of priorities, accountabilities and structures, 'seams well stitched together' might have been a more appropriate goal. The emphasis on clarifying the responsibilities of health and social services in the Department of Health and Social Security's (Cm. 849 1989) White Paper is an important prerequisite for stitching together the seams, but the problem of the boundary between health and social care remains and may have been sharpened by the introduction of purchaser–provider splits.

Collaboration has also been crucial to the wider dimensions of reform in both the NHS and social services in the 1990s. An influential simulation exercise in East Anglia before the introduction of the quasi-market in the NHS came to grief because a cut in the SSD's budget resulted in 'bed blocking' in the hospitals. A substantial degree of collaboration between health and social services was thus recognised to be necessary for the NHS reforms to work at all. Indeed, during the 1990s there has been a significant shift in government's rationale for collaboration, from the user-centred perspective of seamless care, towards an emphasis on the need for both statutory authorities to cooperate in managing the market.

However, there has been a long and none too glorious history of efforts to collaborate. During the 1970s and 1980s, these were referred to as 'joint planning'. The origins of the kind of joint planning carried on in the 1970s were to be found as much in the search for rational comprehensive planning as in the pursuit of collaboration (Webb and Wistow 1986). Planning guidelines were set centrally and focused on service norms rather than on user outcomes or needs, amounting to central resource allocation and the programming of expenditure (Glennerster 1983; Wistow *et al.* 1990). This kind of planning reached its peak at the end of the 1970s.

The division between health and social services was given new emphasis by the NHS reorganisation of 1974 (Lewis 1983), which turned local authority public health departments into SSDs and removed district nurses and health visitors in the process. In the wake of reorganisation, joint planning structures were set up to promote collaboration. Joint consultative committees (JCCs) were established in 1974 and joint care planning teams in 1976; joint finance was introduced at the same time and was described by the Secretary of State as 'collaboration money' (Castle 1975).

The outcomes of what proved to be this rather elaborate and costly machinery were meagre. Planning tended to take place at the margins, around joint finance moneys only. In 1988, the Audit Commission found that 60 per cent of local authorities surveyed had no strategy for resettling people with learning difficulties (Audit Commission 1989). There were problems even with joint finance, because local authorities saw it as a bribe to incur further expenditure (when the joint funding ended) to which they would not otherwise have agreed (Nocon 1994). An increasing amount of joint finance money was spent by health authorities on their own schemes, reaching 19 per cent by the mid-1980s (Wistow *et al.* 1990).

Commentaries on joint planning during the 1970s and 1980s have been almost uniformly critical. Only some attempts at project-based joint working found favour (Hunter *et al.* 1988). The impediments to effective joint planning have been described by Wistow (1990) as structural, procedural, and professional, as well as financial. The budget procedures in local authorities and health authorities are different and they work to different planning cycles. The problem of lack of conterminous boundaries was exacerbated by the NHS reorganisation of 1982, which took out the area health authorities.

Perhaps most important of all, as the Audit Commission (1986) recognised, the professional cultures and patterns of accountability in health and social services are very different. Even their understanding of community care has been different. As Walker (1982, 1989) has pointed out, for the health authority, local authority residential care was community care. Throughout the 1980s, health authorities closed institutions for the mentally ill and people with learning difficulties while community services remained inadequate. On the other hand, the perverse incentives of the social security system led to a vast increase in the number of beds for elderly people, which health authorities were happy to regard as community provision. Thus, in large measure, joint planning amounted to 'tiptoeing through vested interests' (Hunter 1994).

Given this history, mere exhortation to ensure seamless care was unlikely to be successful. In his 1988 report on community care, Sir Roy Griffiths envisaged a specific grant set at 40 or 50 per cent of agreed local spending to be made available to local authorities on the submission of community care plans that were judged to provide evidence of local needs, collaborative planning and the promotion of a mixed economy of care (Department of Health and Social Security 1988). However, the 1989 White Paper abandoned Griffiths' link between planning and resource allocation. Because the implicit objectives of government clearly involved the capping of growth in social security expenditure, it was decided to transfer to local authorities the care element of social security support to residential and nursing homes in the form of the STG.

The 1990 Act obliged local authorities to consult other authorities (district health authorities (DHAs), family health service authorities (FHSAs) and housing authorities), voluntary organisations, and users and carers in the production of community care plans. The 1990 *Policy Guidance* indicated that the emphasis should be on partnership and on the production of planning agreements between authorities grounded in their purchasing functions (Department of Health 1990a: 12). The idea seemed to be to agree who should do what for whom, when, at what cost and who should pay. The House of Commons Social Services Committee (1990c: 93) was not convinced that this was enough: 'We remain to be convinced that without greater incentives to work together the risks associated with the introduction of competition in community care will outweigh the benefits claimed for it by Government.' In the guidance he prepared for the Social Services Inspectorate, Wistow (1990) also wondered about the extent to which 'planning agreements' would differ from joint plans and how, in the absence of the link between resource allocation and planning, they could be delivered. He also pointed out the extent to which the objectives of the new planning agreements had to do with the establishing of processes – to promote enabling, for example – and warned that the tendency in the past had been for structure and process to drive out attention to outcomes.

The 1990 *Policy Guidance* referred to 'joint planning and commissioning' leading to joint operational activity in assessment, individual care planning, service delivery and review. However, our research indicates that it is perfectly possible for achievements with regard to joint planning and/or commissioning to be accompanied by inertia in respect of the formal processes of joint working at the level of the individual user in terms of day-to-day service delivery and vice versa. Collaboration is a many-layered activity and there are limits as to what formal agreements and procedures can achieve.

In fact, action to achieve collaboration in community care has taken a variety of forms in the 1990s. Authorities were faced with the issue of what to do about the elaborate 1980s joint planning machinery. This was not abolished, but reworked in relation to the emergence of purchaser–provider splits and renamed 'joint commissioning'. One of the paradoxes of collaboration is the contrast between the simplicity of purpose behind calls for joint working on the one hand, and the complexity of arrangements and machinery that seem to be necessary to make it work on the other. Much energy has been devoted to putting in place the new structures and processes of joint commissioning, and rather less attention has been paid to outcomes, whether in the form of facilitating joint purchasing or joint work on the part of providers.

Central government's efforts to bring about greater collaboration has encompassed extensive policy guidance, exhortation and monitoring by the Social Services Inspectorate and regional health authorities (EL (93) 48; EL (93) 119/CI (93) 35), and what amounts to financial coercion, whereby the payment of the transferred moneys was linked to local agreements about strategies for placing people in nursing home beds and about hospital discharge arrangements (LASSL (92) 8; LASSL (92) 11). This forced the pace of collaboration in the areas that had always been a source of concern and that were likely to cause the most problems for the working of the health care market. The 1990 Act also demanded that local authorities produce community care plans, the third of which (for 1994/5) was produced in the second year of the research. The 1990 *Policy Guidance* said that these plans would 'evolve', but in many cases the evolution has been slow, with neither the purpose nor the intended audience for the plans being clear.

The formal machinery of collaboration: from joint planning to joint commissioning

Authorities have devoted a lot of time to developing new joint commissioning structures, yet there has been no agreed definition of joint commissioning. Many of the research authorities began with the idea that they would eventually either make purchasing decisions in conjunction with health authorities or actually engage in joint purchasing. It is not evident that joint commissioning in this sense is in sight, but what seems to have happened, paradoxically, is that the new joint commissioning structures have provided a more effective means for joint planning.

In a 1992 article, reproduced by the Department of Health *et al.* (1993a) Knapp and Wistow suggested that joint commissioning was the link between planning and activity. They went on to list a number of tasks that might be involved: the development and agreement of a mission statement; assessment of population needs; the location, assessment, development and stimulation of services that the planning activity suggests are needed; the development of service specifications; the development of contract agreements with providers; performance review; and contract renewal or termination. This was a rather precise list of activities, but it did not include joint purchasing or pooled budgets.

A document on services for people with learning difficulties produced for the county by a national consultancy team in 1994 was more ambitious still. It suggested that joint commissioning incorporated joint planning in the form of developing a strategic framework and carrying out strategic planning, and went beyond it to include operational planning, individual purchasing, and management and review. However, the document acknowledged that the term joint commissioning was used 'very variably' across the country and in situations that were arguably not part of the joint commissioning process at all.

A report by the King's Fund Centre was content to be more vague. It offered a basic definition: joint commissioning occurs when health and social services, 'operating in a defined area, work in a collaborative way to ensure more effective and more efficient use of their available resources', but added that 'the lack of a generally agreed definition is not a major problem' (Poxton 1994: 4–5).

The elaboration of joint commissioning has been a major endeavour for some of the research authorities and the new structures have in two of the five played a major role in the more general implementation of the 1990 Act. However, lack of clarity as to objectives has been a problem for individual authorities and we are not able to be as sanguine about this as Poxton. In fact, during the period of the research, the review and revision of structures for joint commissioning have dominated the agenda on collaborative working in all the authorities. As purchasing emerged more clearly both in terms of the internal structure of SSDs and as a key task, so it became necessary to revisit definitions of joint commissioning and what kind of representation in what kinds of structures was necessary to make it work. Three of the London boroughs, B, C, and D, share a single health authority, which made more detailed comparison possible.

Borough A

Borough A alone of the research authorities had conterminous boundaries with the health authority. This, together with the SSD's thin management structure, served in large part to explain the close relationship between the two statutory authorities in respect of community care implementation.

As with its decision to establish a purchaser–provider split, borough A agreed early on, in July 1991, to move towards joint commissioning. The old joint planning structure consisted, as it did in most places, of a JCC comprising members and officers from the DHA, the FHSA, and the local authority; a senior officers' group below that (the joint care planning team); and finally a number of client-based joint care planning teams. This structure was replaced by: a joint commissioning strategy group (JCSG); a joint commissioning managers' group (JCMG); and joint commissioning teams (JCTs). The membership of these, however, was very similar to the three tiers of the old structure, except that rather more effort was made to include the voluntary sector, which took its turn in chairing the JCSG.

In October 1991 the reasons for the change were stated in a paper presented to the JCC in terms of the new purchasing roles assigned to both health and social services. In other words, at this point joint commissioning was envisaged as macro-commissioning, even though the SSD's only macro-commissioning capacity consisted of a contracts unit focused on administration. The paper implied that initially the commissioning strategy would focus on identifying a framework to provide the direction for each authority's service contracts, identifying areas of duplication and gaps. However, the ambitious final aim of joint purchasing was clearly signalled: 'Over time it may be possible to consider the joint contracting of certain services where each authority will commit funds to a central pool to be managed by joint commissioning teams of each authority.'

In fact, relatively little attention was paid to the question of how to operationalise joint commissioning, but at this point there was very limited information available to authorities on possible ways forward. A joint commissioning project manager was appointed in December 1991. The job was first advertised as 'project manager – joint planning' because the brief for the post was developed before the review of joint commissioning. When the SSD failed to recruit, the job title was changed but not the job description, indicating that the new structure had not moved much beyond a change in nomenclature. Furthermore, the new appointee was asked to draw up terms of reference for the new commissioning structure after being in post for only a week. As a senior manager commented in July 1993:

> Nobody seems to have defined what joint commissioning is. The strategy group feels frustrated because they should be directing strategy, but common sense would tell you that if you have two powerful organisations, the health authority and the local authority, . . . neither will forgo or give up their power to that group. Anything that is determined there has to be a recommendation, it can't be a decision. Basically those recommendations then slot into a whole lot of other priorities.

It is undoubtedly significant that both the health authority and the SSD lacked a director during much of 1992, and, in the case of the SSD, during the first few months of 1993.

In borough A, the impetus towards joint commissioning played a major part in the implementation of community care. The joint commissioning team 1993 was set up in 1992 as a subgroup of the joint commissioning structure and involved members of the health authority, local authority and voluntary organisations, who met fortnightly at the health care provider trust building. This group did a considerable amount of useful task-centred work in respect of the community care changes, including market mapping of residential and nursing home beds, the development of a common assessment form and eligibility criteria for assessment and service, and the production of a community care plan. The existence of the group was important for the way in which it mobilised joint ownership of community care implementation.

However, the development of active joint commissioning faltered. Observation at one of the JCTs during 1993 revealed confusion as to whether the team was to produce 'wish lists' or spending plans. The group met every six weeks, but decision making often could not wait this long. Nor did the group have much by way of financial expertise or administrative back-up. One significant development was the pooling of the health and social services grants budget. All bids were considered by the different client-based teams, and though this did not amount to joint commissioning, it did result in a more democratic procedure for allocating moneys. A number of other initiatives were pursued jointly during the period of study, such as an integrated transport service, a joint occupational therapy (OT) service, and a joint OT store. However, in the case of the joint OT service, negotiations proved difficult because the health authority faced cuts and was therefore uneasy about making funding commitments, and because a local health trust felt unable to share information about its service for fear that this might result in its losing market share. The official guidance denied any possible tension between promoting a mixed economy of care and quasi-market principles on the one hand, and a 'planned economy' on the other (Department of Health and Social Services Inspectorate 1991: para. 2.1.12). However, this example provides some evidence to support Hunter's (1992) warning that increased competition might be inimical to the trust necessary to develop a seamless service.

According to a senior (provider) manager, JCCs had:

> become a dumping ground. People come in and say, 'that is good for joint commissioning, we don't have time to deal with it so we'll put it there'; you write a report but it is to no end, because you make recommendations but they don't get anywhere because there was no money, so you begin to wonder what is the point.

This bleak view was not shared by all senior managers. The SSD purchasers in particular had reason to be grateful to the joint commissioning team 1993 for its work, although health purchasers did not begin to pay serious attention to the JCMG until the middle of 1993. However, there was no doubt that joint commissioning in the sense of the joint purchase of services was not happening. The situation was not improved when the joint commissioning project manager left in the spring of 1993; he was not replaced for nine months, leaving a vacuum. There was also a growing feeling that the 1991 joint commissioning structure was no longer in tune with the changes that had taken place in the SSD since that time, in particular the growing importance of purchasing. JCTs included purchasers *and* providers and senior purchasing managers were no longer convinced that this was desirable. By the middle of 1993, the SSD had decided to review the joint commissioning machinery again. Both health and social services invested considerable resources in a review of the joint commissioning process, employing a consultant and organising several joint meetings to develop a new structure.

At one of the review days held during 1993 the extent to which the approaches of health and social services differed was revealed. Health purchasers had far greater power and larger budgets than their social services counterparts, and were engaged only in macro-commissioning. Participants were asked to consider what they would do if given £3 million for services for people with learning difficulties. Officers from the health authority said that they would go to a provider to see what it could come up with; people from social services talked much more about the need for consultation and about the need to establish trust with new providers, something that was not an issue for the health authority. The more complicated nature of the social services market and the different structures of accountability showed up clearly as points at issue between the two authorities.

The consultant who was asked to review the joint commissioning structure pointed out that the authorities were spending £2.1 million on the process of joint commissioning, £158,000 going on administrative costs alone (this included attendance at meetings). The amount of joint finance allocated by the JCTs, which was the only significant money they handled other than grants to voluntary organisations and the specific grants for mental illness and drugs and alcohol problems, amounted to £129,000. The consultant recommended two possible ways forward: first, a slimmed down JCSG with a purchasing orientation and the disbanding of the JCMG; and second, a more bottom-up proposal whereby the JCTs would become a standing conference with wide membership, chaired by senior purchasers. In the event, neither option was pushed through.

At the JCSG meeting of November 1993, disagreement between health and social services was again evident over the scope of joint commissioning and the extent to which it should include health promotion as well as community care, and over the possibility of devolved budgets, with local authority members expressing grave reservations about these. Thus after several months of discussion, borough A ended up keeping the basic elements of its 1991 structure. It was decided to replace the JCMG by a group comprising the chairs of the JCTs, who would be senior commissioning staff and therefore likely to be quite similar to the previous JCMG members. Providers and purchasers would continue to be represented on the JCTs.

Compared with most other research authorities, borough A was advanced in its determination to come to grips with joint commissioning. The pattern for this authority was, however, somewhat the same as for care management and the creation of a purchaser–provider split. It moved swiftly to implement the change, but then faced second-order problems of definition and process. Nevertheless, while the authority's ambitions with respect to joint commissioning have not been achieved, the long-standing collaboration between health and social services has not been without success. The joint locality care management project used money from health and social services to fund a project manager's post and offered the possibility of moving towards jointly commissioned care packages. This determination to take a project-based focus and start small has been encouraged by such literature as exists on joint commissioning (e.g. Department of Health *et al.* 1993a). The comment of a senior purchaser in the SSD on the review of joint planning early in 1994 was shrewd:

> I think we have joint planning at the moment and not joint commissioning . . . we hooked ourselves on to this ambitious agenda for all sorts of external reasons and I think if we had started off by saying we are going to have some joint planning project work and where possible some sharing of budgetary responsibility, then we would have felt we had achieved more . . . because I think joint planning and joint project work is what we happen to do well . . .

Borough B

Since April 1993, boroughs B, C and D have shared the same health agency. Initially borough B was opposed to the reconfiguration and the new health agency offered to assign designated purchasing staff to each authority. However, the resignation of two senior purchasers within the health agency resulted in this arrangement being abandoned. The benefits of designated personnel were clear in borough B, where in a very short time progress on a number of joint areas of interest for health and social services purchasers became apparent. When the designated staff member left in October 1993, many of his plans were essentially put on ice for the remainder of the research period, and relations seemed to deteriorate.

In contrast to boroughs A and C, borough B did not work closely with the NHS to secure implementation of the new community care policy. The senior officer group overseeing implementation was rarely attended by health authority officers. In part this may be explained by the strength of the SSD's own senior management team and their relatively clear sense of direction. But it may in any case be a mistake to attach too much importance to evidence of collaboration via formal machinery. There were good informal contacts at a senior level in this borough, as well as evidence of joint working, for example on the creation of packages of care for the physically disabled (see below), although the health authority failed to consult fully with social services on its plans for locality purchasing. The record on collaboration is thus harder to assess than for borough A.

In common with all authorities, borough B found it necessary to revamp its joint planning machinery (which took the familiar form of JCC, joint care planning team (JCPT) and local joint planning teams (JPTs)) in the light of the changes since 1990. Unlike borough A, it did not begin to think about this until January 1993, when the JCPT discussed the possibility of moving towards joint commissioning in the light of the reconfiguration of the health authority and changes in the structure and working of the SSD. Frustration with the way in which the joint planning machinery was working meant that a review was generally welcomed by all participants, including the representatives of voluntary organisations, albeit with the proviso that they would be fully involved in discussions related to the changes. Senior SSD managers made it clear that they found the client-based JPTs in particular to be unwieldy, time consuming and unproductive. One expressed concern that too much of the work carried out by the client-based JPTs was 'unfocused and unusable'. The authority was determined to move towards a slimmer structure focused on purchasing. According to one senior officer:

> I think that we have learnt on the ground that tactical joint commissioning for individual clients can work very effectively, so we need to look at how we make services we commission jointly and strategically have that same arrangement.

Purchasers did not have the capacity to back up the large number of client-based JPTs, so in any move to joint commissioning the structure would have to change. It should be noted that the development of joint commissioning in borough B paralleled the growing conviction among senior managers of the merits of a purchaser–provider split within the department.

A day to review joint commissioning was set for April 1993, but this ended up as a series of presentations by and about the SSD to voluntary organisations. Participation by the health authority was slight. A paper written after the review day offered a number of options. This was modified five times. The first draft of the paper set out a range of models for joint commissioning: disbanding the JPTs altogether; making membership of the JPTs provider oriented and their status advisory; retaining the old joint planning machinery but making the work more task focused, concentrating on macro-needs analysis and measurement of user satisfaction; turning the JPTs into joint commissioning teams; and finally a system of provider networks feeding the JCPT, which would be given the task of overseeing purchasing strategy. The paper was clearly grappling with the problem of purchaser and provider representation on the one hand, and that of a strategic planning as against a commissioning role on the other. At the beginning of 1994 a huge cut in the amount available for joint finance made the old joint planning structure seem even more irrelevant.

The last two attempts to elaborate a new model reflected the concerns of purchasers in the SSD. The fourth draft offered the following definition of joint commissioning:

A process of jointly agreeing the range of health and social care services to be provided in the borough and which agency will commission and fund particular services to contribute to the achievement of the community care plan. It is not, as the term joint commissioning might suggest, the delineation of separate health and social service responsibilities by the pooling of both agencies' budgets and the joint signing of contracts, as both social services and health have very separate (as well as overlapping) legal responsibilities.

The aim of joint commissioning was therefore set out clearly as 'compatible commissioning'. The final draft proposed to reduce the membership of the JCPT to health and social services purchasers and to rename it a joint commissioning executive group. The JPTs were to become joint planning provider fora, involving representatives from the voluntary and independent sectors, as well as from health and social services. In other words the idea was to create a small purchasing caucus with provider fora providing advice and guidance on purchasing plans where appropriate.

Responsibility for finalising the arrangements for the new structure and for writing the final draft of the document was given to a multiagency working group comprising purchasers from health and social services and voluntary sector representatives. At this stage it was important to try to secure joint ownership of the changes. The voluntary sector had expressed concern several times during the review process about the way in which they had been consulted. They feared that they were being effectively squeezed out of the new structure. When health and social services managers changed the final report of the working group, it seemed to the voluntary sector representatives that their fears were being realised.

The final document proposed to restrict the voluntary sector to participation in provider fora, with no clear access to purchasers. The voluntary sector representatives expressed 'grave concern' about the document and their dislike at being 'pigeonholed' as providers. As a result, one of the provider fora broke away from the new system and set up its own group. In the case of another forum, a voluntary sector representative said that it was his intention 'to go along to the first couple of meetings and see what is developing'; in other words he felt no ownership of the new arrangements. Nor was the voluntary sector's wish for a full-time 'networks officer' post granted, which would have provided the kind of direction secured from the project manager in borough A. Money was provided for a part-time post only.

While borough B took a year to complete the overhaul of its joint planning machinery, it had a clear vision of what it wanted to achieve and a clear view as to the meaning of joint commissioning. Senior purchasers became convinced that the kind of task-focused joint working they wished to encourage could not be promoted via the old joint planning machinery. As one put it:

> I actually think that fundamentally joint working is about officer-to-officer discussions . . . the idea of putting respite care into one agency's hands – if we had fed that through the old model of joint planning, nothing would have happened; everybody would have put their hands up in horror and said 'you are reducing the service' . . .

However, as another senior social services purchaser said, the authority could not start with 'a blank sheet', rather, 'you are starting with something that has been very rooted and established and it has taken us a year to do something that is really not that radical'. The old joint planning machinery was about involving as many different interest groups as possible. Any attempt to slim it down was bound to be difficult, and while borough B had a clear idea of where it wanted to go, it was not altogether successful in negotiating the change, in that it resulted in the alienation of parts of the voluntary sector.

Borough C

Borough C had the most elaborate joint planning machinery when the new health agency was set up in April 1993. Like borough A, it had revamped its joint planning structure in 1991. In fact, representatives from the NHS were taken into the new community care planning machinery and the old joint planning system was effectively abolished. There had been very little activity in the field of joint planning in the borough during the late 1980s; as one senior manager put it: 'Everyone was quite happy to find something else and leave joint planning behind.' The history of acrimonious relations between health and social services managers came to an end with a change in NHS personnel. The SSD's determination to interpret the new community care policy in terms of user-centred care meant that it was particularly keen to develop collaboration as a means to secure 'seamless care' for users. Indeed, borough C tended to conceptualise the whole purpose of the community care changes in terms of joint working, which, as we have seen in the previous chapter, included the idea of care coordination, whereas an authority like the county put far more emphasis on enabling.

In 1991, 11 inter-agency planning fora were set up on a client-group basis. The large number of these (borough A set up five in 1991) meant that many were staffed by fourth-tier health and social services personnel, who were not in a position to make decisions. Three overarching groups – assessment and care management, aggregate need, and black and minority ethnic groups – were also set up. These reported to a community care planning steering group, which reported to a commissioning group, which in turn reported to

Table 9.1 Joint planning structures in borough C

1991	1993
Joint consultative committee	Joint consultative committee
Commissioning group	Chief officers' group
Community care planning steering group	Coordinating commissioning group
Overarching planning fora	Overarching special focus groups
Inter-agency planning fora	Joint commissioning groups

the joint consultative committee (see Table 9.1). Despite the name 'commissioning group', there was no real intention to give the group a purchasing brief, at least in the short to medium term. Rather, the group was supposed to provide a strategic focus. The creation of the steering group in addition to the commissioning group reflected the difficulty faced by all authorities in terms of reaching a balance between involving as many interested parties as possible and yet establishing a group capable of making decisions. There was in fact substantial overlap between the membership of the two groups. The steering group was the larger of the two and was intended to ensure coordination among the other groups, but it was never clear whether its role was primarily information sharing or decision making. In the event, decision making tended to fall between the two groups.

In the middle of 1992 a meeting of chief executives of health and social services sanctioned the move towards joint purchasing. Senior officers from both authorities had invested time in a two-day simulation event and one assistant director in the SSD was a particularly keen promoter of joint commissioning. A paper on joint commissioning prepared within the SSD set out the steps that would be necessary, including further disaggregation of budgets, devolution of decision-making responsibilities and the pooling of budgets. (By early 1994 this vision of joint commissioning had been recognised as 'utopian' by some senior managers.)

It was decided to turn the inter-agency planning groups into joint commissioning groups (JCGs) during the course of 1993. These were envisaged as being smaller, with mainly third-tier members and chairs, who were all purchasers. The overarching groups were retained, renamed special focus groups, and their numbers increased to include groups on carers, housing, publicity, and monitoring. GPs were included as representatives on some of these. Certainly, central government has exhorted local authorities to involve GPs, but problems of securing a representative GP, together with problems on the GP's part of finding the time to attend meetings that often got procedurally and operationally bogged down made this difficult. The steering group and the commissioning group were replaced by the coordinating commissioning group, and above this the chief officers' group was assigned a rather vague role (see Table 9.1).

Reflecting the formal commitment in borough C to maximising the role of the voluntary sector in the joint machinery, all tiers of the 1993 structure, including the chief officers' group, included voluntary organisation representatives. There was persistent difficulty in securing effective decision making from groups representing a large number of interests. Thus yet another small group, comprising senior officers and a voluntary representative – the commissioning support group – emerged in 1993. There was an effort to make sure that there was liaison between groups, even if only to the extent of circulating minutes. Lack of such liaison had been one of the reasons cited by purchasers in borough B for abandoning the JCTs. However, there were no real mechanisms for feeding the work done by the overarching groups into that of the JCGs.

The new structure also made provision for a jointly funded joint commissioning development officer post, which was filled in the autumn of 1993 by someone from the voluntary sector, demonstrating the close links between the voluntary and statutory sectors in this borough. The existence of the post compared favourably with borough B, although it has probably ended up being more advisory than that of the project manager in borough A.

Borough C has thus shown a huge commitment to joint commissioning. Its hopes in 1992 were as large as those of borough A in 1991. These have not been realised. Work during 1993/4 was described by one senior social services manager as 'shadow joint commissioning'. In fact, no joint commissioning has taken place. At the level of the JCGs, observation revealed providers to be the repositories of both experience and expertise. This was due primarily to a greater continuity in provider staffing at the crucial third-tier manager level. Some of the new purchaser chairs were therefore less experienced than their provider colleagues and less well equipped to give a lead. The difficulties of including purchaser and provider representatives on these groups was initially unacknowledged but real. In the words of one social services' senior manager:

> the move to joint commissioning has always felt like a bit of an idealised notion of collaboration and cooperation, without acknowledgement of reality and different tensions . . . [it] seemed to . . . create an expectation that we would put things in the middle of the table and look at them . . . it felt to me to be very unreal.

This manager felt that because in-house providers consumed the bulk of resources they were under particular scrutiny. Voluntary organisation representatives, on the other hand, felt disadvantaged because they were marginal providers. They also felt the concern common to voluntary organisation representatives in most of the research authorities regarding the confusion between their role as participants and their role as advocates.

The JCGs were poorly resourced in terms of secretarial and administrative support. None had a development budget with which to commission pieces of work and members had no time to undertake work themselves. Observation also revealed a lack of basic information on which to make decisions, for example in respect of the allocation of joint funding. Nor were groups clear as to the kind of decisions they could make. In practice their decision-making capacities appeared severely circumscribed. As one third-tier officer commented at the beginning of 1994: 'Groups have been unsure of the status they have in relation to committing budgets . . . this has caused confusion over the status of the groups: is it decision making, advisory or recommendatory?'

In many respects, this was the key point. Joint commissioning was not happening because the groups had no new budgets to spend, no authority to spend their agencies' budgets, and no development money to commission pieces of work. The gulf between the hopes surrounding joint commissioning and the ability of the groups to deliver was expressed by the chair of one JCG, when he said that it was like a parent asking a child what she or he wanted for Christmas when the present was already bought.

As in borough A, it proved impossible to allow JCGs to commission. There were many reasons for this, including both the need for statutory authorities to manage cuts and the health authority's obligation to manage purchasing across three local authorities. Senior social services managers were reluctant to devolve decision making to third- and fourth-tier officers and no clear direction was given by the coordinating commissioning group. Genuine tensions about accountability existed side by side with organisational and legal constraints.

To senior managers in the health authority in particular, the whole machinery of joint commissioning seemed impossibly protracted. This is probably one reason why decision making was actually as likely to take place outside the formal joint commissioning machinery as within it. This happened in respect of both hospital resettlement and the planned closure of a residential home, a matter that was never brought before the older people's JCG.

Some JCGs seem to have gone through their own learning curve, and in the absence of any firm sense of direction regarding the nature of joint commissioning from the top, arrived at a point where they agreed to undertake project-focused work in a manner not dissimilar to borough A. However, the definition of joint commissioning among senior managers has remained vague.

Like borough B, borough C undertook a further review of its joint commissioning structure, although not until mid-1994 was there a firm proposal to modify the machinery to give providers a new role. It was decided that ultimate decision-making power would in future rest with the chairs of the JCGs, who were purchasers. Unlike the case of borough B, this proved relatively unproblematic. Both providers and voluntary organisations welcomed the move to a more advisory role. Social services providers were, by then, more familiar with the idea of the purchaser–provider split and expressed readiness to seek alliances with providers from health and the independent and voluntary sectors. For voluntary organisation representatives, the proposal offered a solution to the tension they were feeling between their role as participants and their role as advocates. The traditional closeness of the voluntary and statutory sectors in the borough also meant that there was less likelihood of mistrust over such a proposal, although at the time of the review, one voluntary organisation representative voiced her continued feelings of confusion about the meaning of joint commissioning.

The idea that joint commissioning is in essence 'a good thing' seems to have carried the whole project forward in this borough. Despite the failings of the formal machinery, it has contributed to an atmosphere in which informal and bottom-up developments have been able to thrive. There has been a conviction that clarity will emerge out of this positive atmosphere. A health authority manager took this a little further:

> In some ways, the notion of joint commissioning is a bit of a misnomer, and I think it means all things to all people. What it is in real terms is, I think, a process of planning . . . what we actually have is a planning structure into which there have to be clear agreements for certain types of funding over certain periods of time, against a clear specification.

In fact, JCGs have not got this far in borough C, but this manager's vision of what joint commissioning could offer was remarkably similar to that of a senior social services manager in borough A. As of late 1994, borough C's internal commissioning structure was not sufficiently advanced to make even the idea of devising a 'compatible commissioning' strategy work, but in 1992, when the utopian idea of joint commissioning had been put forward, the SSD had had no commissioning capacity at all. Two years later it may, like other authorities, be closer to having an effective planning structure for commissioning, an option outlined in the Department of Health *et al.*'s (1993a) document on joint commissioning.

Borough D

This borough, like the other two sharing the same health authority, reviewed its joint planning structures in autumn 1993 and decided on a new structure that had much in common with the purchasing caucus/provider consultation model adopted in boroughs B and C, although without the opposition encountered in borough B and without having to negotiate the huge structure that existed in borough C. On paper, this borough would seem to have the most promising model. However, it exists in something of a vacuum. When the borough began the process of reviewing its joint planning structure with a view to moving to joint commissioning in October 1993, the SSD had no purchasers in place. In addition, given the lack of an ethos of change in this borough, the informal commitment to joint working, which proved so important elsewhere, was lacking.

Borough D's joint planning structure was the usual one of JCC, JCPT and local joint planning teams (LJPTs). There was no attempt at liaison between these, aside from reporting systems established at the level of the JCPT, unlike the albeit not very successful attempts at inter-group linkages in borough C. The LJPTs were not resourced in any meaningful way and health representatives did not usually attend. In other words, the problems of the LJPTs were not dissimilar to those experienced elsewhere. At the top of the joint planning structure, the SSD was quite dependent on the health authority because it lacked planning and strategic staff of its own. In January 1992, a senior managers' group was set up, ostensibly to look at the social/health care boundary, but this group tended to share information more than make decisions. Issues such as the possibility of a joint OT service remained on the agenda for more than a year between 1992 and 1993 without reaching any resolution.

The need to review the structure was set out in a September 1993 paper as being:

> in line with the majority of authorities throughout the country who have found that structures set up previously are no longer appropriate to the current differentiation of functions in all agencies to purchaser/ commissioner and provider/operational roles in a community care setting.

Despite not having implemented the purchaser–provider split, the borough recognised the need not to be left behind. It was also very aware of forthcoming budget cuts for social services and the need to join forces where possible with the health authority. However, it was necessarily cautious about moving towards joint commissioning in the sense of actual joint purchasing. As a senior manager pointed out, members would not allow officers that kind of freedom in an authority 'where members like to know whether it is going to be sago or tapioca for pudding'. Health authority officers took the lead in pushing the idea of joint commissioning.

The review of the structure took place in two workshops held in October 1993 and January 1994, facilitated by an external consultant. Out of these emerged a model of a purchasing caucus and provider forums not dissimilar to the shift in the other two boroughs sharing the same health authority. At the meeting in October, voluntary organisations feared that such a change would mean a more hierarchical structure and would involve them giving up their hard-won place in the joint planning structures, but social services managers stressed the idea of differentiated roles together with equal partnership. According to the report from the second review day, the challenge of the new system was:

To grasp the present opportunity to assist the community in [borough D] to understand and recognise the new ways in which the statutory and voluntary bodies can operate in partnership with users, carers and consumers within (a) a clear purchaser/provider split, (b) with maximum joint collaboration between budget holders, commissioners and members of the statutory bodies.

As in borough B, a working group was set up to work out the detail of the new arrangements, but with first- and second-tier staff rather than the third- and fourth-tier officers included by borough B. The work of the group was usefully steered in borough D by the SSD's health liaison officer, a primarily administrative post that had existed under the old joint planning structure. While the new joint commissioning structures require a shift in focus towards project management (as in borough A), the presence of the administrative officer was nevertheless important in achieving a smoother transition to the new system in borough D than was the case in borough B.

The new structure replaced the JCPT with a joint health strategy group comprised of purchasers, with a brief to set the decision-making agenda for the JCC, to share information, and to develop two or three priority areas. The LJPTs were replaced by client-focused groups comprised of providers, whose job was to propose key priorities, monitor services and identify areas for innovation. The borough also introduced a customer consultation group to look at ways of involving users and carers. In line with the idea of partnership rather than hierarchy, the structure was described by the SSD in terms of promoting 'circular relationships' between the different levels. This did much to win over voluntary organisation opinion, as did the effort to include users and carers in the process. How the relationships will work out in practice remains to be seen.

The county

The county worked with two health authorities until these merged in October 1993. The process of merger, followed by a restructuring of the joint planning machinery, has meant that there was something of a hiatus in terms of formal joint planning/commissioning during much of the life of the research project. Nevertheless, the new structure that has emerged has some interesting points of contrast with the London boroughs, especially in terms of the meaning of joint commissioning.

Before October 1993, the two sets of joint planning machinery were rather different. In the eastern part of the county there was a more formal structure, consisting of a JCC, a joint planning and purchasing team, client planning teams and local development groups (LDGs). The client planning teams drew their representatives from the whole of the eastern part of the county, while the LDGs were much more localised, based, for example, on a particular town. As in the other authorities, both sets of groups produced work of variable quality. In the west of the county the structure consisted of a JCC, a JCPT and a range of fora and short-life working groups. In other words, the bottom of the structure was considerably less formalised.

The review of the structure that began in the summer of 1993 was a sensitive process and was dominated by the new health authority. The model was a purchasing one, although the term purchasing appeared in the title of only one tier in the new machinery and the term commissioning did not appear at all. The new structure consisted of: the JCC, a chief officers' group, a joint strategy group (JSG), a joint purchasing group (JPG), and locality planning groups (based on the 9 health localities rather than the 15 SSD localities). The chief officers' group was left deliberately informal, but appeared to deal with a wide range of issues, covering both major points of joint strategic direction and the resolution of particular disputes about financing aspects of a particular user's care. The creation of two groups below this, effectively separating strategy from purchasing, appears odd. The explanation lies in the old dilemma: how to maximise the representation of stakeholders while securing a group that is sufficiently cohesive to make decisions. Thus the JSG was large and included representatives from the district councils, whereas the JPG was much smaller. The establishment of both was a not dissimilar development to the setting up of the commissioning support group in addition to the coordinating commissioning group in borough C. Even with both these groups, it is still the case that informal inter-agency meetings of purchasers probably played the most important role of all in securing collaboration. In the county very small numbers of purchasers of equivalent grades met for what were frank discussions; in the formal structure the status of the non-statutory representatives tended to be lower than that of the two statutory agencies, which made strategic decision making difficult.

The use of the new health locality planning groups at the bottom of the structure meant that the client planning teams and the LDGs in the east of the county were asked to stand down. As in borough B, this met with considerable opposition from voluntary organisations and some LDGs decided to change their names and carry on. Locality planning provides no formal places for voluntary sector representatives. Voluntary organisations were represented at the top of the structure, but according to one representative the new structures felt 'pretty terrible', while another felt that she was placed 'lower than the salt'. The new structure therefore marginalised the voluntary sector and there was no provider input either.

Despite being dominated by purchasers, the new structure had not got as far as engaging in joint purchasing by the end of 1994. Instead, the JPG tended to continue to confine its decisions to joint finance. However, the authorities made a commitment to move forward to joint purchasing in respect of people with learning difficulties and people with mental health problems. What is interesting is the extent to which this progress was due to factors other than the attributes of the new structures, such as personalities. This is perhaps not surprising, given the complicated nature of the purchasing structure in the county. As well as the layers of purchasing possible within the SSD, there is also the possibility in the future of cross-agency purchasing at a locality level, or indeed cross-consortia/cross-agency purchasing. The picture is additionally complicated by the fact that 50 per cent of the population is registered with GPs who are fundholders, and who must agree individually to any joint commissioning strategy. Both health and social services were struggling to find the appropriate scale for purchasing.

In this context, it seems that the county decided to take an open-ended approach to joint commissioning. In one of the clearest statements by a senior manager, joint commissioning was defined in terms of each agency declaring its purchasing intentions and then coming together to explore the areas of overlap. This provides a simple starting point and does not assume that the process will result in joint purchasing, joint specifications, or joint anything in particular. In practice, the county has been successful in pursuing a variation on the theme of project-related work. The JSG set itself the task of reviewing strategy in respect of client groups on a rolling basis and had completed work on people with learning difficulties at the end of 1994. Aside from the formal strategy review work of the JSG, the county introduced a series of joint initiatives and proposals.

Before the start of the research, health staff had been trained in care management procedures, enabling them to access SSD resources for individual clients. During the research period, initiatives were undertaken in respect of making information systems compatible, joint commissioning for mental health, and an SSD purchaser–health provider relationship established under formal contract using STG moneys. This approach is reminiscent of what Gostick (1993) described as 'specialist group commissioning'. In an extremely complicated purchasing environment, it has the great advantage of providing a pragmatic approach. Once again, it is the case that while the new structure has not resulted in the kind of joint commissioning outlined by Knapp and Wistow (Department of Health *et al.* 1993a), it has provided the means for effective joint planning in the sense of agreeing strategy and priorities.

The new joint commissioning structures – issues

It is possible to observe convergence in all the research authorities towards an understanding of joint commissioning in terms of 'compatible commissioning', collaboration that involves agreement on the framework within which purchasers from the statutory authorities will purchase. Early, rather utopian hopes on the part of two authorities – boroughs A and C – regarding the possibility of actual joint purchasing have faded. In the best case, what seems to be emerging is, paradoxically, structures that make effective joint planning more possible, together with the possibility of more project-focused work.

All the research authorities were prompted to move towards making their formal structures more oriented towards purchasing; only borough A did not in the end change the composition of its groups, but it has nevertheless been committed from an early stage to facilitating joint commissioning. Borough B and the county were, as ever, clearest in their vision of what could and could not be aimed for in terms of joint commissioning, but it is perhaps symptomatic of the difficulties in achieving effective joint commissioning structures that both these authorities experienced problems in reconciling stakeholders to the new structures, particularly voluntary sector representatives. Statutory agencies had tended to define voluntary organisations as providers and hence to 'relegate' them to a consultative role in the machinery, which many do not regard as in any way an 'equal' part.

All authorities have faced an additional difficulty in securing groups that are fully representative of all interests and yet small enough to reach decisions. Securing liaison between the different levels of joint commissioning machinery has also been difficult. And the new structures have faced the same problems as the old joint planning machinery regarding the difference in accountability structures and cycles between health and social services, for example in respect of budgetary planning. In some local authorities members were very suspicious of joint commissioning. However, in the county the new machinery was beginning to overcome some of the structural impediments to collaboration, for example in respect of the alignment of planning cycles. Nevertheless, the very real problems in achieving effective collaborative structures have persisted and it is therefore not surprising that decisions continue to be made using informal channels. This was true of four of the five research authorities and means that there must still be something of a question mark over the time and money devoted to the elaborate formal structures.

Overcoming the barriers to formal collaboration requires commitment from senior management staff and the establishment of dedicated joint commissioning posts. Comparison of the London boroughs showed that those departments with a joint commissioning officer managed the shift to joint commissioning rather better and revealed the extent to which such a person is important in pushing collaborative work along. It is also the case that the administrative liaison officers commonly found in the old joint planning structures have had to take a rather different view of their responsibilities in the new structures and become more project focused.

The new joint commissioning structures hold out more promise of effective joint planning than their predecessors, but it would be a mistake to rest any assessment of collaboration on the work of these structures alone. The fundamental conflicts between agencies that are financed separately, administered separately, staffed by different professions and run within different statutory frameworks are so great that no joint commissioning or joint planning has much hope of succeeding. In essence, nothing has changed since one of the authors studied the issue 15 years ago (Glennerster 1983). Then, as now, informal working was just as or more important than formal structures in many of the authorities.

One of the problems with the new machinery is that in the context of the social care market, purchasing has tended to assume the greater importance; providers have been allocated a consultative role. While this makes sense in terms of determining strategies and priorities, there is a danger that collaborative achievements that are not part of the commissioning process but depend rather on joint working between providers will be crowded out.

Joint working by providers

'Seamless care' depends on joint working. Both health and social services carry out assessments and provide care, and this effort has to be coordinated. There were examples of joint working to be found in all the research authorities, but very few had any links to the formal joint commissioning structures. Such collaboration had usually grown up from cooperation at the level of front-line providers. It was not subjected to any central steering and tended to be very disparate.

Only borough A developed a 'seamless care' project using the formal joint commissioning machinery. The joint locality care management project was set up to evaluate assessment and provision, and involved one care management team and six GP practices. It ran into problems over differences between both the hierarchical structures operating in health and social services, and the eligibility criteria employed. The project leader felt that one of the major obstacles to developing a joint assessment process was that people were not willing to provide resources on the basis of another agency's assessment and she therefore recommended the devolution of budgets to one locality as a pilot project. But the move to creating a joint budget was firmly resisted by local authority members.

More common have been 'pockets' of joint working divorced from the formal planning machinery. For example, in borough B cooperation between health and social services was secured informally whereby the health authority stopped discharging physically disabled people from hospital into nursing home care and worked instead with social services to develop packages of care.

Many authorities have endeavoured to work out a scheme of common assessment, but it proved extremely difficult to devise a common assessment form. Some of the county's inter-agency teams have managed to secure acceptance of one professional group's assessment by another, although in

many places this has proved problematic. However, agreement over the
process of assessment should be a priority for future work. In the past,
tensions over needs and resources were resolved at the level of provision, by
providers agreeing more or less amicably about who did what. But as
contracts develop further and become more specific, it is likely that the issue
as to who does what will disappear. The mediation of resources will then take
place at the site of assessment rather than provision.

To some extent, the development of purchasing has raised additional
difficulties for providers attempting joint working. In the case of the mental
health multidisciplinary teams in the county, it is possible that at some time in
the future GP fundholders may elect to pull community psychiatric nurses out
of the teams and attach them instead to practices. As it is, GP fundholders
have tended to pass their 'worried well' patients wanting assessment by CPNs
over to the SSD's multidisciplinary teams, swelling the waiting list. The
problem of engaging with large numbers of fundholders in the county is
considerable.

While the purchaser–provider split has the advantage of making the gap
between health and social care transparent, many home care and district
nursing respondents referred to the difficulties they experienced as a result of
their interactions being mediated by care managers; in certain respects home
care workers tended to feel more allegiance to district nurses than to social
workers/care managers. While lack of conterminous boundaries between
health and social services has always been an impediment to the delivery of
seamless care, the added dimension of purchaser–provider splits, together
with the additional geographical subdivisions of health and social services
purchasers, have posed further challenges. Providers in the county, for
example, have been faced with different purchasing policies in different
localities.

One district nurse working in borough A referred to a 'golden age' before
the 1974 reorganisation of the NHS, when both the district nursing and home
help services had been controlled by the medical officer of health in the local
authority and, according to her account, good cooperation resulted:

> When we first came into district nursing that is how we worked . . .
> whoever got there started first; the patient might need a cup of tea,
> we would put the kettle on, we did the dressing, then the home help
> might come and take over. . . . We were all employed by the same
> authority. . . . If someone was heavy, we didn't bring another nurse in,
> now we're having to provide two nurses; personal care or home help
> would help you, you knew the home help would attend to your client
> and you worked together . . .

Borough A was endeavouring to operate a 'shared care' arrangement between
home care workers and district nurses, which this nurse saw as an effort to
return to the kind of cooperation she had experienced some 20 years

previously. However, workers from the two statutory agencies are now employed on a different basis, social care workers being allocated to clients on the basis of units of time and health care workers on a capitation basis. Problems therefore arose for the home carer if the district nurse was late. It is also more problematic to secure good cooperation between these groups of workers at a time of budgetary contraction, when most health authorities in particular are trying to withdraw from those tasks on the borderline between health and social care.

Indeed, as the Audit Commission (1992a: 10) pointed out, it has proved very difficult to define the boundary between health and social care. In borough D, a seamless care project designed to promote the development of a generic worker to cover the grey area between health and social services (an idea also discussed in two other boroughs) came into being as a result of an initiative taken by a health provider. In practice, it proved difficult to identify suitable clients for this project. This scheme and a similar one in the county proved both hard to negotiate and expensive. The classic 'grey areas', such as bathing, matter enormously to users, but less so to the statutory authorities because they tend not to be associated with high risk. As a social services manager in borough D put it:

> I think in terms of our relationship with health and the grey area, bathing has to be the most obvious, the sort of smaller tasks . . . little things that . . . are not a priority for us, because the person won't collapse. The short way to say it [define the grey area] is the things that none of us can offer any more because of finance.

In the absence of anything but anecdotal evidence as to how much the dependency levels of people being cared for in the community have increased, it is hard for authorities to discuss the grey area between health and social care and how to cover it. In borough B, the authorities moved quickly after April 1993 to identify the grey area, but trade union resistance on the part of home care staff has meant that there has been little progress in extending the practice of home carers to include more tasks hitherto defined as being on the borderline of nursing care.

In the county, the contracts to purchase community nursing have been vague and some health managers have said that they have left negotiation of the boundary to front-line workers:

> For example, you give a chap insulin and that's probably the only visitor he gets. He needs perhaps toast and tea. This is not a health task, but of course on an individual level she [the nurse] will. She has to weigh up her own priorities and come to a decision . . . I don't want to take away my nurses' discretion to make decisions like this.

However, it is not necessarily easy for the nurse to make such decisions. In one of the research authorities, nurses said that they were picking up social care tasks for patients who were waiting for assessment, but they felt that this would have met with the disapproval of their managers.

Hunter *et al.* (1988) were much more optimistic about joint working than about joint planning, although Hardy *et al.*'s (1992) investigation into inter-agency cooperation stressed the vulnerability of jointly managed projects. The encouragement given to statutory authorities by the guidance to 'start small' and to think in terms of project-based work may well promote joint working, but the fact that many of the current endeavours bear no relation to the formal joint commissioning machinery may be a sign that insufficient attention is being paid by senior managers to provider-centred aspects of collaborative work. It may also be that both senior purchasers and senior providers know little about aspects of collaborative working between providers at lower levels. This raises the larger issue of the valuable strategic input that providers could make and how this may best be achieved.

Obligatory collaboration

Community care plans

The production of a community care plan was one of two areas of collaboration that was dictated by government. The original impetus behind the idea of community care plans had been Griffiths' proposals to link them to the allocation of resources (Department of Health and Social Security 1988). When the 1990 legislation failed to make such a link, the precise purpose of the plans was no longer clear. The 1990 official guidance advised that the plans did not have to be jointly produced, but that they should be based on shared principles and show how the authorities were going to promote the aims of the legislation in respect of assessing need, clarifying the responsibilities of the agencies involved, securing better value for money, ensuring support for carers and promoting a flourishing independent sector (Department of Health, 1990b). In the research authorities, plans varied considerably in terms of the means used to produce them and in their form, both between authorities and within a single authority over the three years of their production (1992/3, 1993/4 and 1994/5).

Hardy *et al.*'s (1993) analysis of 25 community care plans found that only 50 per cent were jointly owned by health and local authorities. Boroughs A, C and D all produced their plans jointly, using the joint planning machinery, although borough D established a special inter-agency group to oversee the production of the plan. In borough B, the SSD took responsibility for the production of the plan, with the JPTs contributing sections on the different client groups. From 1993/4 it was jointly signed. In the county, while the plan was jointly owned from the first, the bulk of the work involved in its production was carried out by the SSD in the first two years.

The 1990 legislation obliged authorities to consult widely in the production of plans, and in 1993 a new circular instructed local authorities to consult representatives of the independent sector (LAC (93) 4). Hardy *et al.* (1993) found that of their 25 authorities, 64 per cent had consulted the private sector and 84 per cent the voluntary sector. As Phaure (1992) commented in his review of plans produced in London, authorities interpreted the injunction to consult very differently. Indeed, consultation tended to be most elaborate in the first and second years of community care planning. In borough C, the experience of getting somewhat similar replies over the first two years of consultation on the draft plan resulted in a decision to change the process. Asking about gaps meant that a huge range of needs were identified, which could not possibly be met. One senior manager acknowledged that by the second and third years, users and carers were beginning to say: 'you keep asking, but very little is getting delivered'. In this authority the aim for the two to three years after 1995 was therefore to focus on priorities and on plans for commissioning.

Hardy *et al.* (1993: para. 5.1) advised that authorities needed to recognise the 'changed planning context' and should see community care plans as purchasing documents. In a sense this had always been implicit in the idea of community care planning after 1990. Clarifying the role of agencies in the context of the development of a social care market necessarily involved deciding who would do what, at what cost. However, the evolution of purchasing structures took considerable time and in many places was by no means complete at the end of 1994. In addition, the community care plan was intended to be a public document, which tended to conflict with any idea of making it a sophisticated purchasing plan. It is therefore not surprising that the purpose and hence the form of community care plans remained unclear in most places.

The first plan in all the research authorities tended to be descriptive, focusing on what was available rather than what authorities planned to purchase. In borough D this remained the case in 1994/5. Indeed, most authorities lacked the planning capacity to do much more than this. In borough B, the 1994/5 plan contained more on resources and eligibility criteria and to this extent moved in the direction of becoming a purchasing plan, although much of the content still amounted to a directory of services. Borough A produced a very short plan in 1994/5, which was coordinated by a voluntary sector representative. This borough decided to put its efforts into getting the joint commissioning machinery right in 1994, rather than into the community care plan.

Borough C changed the form of its plan dramatically over the three years. The 1992/3 plan consisted of a 100-page document, accompanied by a short summary document, and included chapters on different client groups prepared by the joint planning group machinery. The plan for 1993/4 consisted of a bulky folder compiled in a similar way, but that for 1994/5 was both brief and rather vague. The aim continued to be to produce something for public consumption, which helps to explain the rather bland character of the plan. Thus under 'Priorities for 1994', the chapter on older people listed areas of desired developments – respite care, services for older people with mental health problems, services for black and ethnic minority communities, residential and nursing home provision, and provision to enable people to remain at home – with no reference to the state of current provision, the funding available, or precise purchasing plans.

The county has perhaps gone furthest in resolving the conflicting pressures affecting the production of community care plans. In years two and three it began to produce locality plans, which consisted of information useful to local residents, together with a centrally produced plan that has become much more of an SSD strategy document. It was decided that the 1994/5 plan would be based on the 9 health localities, rather than the 15 SSD localities.

A considerable amount of effort was devoted to the production of community care plans, not least because the Act made them obligatory. However, the impact of these documents has been rather limited. Borough A's decision to concentrate on getting its joint commissioning machinery in order before putting more effort into its plan was surely logical if the plan is to become more of a commissioning document. But most authorities have yet to decide how to reconcile the emphasis on commissioning with the plan's official role as a publicly accessible document.

Nursing home and hospital discharge agreements

Unlike community care plans, which were supposed to set a new planning framework, government's requirement that authorities reach agreement about the integration of hospital discharge arrangements with assessment procedures, and about strategies governing their responsibilities for placing people in nursing homes, addressed long-standing problems that were brought to a head by the full implementation of the new community care policy in April 1993. In 1993, the Audit Commission signalled a possible area of conflict between the aims of health and social services when it pointed out that the choice directive on residential care was slowing down discharge from hospital. Good care management required time for both proper assessment and choice; hospitals wanted rapid discharge.

Thus local authorities were required to reach agreement with health authorities by the end of 1992 or forfeit a substantial proportion of their STG moneys. Agreements were renewed at the end of 1993, and government required that they become more detailed the second time round, including likely numbers of people needing residential and combined health and social services support at home, as well as the number who would be entering nursing homes. As one senior manager in borough A commented:

> I think one of the slickest things that the Department of Health did was to say there must be a signed agreement before they hand over the transitional grant. That was a really wonderful thing for them to do because they achieved a whole load of things they hadn't managed to achieve over the years . . . it's forced health providers, social services and health commissioners to come together.

All local authorities reached agreement by the end of 1992. However, there is some doubt as to how robust these agreements actually were (see also Henwood and Wistow 1993). Discussion about the agreements in borough D revealed that no one was sure about the precise nature of the agreement, for example in respect of the timescales for hospital discharge. In borough C it was acknowledged that the 1992 agreement was drawn up to enable the local authority to get its full STG allocation, but that the 1993 agreement would have to be more of a living document.

In some authorities the number of placements in nursing homes was rather crudely estimated in both 1992 and 1993. This was true of borough C and contrasts with the more careful approach in the county, where numbers for the 1993 agreement were based on the actual level of demand for placements and were therefore lower than the estimates included in the 1992 agreement. The major change in practice resulting from the agreements over nursing home beds was the effective passing of the power to place clients from hospital consultants acting in isolation to the collective decision of the SSD/health panels. This happened in all authorities except borough D, which allowed the health authority access to its STG money in order to make placements, which in turn resulted in the money being quickly spent.

The main issue in respect of hospital discharge procedures related to timescales. The health authority shared by three of the London boroughs wanted to include a penalty clause in respect of clients not placed within 28 days. This was not included in the final 1993 agreement, but a target time of 28 days was agreed. Given that placement had previously taken longer, this meant that social services were effectively picking up extra care costs. In borough A, where a 28-day timescale was also set, the main concern of the SSD was to ensure that the client was stable before being assessed, which was agreed. This concern also reflected the problem of the conflict between the health authority's desire for speedy discharge and social services' need to make sure that assessment was meaningful.

Yet in all the research authorities agreement was reached in both 1992 and 1993 relatively amicably. In borough A, the health authority tried to get social services to reach agreement about policies unrelated to the agreement before it would sign, and in one half of the county the two health authorities at first refused to sign the 1992 agreement because they disputed some of the numbers. But given the potentially dramatic divergence in the interests of health and social services, especially in the arena of hospital discharge arrangements, these hiccoughs were minor. Nor did agreements break down in 1993/4. However, this is probably a reflection of the fact that no authority ran out of money. As some shire counties began to run out of funds towards the end of 1994, so the spectre of 'bed blocking' became more real and relationships between health and social services became more tense.

Conclusion

The injunction to collaborate and to achieve seamless care is deceptively simple. First, there are many aspects of collaboration, and it is possible for there to be successful pockets of, say, joint working going on in the absence of any thoroughgoing collaboration in other areas. The emphasis has tended to be put on formal joint machinery, which is in many respects a hangover from the 1970s. For the most part, it has not proved possible to jettison this machinery and start afresh.

Second, the impediments to collaboration between health and social services in the form of differing work cultures, patterns of accountability, imperatives, and timescales have not disappeared, although there is some evidence that the more practical problems – for example, in terms of different planning cycles – are being addressed by the new joint commissioning machinery.

Third, there are new impediments to collaboration inherent within the move to quasi-markets that highlight competition rather than collaboration and can make trust harder to achieve. In addition, the whole nature of the new purchasing structures is very different for health as opposed to social services, which makes it difficult to achieve matching representation in joint commissioning structures, and agreement on ways of approaching decisions regarding a compatible commissioning.

Fourth, and in the long term probably most important, the imperatives facing health and social services are very different in the new order. Health authorities are under growing pressure to move patients out of beds as fast as possible. Indeed, a senior health purchaser in one of the research authorities was frank about wishing to see an end to an NHS commitment to continuing care in the long run. But if social services are to undertake sound assessment and care management, they cannot move too quickly.

Perhaps for these reasons the imposition of collaboration by government fiat may not be wholly successful. Nursing home and hospital discharge agreements can only hold as long as there is no conspicuous shortage of resources. Community care plans have thus far tended to be rather mechanistic exercises, and their purpose has tended to remain unclear. It is not possible to make them do what the guidance intended until assessment and care management and purchasing structures are fully sorted out on the social services side, which, at the end of 1994, was far from being the case in most places.

After that, authorities face the same question of purpose that hovers over joint commissioning machinery. This chapter has suggested that authorities have not been successful in accomplishing actual joint commissioning, but, in what is an unintended outcome, the new machinery has begun to provide a more effective framework for joint planning. It nevertheless remains the case that planning for compatible commissioning cannot assume any real importance until there is a much greater range of domiciliary as well as institutional care to buy. Yet it is impossible to deny the importance of collaboration. Borough C's stress on building a positive attitude to collaboration has merit in this regard. There is a danger that collaboration might be abandoned – because it is so difficult – in the name of waiting for the effective integration of health and social services.

The most recent guidance on collaboration stressed the importance of fostering small projects. On the whole, the value of this advice was borne out by the experience of the research authorities, which makes the relative lack of attention paid to joint working by providers as opposed to joint commissioning a matter for concern. How far elaborate joint commissioning structures are necessary, either for effective planning or for undertaking project-managed work, is unclear. Much of what has actually been accomplished in the research authorities has been the product of informal inter-agency groups.

With regard to the formal joint commissioning machinery, the focus during 1993/4 has been very much on structure and process rather than on outcomes. And yet it is difficult to achieve trust without having a large formal structure that symbolically represents all the interest groups. This is why the slimming down of the new purchasing caucuses, such that the voluntary sector tended to be excluded, caused so much fuss in two authorities.

Collaboration requires time, commitment and energy at a senior level, and money, particularly for dedicated posts. All are difficult to achieve and it is likely that authorities will collaborate only as much as they have to. Yet, past experience has shown that collaboration at the margins produces very little. However much is achieved in informal ways, it can never amount to the fully fledged collaboration that is arguably necessary at both the strategic and individual-user levels.

10

Conclusion: what has changed?

The core policy

We have seen that there is nothing new about government's pursuit of community care. Nor was there anything new about the problems that derive from the split system of funding and administration of what should be a seamless web of services for vulnerable people. What was new in the 1980s was the runaway cost of giving families what amounted to an open cheque to buy residential and nursing home care – the most expensive kind of alternatives available. No government could have let such a situation continue. In the end stopping it was the Conservative government's prime concern. We, therefore, called this the 'deep normative core' of the government's policy.

It succeeded on several levels. First, the escalation in spending ceased. Second, a sum was transferred to local authorities that looked as if it would achieve long-term savings to the Treasury. Third, the policy of making one budget holder responsible for rationing all social care spending for those in need of community support had its intended effect. Care managers were relying less on residential care and more on a range of domiciliary services. This trend was limited by the arbitrary rule that 85 per cent of the 'new money' had to be spent on private or voluntary organisations. We saw that this policy originated from a secondary but important short-term goal of appeasing the private-homes lobby. There was also the long-term goal of fostering a larger private sector in this field. Faced with the 85 per cent rule, local authorities sought to develop an independent domiciliary sector, but this proved extremely difficult, as we discuss below. The rule could be justified on an argument akin to the economists' infant industry case for tariffs, but the long-term case for such a limit is extremely dubious. When all the transfer money becomes part of the general revenue support grant in 1996, this provision will automatically lapse.

We conclude that the normative core of the policy was a success on its own terms. Our prediction that the government would make sure it won on its core policy proved correct. Moreover, it was achieved without the central government being faced with major political fallout. This was not merely because the problems were devolved to local authorities, but also because the financial transfers to most authorities were quite generous. The demands put on authorities by new clients were less than many feared. The ring-fencing clearly worked to the advantage of SSDs. Without it, the financial pressures exerted by central government on the parent authorities would have had an even greater effect. Those authorities that had a very poor deal in the first year did so because the grant reflected the rule that money should go to those areas that had gained most from the social security money. This was abandoned for a more logical needs-based allocation in year two, which, while it produced only winners and no conspicuous losers among the research authorities, caused major problems for some shire counties during 1995.

Near core policies

Second only to the goal of reducing spending was the government's aim of extending the independent provision of care. This was never as fully spelled out, beyond the 85 per cent rule. For example, the depth and extent of the purchaser–provider split was left vague. Not surprisingly, the authorities interpreted this very differently. Yet because the Conservative government did see it as a near core element in its ideology, its inspectorate required authorities to report on progress in achieving the split. Officers therefore devoted a great deal of senior staff time and intellectual energy to the question. Similarly, collaboration was also interpreted very differently. Like enabling, some aspects of collaboration were sufficiently important to government to warrant direct intervention in the form of regulation (on hospital discharge) after the passing of the 1990 legislation.

Central to the rhetoric, but, we hypothesised, less to the reality of government concern, was care management and assessment. The government had views on how that was to be done, but local authorities were left free to interpret who should do it and how far budgets should be devolved. Local managers restructured the models that government had in mind in the White Paper (Cm. 849, 1989) and elaborated in the guidance (Department of Health 1990a). They were adapted to local organisational traditions which played a more important part than pure party politics. We had worked with more than one of the authorities before, in one case many years ago. What was remarkable was how persistent the organisational culture proved to be. A very traditional authority interpreted the legislation with minimal changes to its core culture. The authorities that had been most keen to move to a purchaser–provider split moved fast here too. Yet by the end of the research period, the inherent problems of the local social care market and the task of meeting the needs of very vulnerable people forced a degree of convergence between the hares and the tortoises.

Probably some of the most significant unintended consequences concerned the organisational changes to the SSDs themselves and the hastened death of the Seebohm model. Or was it all a case of 'all change, no change', as some authors have suggested (Robinson and Wistow 1993)? Certainly, the issues concerning the finance of long-term care and the perverse forms of funding between health authorities and the local councils remained and became even more of a political issue by the end of the research period.

The local response: diversity

On the whole, the new community care policy received a positive reception by most staff in SSDs because it was perceived as promising a more user-centred practice. The managers who were interpreting the government's wishes brought with them a tradition of user-centred training. Nearly all were social workers. They mostly did not share the belief that markets and competition would achieve this goal, but they did accept that the client should be put more at the centre of the services than had often been the case. The assumption that lay behind many of the reforms of this period, that professionals' and clients' interests are opposed in a public bureaucracy, tends to ignore the values that lie at the heart of much of the training and motivation that social workers bring to their job. That is not to say that self-interest and bureaucratic advancement are not present too! It was common for authorities to take up the more explicitly user-focused aspects of the new policy first. Attention was usually turned to care management before enabling.

We observed a significant difference between authorities that implemented the new policy in line with an interpretation of it that fitted an already existing desire to be user centred, and those that responded to a greater or lesser extent to the need to implement the mechanisms that were required, whether of assessment or purchaser–provider splits. The county embraced the new policy as something that could improve the position of users and from the beginning sought to link the emphasis on needs-based rather than provider-led services to *both* care management and commissioning. Thus it proposed that every user would come into contact with a care manager, who would draw on the services commissioned by the multilayered purchasing structure in order to change the pattern of services provision for all users. It is possible to see the county's idea of assessment as a continuum as being less led by resources than the more common development of several levels of assessment, in the manner advocated by the official guidance. In other words, the county developed a rationale for the changes that was compatible with its commitment to user centredness.

From the first the county had what Leach *et al.* (1994) have termed a 'wider' concept of enabling, meaning that its emphasis was not merely on contracting out services, but rather on considering a wider range of ways of meeting community needs and problems. Following Leach *et al.*'s typology, no SSD found that it was able to confine itself to the role of a 'residual enabler', adopting narrowly defined business values, even though initially it appeared that members in borough A and the county leaned towards this approach. The work of the personal social services meant that the user had to be accorded a central place, but whether as a customer in the social care marketplace or as a participative citizen has been more difficult to determine. Arguably, even those authorities that sought to implement the changes in a user-centred way still tended to an approach that set out to make things better for users rather than empowering them. This is not so surprising given the internal conflict in the guidance on this central issue. While the guidance on assessment and care management talked about empowerment, the rest of the guidance, on enabling and community care planning, talked about imple- menting structures and strategies that would result in better services for users rather than directly involving them. Even within the assessment and care management guidance there was a tension between empowering the user in respect of the process of assessment, while adopting top-down procedures to establish eligibility for services.

At the opposite end of the spectrum from the county, borough D took a reactive approach to the changes, implementing only an assessment system and preparing a community care plan, as the legislation demanded. External consultants were asked to prepare a care management system and to recommend a purchaser–provider split, but the first of these remained largely a paper plan and the latter had been only partially implemented by the end of 1994. Thus while there had been some change in procedures and a change of staff at second-tier level, the actual ways in which the SSD operated had not changed significantly. This borough did not think through the changes and did not arrive at a conceptualisation of them that could serve to chart the authority's strategic direction. Thus even if and when all aspects of the reforms are implemented, it is not clear how much will actually change. This is probably what voluntary sector respondents were getting at when they said that there was no culture of change in the borough; certainly there has been little working through of the changes internally.

Borough B responded more like the county in terms of shaping the requirements to accord with the particular vision of senior officers. It did not proceed to develop a purchasing function until senior managers were persuaded that the establishment of a purchaser–provider split would benefit users. However, this borough has taken a more limited approach to the reforms, confining innovation to expenditure of the STG and hence new clients, and confining care management to the heavily dependent. This may be explained in part by its need for caution in the light of its very poor STG settlement in the first year of implementation. It is also the sort of approach to assessment and care management that was recommended in the guidance.

The county was alone in both working out its own understanding of the changes and arriving at its own ways of implementing them.

In borough C, the SSD had a firm commitment to user centredness, but found that some aspects of the changes required by the new community care policy were at odds with the scheme of care coordination that it had just implemented, and difficult to implement using the joint machinery to which it was committed.

In borough A, the SSD moved fairly rapidly away from seeing the reforms as another step along the road to simple privatisation, to which members were committed. But there remained a tendency in this borough to relabel staff and functions before establishing a firm understanding of the meaning of the reforms, which has resulted in a need for further review and a lack of cohesion.

The responses to the reforms have therefore been very different, depending, we would suggest, mainly on whether the authority was able and willing to interpret the changes in a manner that made sense to it. The guidance set out the changes as a series of logical steps, but any mechanistic approach to them, in the sense of going through the motions of setting up new structures and functions without a firm idea as to how these would come together, was unlikely to result in significant change. Because the guidance was not prescriptive and because it was fragmented, implementation *required* a bottom-up input.

Making strategic change is difficult

It is not easy to explain why some authorities were more able and willing to think through the changes than others. First, the connection with political control of the authorities is not clear. While the SSD in borough A began the process of implementation by reflecting members' views about privatisation and contracting out, staff in the county managed to work alongside members who were equally determined to externalise and to secure a very different interpretation of enabling. The SSD in borough B came to view the possibilities of commissioning favourably with no encouragement from members.

Second, the response to the legislation certainly had something to do with the position in which the SSD found itself; for example, borough C had to juggle the new demands for purchasing and care management alongside its prior commitments to joint working and care coordination.

Third, and most important, seems to have been the strategic capacity of the authority and the commitment of senior managers to change and to disseminating the need for change, a finding not dissimilar to much earlier studies of local government (e.g. Haynes 1980). Managers with vision in the right place to achieve change were important to implementation in both the county and borough B, as was a critical mass of such people in these two authorities. In both boroughs A and C the lack of strategic back-up for the very few individuals with a sense of direction meant that they were frequently overwhelmed. In borough D decision making about the process of implementation was farmed out to consultants, making ownership of the changes difficult to achieve. Other authorities used external consultants, but not to decide the central framework for implementation.

Even though we would argue that implementing the changes required a significant input from authorities themselves, this does not mean that implementation was straightforward. Indeed, one of the most striking aspects of the process of implementation in the first 18 months was the extent to which an authority like the county, which had a clear sense of direction and which made an early start, encountered second-order problems. The guidance's portrayal of implementation as an orderly and rational process was far removed from actual experience. Again, this had much to do with the fact that authorities were responsible for bringing together the different aspects of the changes; thus, for example, the establishment of firm care management procedures in the county was delayed by the setting up of the purchasing structure and by the need to rethink procedures in line with IT requirements. It was also the case that authorities had the responsibility of reconciling the tensions inherent within central government's policy, particularly that between need and resources.

Finally, authorities had also to contend with the intervention of central government after 1990. While the guidance was not prescriptive, intervention in the form of government directives after 1990 meant either that authorities had to modify or change their procedures, or that they had to negotiate and make allowance for unanticipated policy constraints. Harrison *et al.* (1992) were prescient in their comments regarding the NHS, to the effect that while it was likely that central government would give rhetorical support to decentralised local management, it would intervene fairly often to attempt to deal with issues that became politically difficult.

The most significant central government intervention in the field of community care was the imposition of the 85 per cent rule late in 1992, which had the effect of forcing authorities to continue spending more on institutional care because that was where the bulk of independent provision lay, and which limited the investment possible in in-house services, thereby inhibiting their capacity to change. The 'choice directive', regarding the user's right freely to choose a residential care home, was also issued late in 1992, and made staff in the county wonder whether it was worthwhile continuing the programme of accreditation.

Government intervention was often double edged from the point of view of users. Thus choice of residential home was secured at the price of quality control. Similarly, the forced collaboration between health and social services over discharge from hospitals secured an agreed time limit for assessment, but there is evidence that the inherent tensions between the different imperatives facing health and social services have been resolved in favour of the hospital, making it more difficult to carry out proper care management. Lack of clarity from central government has also proved problematic, for example in respect of guidelines regarding the provision of continuing care under the NHS, which were not set out until 1995.

What had changed for SSDs?

During 1993 and 1994, SSDs have tended to be preoccupied with putting in place the structures and processes required to implement the changes: purchaser–provider splits and assessment and care management systems. This is despite the emphasis that was placed in the 1989 White Paper on the importance of outcomes. Nevertheless, central government monitoring has tended to take measures of process, for example evidence of progress towards a social care market, as proxies, reflecting the ideological belief of government that the insertion of market principles into the public sector will indeed produce desirable outcomes. Local authorities have therefore been encouraged to pay close attention to structures and processes. As Wistow et al. (1994b: 146) have observed, 'unless those objectives [of the white paper] are reinforced and form the basis for monitoring the mixed economy, the new framework is more likely to be driven by resource and process factors than by needs and outcomes'.

Irrespective of the implications for the success or failure of community care, the need to implement new structures and processes has meant that there has been a considerable amount of change for SSDs. Indeed, one of the unintended, or at least unadvertised, outcomes of the legislation has been the demise of the Seebohm departments in two crucial respects.

(i) There have been problems in treating children within the framework of the purchaser–provider split. Indeed, work with children has tended to remain separate. To some extent this reflects the different preoccupations of the Children Act (with partnership and prevention) from those of the community care legislation (with creating a social care market and with targeting). While it seems that the community care legislation has raised the profile of work with adults, some bifurcation of departments along lines more familiar after 1948 than after Seebohm seems likely.

(ii) Departments have abandoned universalism. In fact, provision was always rationed; nevertheless, the explicit retreat from universalism manifest in the language of targeting, service substitution, cost-efficiency and outcome measurement is new. The Seebohm report intended that personal social services should have an organisational structure that provided an open-door service (Cmnd. 3703, 1968). Some of the research authorities were determined to maintain that commitment, but had nonetheless to apply explicit eligibility criteria for services for the first time. Arguably this transparent approach is fairer, but it nevertheless represents a significant change in the perceptions of staff as to how departments operate.

There is room within the new structures for old divisions to live on; for example, that between field work and residential care staff has been given a new rationale by the purchaser–provider split, as field workers have for the most part become care managers and purchasers, while residential staff have remained providers. However, the balance has been towards change rather than continuity, with the new functional division between purchasing and providing dominating implementation.

The attempt to create and manage a social care market has proved both difficult and time consuming. While alternative providers may provide additional choice for users, or, as in the case of independent domiciliary providers, a service such as night sitting that was not previously available at all, the increased fragmentation of provision has, as Rhodes (1994) suggested, proved hard to manage. In particular, purchasers have found it difficult to get and organise the kind of information they need. Furthermore, in respect of external providers, SSDs that have tried to be proactive in the marketplace have encountered a range of challenges associated with stimulating and managing private suppliers. The attention given the voluntary and informal provision of care in the literature of the 1980s has not been carried through in implementing the 1990 legislation. Central government's guidance has also focused increasingly on the importance of managing the market. This has been particularly noteworthy in the guidance relating to community care planning; however, the increased fragmentation caused by the purchaser–provider split has made it harder to organise stakeholders in collaborative planning.

It has proved difficult to stimulate the independent provision of domiciliary care. The experience of the research authorities indicated that the domiciliary care market is not stable and in some instances only large block contracts elicited a strong response. In the case of residential care providers, many authorities have sought to avoid market failure, in line with the wishes of central government, which means that these suppliers may yet have to experience the full force of the market. In the county, residential placements did drop substantially, but it seems likely that private suppliers may be able to sustain their operations in the short to medium term. After that they may resort to cost-cutting measures that may in turn raise issues about quality.

Government guidance claimed an extraordinary amount for the separation of assessment and purchasing from providing: greater choice, flexibility, responsiveness, quality and cost-effectiveness (see also the Audit Commission 1992b). However, when we looked at one example of responsiveness – whether a user could now be put to bed at a later hour – we found that the role of the purchaser–provider split in achieving this, as opposed to the threat or reality of external competition, was far from clear. Certainly in borough B a more flexible external provider had made it more likely that new and highly dependent clients would be put to bed when they wished, and in the county the threat of competition had helped (together with the push provided by the 1988 recommendations from the Social Services Inspectorate on home care and the initiative of provider managers) to make in-house providers more flexible. Yet the existence of an independent provider had not had the same stimulating effect on in-house providers in borough B. The precise way in which the move to enabling will affect the nature of service provision seems therefore to be hard to predict.

In respect of choice, no authority has found it possible or desirable to devolve budgets to those closest to the users, that is, the care managers. Moreover, while some very complicated packages of care have been put together, services tend to remain a 'set list'. The spot purchase of a pub meal or a trip to the opera instead of day care that would constitute a truly individually tailored response to need has not happened. There are good reasons for this: such responses raise problems in respect of health and safety legislation and are costly in terms of both money and staff time. Nevertheless, an enormous investment has been made in terms of the development of purchasing structures and procedures, which have produced a considerable increase in bureaucracy for front-line workers, in order to produce change in the pattern of provision for what may turn out to be relatively few users.

In respect of quality, it is for the most part too early to comment on this issue, but how authorities monitor and deal with departures from service specifications will be of crucial importance.

Potential for good

The changes entailed in enabling may nevertheless be worthwhile in terms of their *potential* to change the situation for more users, although the problem of the costs of intensive care packages relative to residential care has been raised in some authorities. As we noted, packages were not being fully costed in borough B. More broadly still, the move to enabling may have succeeded in changing the culture of SSDs. In the first instance, it is not clear that the internal rivalry between purchasers and providers was particularly helpful, and it is possible that competitiveness between providers in the independent and statutory sectors will yet prove inimical to the trust that has been shown to be so important to successful transactions in the private as well as the public sector (Sako 1992). Nevertheless, the move to enabling has promoted more attention to the needs of the user. As a senior manager in borough C put it:

> We've published three community care plans now and I struggle to put my hand on my heart and say what it is that the production of those plans changed. I think you can say that it's changed the culture, I think

you can say that it's made us look more open, I think you can say that it's changed our way of examining our responsibilities. It's allowed for a lot more voices to be heard. But if you take it down to 'how has it produced a different welfare system for individual customers?' I am by no means convinced that we've managed to do that.

On the other hand, changing the culture is probably a fundamental step towards changing practice. As Brown (1973) noted in respect of the first major reorganisation of the NHS, it was all too possible for old wine to be poured into new bottles; in other words, for structures to change but not the people. In particular the observation in the quotation that 'more voices' have been heard is important. Ramon's (1994) study of mental health social workers showed that 18 months after the changes the social workers felt that both their views and those of users were more likely to be listened to.

All but one of the research authorities have undergone a substantial change in culture, largely because of their hope that the changes would empower users, which in itself speaks against any simple notion of provider opposition. However, it is difficult to pinpoint the extent to which a generalised commitment to users, which may to a large extent always have been present, has been translated into flexible and responsive services. It is not possible to generalise about the different ways in which the changes have been received at different levels in SSDs.

In the county in particular, there has been evidence of real change on the part of in-house home care providers, but not all the other in-house services in this authority have shown as much inclination to change their pattern of service delivery. This demonstrates how elusive the particular conjuncture necessary to produce change is. Any one structural change, such as the establishment of a purchaser–provider split, no matter how radical, is unlikely to be sufficient. In the instance of home care in the county, we observed again how important it was to have highly competent managers with a clear vision. One of the 'ifs' of the changes may be 'what would have happened if there had been no purchaser–provider split, but budgets had been devolved to go-ahead provider managers?' In essence this is what had happened in the late 1980s in the county and the home care service did change, although we accept that this would not have been sufficient to change a service in the absence of high-quality managers, in which case, it is probably mistaken to expect the purchaser–provider split alone to deliver change.

From professionals to managers

The new structures in SSDs have shifted the centre of gravity from professional to managerial control. As James (1994) has noted, historically a managerial ethos was confined to the finance and administration divisions of SSDs. Operational divisions were dominated by the ethos of professionalism. It is common in social services for large numbers of managers to be trained social workers, rather than a separate cadre as in the NHS. It might be expected, therefore, that there would be a somewhat mixed reaction to the changes. In those research authorities in the forefront of the changes, senior managers have exhibited a strong commitment to the new policy of community care. Nixon (1993) has suggested that the new arrangements give managers the opportunity to take control and become 'bureau-shapers' (to use Dunleavy's (1991) term). She further suggests that managers who have wanted to shed their professional association with social work have had reason to welcome the changes. While we observed some impatience with the professional culture of social work among some managers in the London boroughs, this was not true of all and was quite at odds with the assumptive worlds of managers in the county, despite the fact that not all senior officers had a social work background. However, a belief in the need for a different, more managerial approach did characterise those managers espousing the changes.

Managerialism has had an effect on the exercise of professional discretion. The fear among practising social workers, whose professional dominance was disproportionate to their numbers, was that a system such as care management would make their work routine and mechanistic. On the whole, these extreme fears have not been realised. But the transparency of the new transactions, for example the visibility of assessment and the resulting service decisions, and the need to achieve consistency, for example in respect of eligibility criteria and response times, have inevitably required more standardisation of professional practice. Schorr (1992), observing the changes under way in the personal social services, warned of the need to avoid the kind of routinisation of tasks that had followed similar changes in the United States. Thus far, there is not much cause for concern on this score.

Some aspects of the standardisation of procedures, such as the filling in of assessment forms, have revealed bad practice, which managers have been able to correct. Other aspects, such as the formal methods employed to decide eligibility for services, have protected social workers from taking responsibility for decisions dictated by finite resources, as well as limiting their discretion. However, morale among practitioners has been seriously lowered by the bureaucratic demands of the new systems in the shape of form filling.

The changes have raised issues about the nature of social work practice with respect to direct versus indirect work with clients. It is also the case that while SSDs continue to be resistant to the idea of mixing social work practice with money, some senior practitioners, at what was the team leader level, are likely in the new systems to find themselves responsible for authorising expenditure and stimulating the local social care market. To this extent the clear delineation between 'street-level bureaucrats' (Lipsky 1980) and managers has become blurred. These kinds of changes, together with the increasing dependency of clients, which resulted from the way in which the community care changes interlink with the running down of continuing care under the NHS, amount to a significant change in social work practice.

It is more difficult to decide whether such changes will result in practice that is user led, let alone whether they will empower users. The reforms were supposed to focus on outcomes, but the first 18 months saw a radical change in structures within SSDs. It is presumed that separating purchasing and providing will in and of itself bring changes in services that will benefit users. Many SSD workers were enthusiastic about the possibility of user empowerment, but have found it difficult to separate needs-based assessment from the ever-present issue of resources and what services are actually available, and have been subjected to a vast increase in bureaucracy. Thus from a bottom-up perspective, it is less clear that such a managerial and organisational approach to change has been successful.

What has changed for users?

The focus of our study was the implementation of the changes. We were not able to look at outcomes for users; however, it is possible for us to make some general observations. In general, the community care changes have served to raise the profile of work with elderly people, which may in and of itself have a positive effect on the services offered to that client group. The reforms were intended to promote greater choice, flexibility and responsiveness, and higher-quality services. Schorr (1992) noted the 'cognitive dissonance' surrounding the idea of choice: it is not in fact the user who chooses; choice consists rather in plurality of supply. While there is usually a range of residential care homes to choose from, previous studies have shown that entry into residential care often takes place at a time of crisis for the client (e.g. Bradshaw and Gibbs 1988), which means that in practice there may be little choice. In contrast to residential care, there is as yet very little choice in respect of domiciliary care. For the future, there is additionally some concern about the extent to which the large care homes will drive out the smaller, family-run enterprises and reduce choice.

Political scientists and lawyers have stressed the extent to which the introduction of market principles into public service has effectively conceptualised the service user as a consumer rather than a citizen (Deakin and Wright 1990; Stewart and Walsh 1992; Harden 1993). In other words, the 'contract state' is by its nature unlikely to provide much space for the service user to participate in making decisions and choices about services. The extent to which users have been 'empowered' in terms of being actively involved in both the process of assessment and decisions about services at the individual level, and in strategic planning at the aggregate level, through, for example, formal collaborative machinery, has varied. Even if procedures are put in place to secure user participation, it is by no means certain that the circumstances will permit participation on *equal* terms. In any case, the 1990 legislation is quite clear about giving the responsibility for assessing need and deciding on service provision to the local authority. It seems that there has been progress, especially in terms of hearing the voice of the individual user. All the research authorities had endeavoured to provide a space for recording the views of users and carers on assessment forms and at the least these had to be filled in. In other words, the new system provided a means of checking what was already established as good social work practice, but was far from uniform. Authorities will need to take ahead the work of review in order to maintain a role for clients in determining the nature of their care.

It remains the case that needs-led services are not the same as user-led services. The legislation was never intended to provide the latter. Need is an essentially contested concept, sometimes between user and carer, as well as between user and professional. In their discussion of health professionals, Harrison and Pollitt (1994) pointed out that the purchaser–provider split allows other judgements of need to compete with or take precedence over professional judgements. In a sense this is less true of social services, where it is the care manager who must contain the conflict between needs and resources. This has been accomplished in the main by defining need in terms of a combination of risk, need and statutory responsibility. Arguably, SSDs have always had to do this. Now the process has been made explicit. However, the insistence in the legislation on separating the consideration of need from service provision, together with the injunction to promote independent living, has resulted in some shift of resources from institutional to domiciliary care. New and highly dependent clients are in some places likely to get sophisticated packages of domiciliary care. However, clients who are not at high risk and whose needs are for services like shopping or cleaning are more likely not to have their needs met at all. Indeed, the rhetoric of 'needs-led services' has led to the formalisation of *hierarchies* of need, which legitimise not meeting lower-level needs.

As Lipsky (1980) observed, 'street-level bureaucrats' have been consistently criticised for their inability to provide a responsive and appropriate service. He suggested that problems in this respect arose from professional discretion being exercised in a particular work context, namely one in which demand exceeded supply, resources were scarce, and goal expectations were ambiguous. Thus, Lipsky did not blame the self-interest of professionals, but rather focused on the problems social workers faced in reconciling needs and resources on the one hand, and ambiguous aims on the other. More explicit targeting of services was intended to address the latter. However, even apparently simple policy goals can remain difficult to achieve. As we saw in the case of a client wishing to be put to bed at a normal hour, success depends on the availability of supply, but what in turn determines that has been very different from authority to authority.

There are finally the issues of quality and accountability, which take on new significance for users in a social care market. Accountability will in all likelihood be blurred when care is contracted from an external supplier. Voluntary organisations have expressed concern about how far they can be responsible for the work of volunteers, besides which the directors of voluntary agencies are accountable to members and management boards, as well as to the SSD contractor. Our study did not look at complaints procedures, but the extent to which the SSD knows about and takes responsibility for complaints made to an external provider would seem to be important, especially given the difficulties SSDs are likely to encounter (if the American experience is anything to go by) in respect of quality control. Like review of individual clients, monitoring of contracts is a major task for authorities and for the most part has not been fully implemented.

The 1990 reforms were distinguished by their ambition to measure outcomes for users. It was not clear at the end of 1994 that that was actually happening. Central government monitoring has been intense and the overall impression to emerge from it has been one of relatively smooth progress. But as Henwood and Wistow (1995) have pointed out, the template against which the Department of Health evaluated progress was a minimal one. The eight key tasks (see Chapter 1) were the basic necessities for administering and managing change. Thus monitoring has been concerned with means rather than ends. The complications of introducing the purchaser–provider split in particular, together with the effort required to create more of a market in social care, led to central government monitoring that focused more on process and structures and an emphasis in government guidance and circulars on the importance of 'managing the market'. Nowhere has this been clearer than in respect of the issue of collaborative work, where central government documents have moved clearly from stressing the importance of 'seamless care' for users to that of managing the market.

The future finance of long-term care

As the number of people over the age of 80 rises and the number of those with learning difficulties who live a full life span grows and the scale of long-term mental illness in the community grows too, so will the funding problem. The injection of new money that the social security system provided in the 1980s and 1990s came to the rescue in an unplanned way. In the late 1990s the problem will reappear if the sum transferred to local authorities remains capped.

It is clear that the finance of long-term care is going to become one of the key national policy issues by the turn of the century. Local authorities will be under growing pressure to provide better education and preschool provision too. There may be a case for more explicit funding of community care services. This could be done by adding one per cent to the social security contribution and using the receipts as an assigned revenue to local authorities to spend on community care. Tax reliefs might encourage more private insurance policies covering long-term care.

There will be many competing models discussed in the next few years. What few proponents do is face up to the fundamental illogicality of the present divide between NHS and local authority funding and all the petty boundary disputes to which this gives rise, of the kind we saw in this study and have documented in a previous study of well over a decade ago (Glennerster *et al.* 1983). It is not merely more money, public and private, that the services need, but a saner way of bridging the divide between 'free' (centrally tax-funded) health care and means-tested and locally funded social care.

One way to do this would be to create separate centrally funded long-term care agencies, with health and social care staff. Another would be to transfer all such care to the local authorities. Another solution would be to provide all social as well as medical and nursing care free, but to charge for accommodation and food in both the residential homes and the hospitals. This is not the place to explore all these alternatives, but the long-running nonsense of the false divide between health and social care and its finance must be brought to an end.

Bibliography

Note: Many of the Department of Health's monitoring studies of community care were issued undated. We have nevertheless put in the year of publication.

Allen, I., Hogg, D. and Pearce, S. (1992) *Elderly People: Choice, Participation and Satisfaction*. London: Policy Studies Institute.

Ascher, K. (1987) *The Politics of Privatisation. Contracting out Public Services*. London: Macmillan.

Association of Metropolitan Authorities (1990) *Contracts for Social Care. The Local Authority View*. London: AMA.

Association of Metropolitan Authorities (1994) *A Survey of Social Services' Charging Policies 1992–4*. London: AMA.

Audit Commission (1986) *Making a Reality of Community Care*. London: HMSO.

Audit Commission (1989) *Developing Community Care for Adults with a Mental Handicap*, Occasional Paper No. 9. London: HMSO.

Audit Commission (1992a) *The Community Revolution: The Personal Social Services and Community Care*. London: HMSO.

Audit Commission (1992b) *Community Care: The Cascade of Change*. London: HMSO.

Audit Commission (1993) *Taking Care: Progress with Care in the Community*. London: Audit Commission.

Audit Commission (1994) *Taking Stock: Progress with Community Care*. London: Audit Commission.

Audit Commission (1995) *Local Authority Performance Indicators*. Appendix to vols I and II. London: Audit Commission.

Baldock, J. (1994) The personal social services: the politics of care, in V. George and S. Millar (eds) *Social Policy Towards 2000. Squaring the Welfare Circle*. London: Routledge.

Baldock, J. and Evers, A. (1991) Citizenship and frail old people: changing patterns of provision in Europe, in N. Manning and C. Ungerson (eds), *Social Policy Review, 1990–1*, pp. 101–27. London: Longman.

Baldock, J. and Ungerson, C. (1994) *Becoming Consumers of Community Care*. York: Joseph Rowntree Foundation.

Bamford, T. (1990) *The Future of Social Work*. Basingstoke: Macmillan.

Barrett, S. and Fudge, C. (1981) *Policy and Action*. London: Methuen.

Barry, N. (1990) *Welfare*. Buckingham: Open University Press.

Bebbington, A. and Davies, B. (1993) Efficient targeting of community care: the case of the home help service. *Journal of Social Policy*, 22(3): 373–91.

Bebbington, A. and Miles, J. (1988) A need indicator of in care services for children. PSSRU Discussion Paper No. 574. Canterbury: University of Kent.

Bellamy, C. and Taylor, J. A. (1994) Introduction – towards the information polity. *Public Administration*, 72(1): 1–12.

Billis, D. (1984) *Welfare Bureaucracies: Their Design and Change in Response to Social Problems*. London: Heinemann.

Billis, D. (1989) *A Theory of the Voluntary Sector. Implications for Policy and Practice*, Working Paper No. 5. London: LSE, Centre for Voluntary Organisation.

Billis, D. (1993) *Organising Public and Voluntary Agencies*. London: Routledge.

Bradshaw, J. and Gibbs, I. (1988) *Public Support for Private Residential Care*. Aldershot: Avebury.

Braye, S. and Preston-Shoot, M. (1995) *Empowering Practice in Social Care*. Buckingham: Open University Press.

Brown, R. G. S. (1973) *The Changing National Health Service*. London: Routledge and Kegan Paul.

Butler, D., Adonis, A. and Travers, T. (1994) *Failure in British Government. The Politics of the Poll Tax*. Oxford: Oxford University Press.

Carpenter, M. (1994) *Normality is Hard Work. Trade Unions and the Politics of Community Care*. London: Lawrence and Wishart.

Castle, B. (1975) Speech at the Local Authority Social Services Conference, 28 November.

Challis, D. (1992) The Community Care of Elderly People: Bringing Together Scarcity and Choice, Needs and Costs, PSSRU Discussion Paper No. 813, pp. 135–46. Canterbury: University of Kent.

Challis, D. (1994a) Case management: a review of UK developments and issues, in M. Titterton (ed.) *Caring for People in the Community. The New Welfare*. London: Jessica Kingsley.

Challis, D. (1994b) Care management, in N. Malin (ed.) *Implementing Community Care*. Buckingham: Open University Press.

Challis, D. (1994c) *Care Management: Factors Influencing its Development in the Implementation of Community Care*. London: Department of Health.

Challis, D. and Davies, B. (1986) *Case Management in Community Care*. Aldershot: Gower.

Challis, D. and Ferlie, E. (1987) The myth of generic practice: specialization in social work. *British Journal of Social Work*, 17(2): 135–46.

Challis, D., Darton, R., Johnson, L., Stone, M. and Trashe, K. (1995) *Care Management and the Home Care of Older People*. Aldershot: Arena.

Challis, L. (1990) *Organising Public Social Services*. London: Longman.

Chandler, J. A. (1991) Public administration and private management. Is there a difference? *Public Administration*, 69: 385–91.

Chartered Institute of Public Finance and Accountancy/Association of Directors of

Social Services (CIPFA/ADSS) Financial Management Partnership (1991) *Community Care 1991 – Information Strategy*. London: CIPFA/ADSS.

Chartered Institute of Public Finance and Accountancy (CIPFA) (1994) *Personal Social Services Statistics 1992–93 Actuals*. London: CIPFA.

Chartered Institute of Public Finance and Accountancy (CIPFA) (1995) *Personal Social Services Statistics 1993–94 Actuals*. London: CIPFA.

Cheetham, J. (1993) Social work and community care in the 1990s: pitfalls and potentials, in R. Page and J. Baldock (eds) *Social Policy Review 5*, pp. 155–76. London: Social Policy Association.

CI (92) 34. Letter from Herbert Laming, Chief Social Services Inspector, on Assessment, 14 December 1992. London: DH.

Cm. 849 (1989) *Caring for People. Community Care in the Next Decade and Beyond*. London: HMSO.

Cmd. 9663 (1956) *Report of the Committee of Enquiry into the Cost of the National Health Service* (Guillebaud enquiry). London: HMSO.

Cmnd. 3703 (1968) *Report of the Committee on Local Authority and Allied Personal Social Services* (Seebohm report). London: HMSO.

Cmnd. 8173 (1981) *Growing Older*. London: HMSO.

Committee of Public Accounts (1988) *Twenty-sixth Report*. London: HMSO.

Common, R. and Flynn, N. (1992) *Contracting for Care*. York: Joseph Rowntree Foundation.

Community Care Support Force (1992) *Implementing Community Care. Delivering the Key Tasks. A Guide for Health Authorities*. London: Price Waterhouse.

Davies, B. (1992) Care management and the social sevices: on breeding the best chameleons. *Generations Review* 2(2): 18–21.

Davies, B. (1994) Maintaining the pressure in community care reform. *Social Policy and Administration*, 28(3): 197–205.

Davies, B., Bebbington, A. and Charnley, H. (1990) *Resources, Needs and Outcomes in Community-Based Care*. Aldershot: Avebury.

Davies, B. and Knapp, M. (1994) Improving equity and efficiency in British community care. *Social Policy and Administration*, 28(3): 262–85.

Davis Smith, J. and Hedley, R. (1993) *Volunteering and the Contract Culture*. Berkhamsted: Volunteer Centre.

Deakin, N. and Wright, A. (1990) *Consuming Public Services*. London: Routledge.

Department of Health (1990a) *Community Care in the Next Decade and Beyond. Policy Guidance*. London: HMSO.

Department of Health (1990b) *Planning. Draft Guidance*, CCI 6. London: DH.

Department of Health (1990c) *Key Indicators of Local Authority Social Services 1989–90*. London: DH.

Department of Health (1992) Memorandum on the Financing of Community Care, 2 October. London: DH.

Department of Health (1993a) *Community Care Monitoring. Special Study. Mental Health Services*. London: DH.

Department of Health (1993b) *Monitoring and Development. First Impressions*. London: DH.

Department of Health (1993c) *Key Indicators of Local Authority Social Services 1992–93*. London: DH.

Department of Health (1994a) *Implementing Caring for People. The Role of the GP and Primary Healthcare Team*. London: DH.

Department of Health (1994b) *Implementing Caring for People. Care Management*. London: DH.

Department of Health (1994c) *Residential Accommodation for Elderly and for Younger Physically Disabled People. All Residents in LA, Voluntary and Private Homes Year Ending 31 March 1988 to Year Ending 31 March 1993*. London: DH.

Department of Health (1995) *Government Expenditure Plans 1995–6 to 1996–7* (Cm. 2812). London: DH.

Department of Health and Peat Marwick (1994) *Informing Users and Carers*. London: DH.

Department of Health and Price Waterhouse (1991) *Purchaser, Commissioner and Provider Roles*. London: HMSO.

Department of Health and Price Waterhouse (1992) *Feedback on Purchase of Service and Purchaser/Provider Workshops*. London: DH.

Department of Health and Price Waterhouse (1993) *Population Needs Assessment. Good Practice Guidance*. London: DH.

Department of Health and Social Security (1981) *Growing Older*. London: HMSO.

Department of Health and Social Security (1988) *Community Care: An Agenda for Action*. London: HMSO.

Department of Health and Social Services Inspectorate (1991a) *Purchase of Service Guidance*. London: DH.

Department of Health and Social Services Inspectorate (1991b) *Assessment Systems and Community Care*. London: HMSO.

Department of Health, Social Services Inspectorate and NHS Management Executive (1993a) *Joint Commissioning for Community Care. 'A Slice Through Time.'* London: DH.

Department of Health, Social Services Inspectorate and NHS Management Executive (1993b) *Assessment Special Study*. London: DH.

Department of Health, Social Services Inspectorate, NHS Management Executive and Price Waterhouse (1992) *Model for Purchasing Care for Elderly People*. London: DH.

Department of Health, Social Services Inspectorate and Scottish Office Social Work Services Group (1991a) *Care Management and Assessment. Managers' Guide*. London: HMSO.

Department of Health, Social Services Inspectorate and Scottish Office Social Work Services Group (1991b) *Care Management and Assessment. Practitioners' Guide*. London: HMSO.

Derthick, M. (1972) *New Towns in Town*. Washington, DC: Urban Institute.

DiMaggio, P. and Powell, W. W. (1991) The iron cage revisited: institutional isomorphism and collective rationality in organisational fields, in W. W. Powell and P. DiMaggio (eds) *The New Institutionalism in Organizational Analysis*. Chicago, IL: University of Chicago Press.

District Audit Service (1992) *Constructing Budgets for Purchasing Community Care*. London: Audit Commission.

Donnison, D. V. (1965) *Social Policy and Administration*. London: Allen and Unwin.

Dunleavy, P. (1986) Explaining the privatisation boom: public choice versus radical approaches. *Public Administration*, 64: 13–44.

Dunleavy, P. (1991) *Democracy, Bureaucracy and Public Choice. Economic Explanations in Political Science*. Hemel Hempstead: Harvester Wheatsheaf.

Dunleavy, P. and Hood, C. (1994) From old public administration to new public management. *Public Money and Management*, July–September: 9–16.

Dunsire, A. (1978a) *Implementation: The Execution Process, I*. Oxford: Martin Robertson.

Dunsire, A. (1978b) *Implementation: The Execution Process, II*. Oxford: Martin Robertson.

EL (92) 13 Implementing Caring for People ('Key Tasks'). 25 September 1992.

EL (92) 65 Implementing Caring for People. 11 march 1993.

EL (93) 48 Community Care Implementation and Monitoring. 26 May 1993.

EL (93) 119/CI (93) 35 Community Care. 23 December 1993.

Ellis, K. (1993) *Squaring the Circle. User and Carer Participation in Needs Assessment*. York: Joseph Rowntree Foundation.

Elmore, R. F. (1978) Organisational models of social program implementation. *Public Policy*, 26 (spring): 185–228.

Elmore, R. F. (1982) Backward mapping: implementation research and policy decisions, in W. Williams *et al.* (eds) *Studying Implementation*. Chatham, NJ: Chatham House.

Finch, J. and Groves, D. (eds) (1983) *A Labour of Love*. London: Routledge.

Flynn, N. and Common, R. (1990) *Contracts for Community Care*, CC 14. London: DH.

Flynn, N. and Hurley, D. (1993) *The Market for Care*. London: LSE Public Sector Management.

Fraser, N. (1989) Women, welfare and the politics of need interpretation, in P. Lassman (ed.) *Politics and Social Theory*. London: Routledge.

Glennerster, H. (with Korman, N. and Marsden-Wilson, F.) (1983) *Planning for Priority Groups*. Oxford: Martin Robertson.

Glennerster, H. and Le Grand, J. (1995) The development of quasi markets in welfare provision in the United Kingdom. *International Journal of Health Services*, 25(2): 203–18.

Glennerster, H., Matsaganis, M. and Owens, P. (1994) *Implementing GP Fundholding*. Buckingham: Open University Press.

Glennerster, H., Power, A. and Travers, T. (1989) A new era for social policy. A new enlightenment or a new Leviathan? STICERD, WSP/39. London: London School of Economics.

Gostick, C. (1993) *Collaborative Commissioning*. London: NW Thames RHA.

Gray, A. and Jenkins, B. (1993) Markets, managers and the public service. The changing of a culture, in P. Taylor Gooby and R. Lawson (eds) *Markets and Managers. New Issues in the Development of Welfare*. Buckingham: Open University Press.

Griffiths, R. (1992) With the past behind us. *Community Care*, 16 January: 18–21.

Gutch, R. (1992) *Contracting Lessons from the US*. London: NCVO.

Hadley, R. and Hatch, S. (1981) *Social Welfare and the Failure of the State*. London: George Allen and Unwin.

Ham, C. and Hill, M. (1993) *The Policy Process in the Modern Capitalist State*. Hemel Hempstead: Harvester Wheatsheaf.

Harden, I. (1993) *The Contracting State*. Buckingham: Open University Press.

Hardy, B., Turrell, A. and Wistow, G. (eds) (1992) *Innovations in Community Care Management*. Aldershot: Avebury.

Hardy, B., Wistow, G. and Leedham, I. (1993) *Analysis of a Sample of English Community Care Plans 1993/4*. London: DH.

Harris, M. (1987) *Management Committees: Roles and Tasks*, Working Paper No. 4. London: Centre for Voluntary Organisation, LSE.

Harris, M. (1989) *Management Committees in Practice: A Study in Local Voluntary Leadership*, Working Paper No. 7. London: Centre for Voluntary Organisation, LSE.

Harris, M. (1991) *Exploring the Role of Voluntary Management Committees: A New Approach*, Working Paper No. 10. London: Centre for Voluntary Organisation, LSE.

Harrison, S. and Pollitt, C. (1994) *Controlling Health Professionals. The Future of Work and Organization in the NHS*. Buckingham: Open University Press.

Harrison, S., Hunter, D. J., Marnoch, G. and Pollitt, C. (1992) *Just Managing: Power and Culture in the NHS*. London: Macmillan.

Hawtin, M., Percy-Smith, J., Hughes, G. and Foreman, A. (1994) *Community Profiling. Auditing Social Needs*. Buckingham: Open University Press.

Haynes, R. (1980) *Organisational Theory and Local Government*. London: Allen and Unwin.

Henwood, M. (1992) *Through a Glass Darkly. Community Care and Elderly People*, Research Report 14. London: King's Fund Institute.

Henwood, M. (1994) *Fit for Change? Snapshots of the Community Care Reforms One Year On*. London/Leeds: King's Fund Centre/Nuffield Institute for Health.

Henwood, M. and Wistow, G. (1993) Discharge: the time and the space. *Community Care*, 4 November: 24–5.

Henwood, M. and Wistow, G. (1995) The tasks in hand. *Health Service Journal*, 13 April: 24–5.

Hill, M. (1972) *The Sociology of Public Administration*. London: Weidenfeld and Nicolson.

Hill, M. (1981) The policy implementation distinction: a quest for rational control, in S. Barrett and C. Fudge (eds) *Policy and Action*. London: Methuen.

Hoggett, P. (1990) *Modernisation, Political Strategy and the Welfare State. An Organisational Perspective*. Bristol: SAUS.

Home Office (1990) *Efficiency Scrutiny of Government Funding of the Voluntary Sector. Profiting from Partnership*. London: HO.

Hood, C. (1991) A public management for all seasons? *Public Administration* 69(1): 3–19.

House of Commons Health Committee (1993) 482-I. *Sixth Report. Community Care: The Way Forward, Vol. I*. London: HMSO.

House of Commons Social Services Committee (1990a) (277) *Third Report. Community Care: Funding for Local Authorities*. London: HMSO.

House of Commons Social Services Committee (1990b) (444) *Sixth Report. Community Care: Choice for Service Users*. London: HMSO.

House of Commons Social Services Committee (1990c) (580-1) *Eighth Report. Community Care Planning and Cooperation*. London: HMSO.

Hoyes, L., Lart, R., Means, R. and Taylor, M. (1994) *Community Care in Transition*. York: Joseph Rowntree Foundation.

Hudson, B. (1994) *Making Sense of Markets in Health and Social Care.* Sunderland: Business Education.

Hunter, D. J. (1980) *Coping with Uncertainty.* Letchworth: Research Studies Press.

Hunter, D. J. (1992) To market! To market! A new dawn for community care? *Health and Social Care,* 1: 3–10.

Hunter, D. J. (1994) From joint planning to community care planning – some tensions, in R. Davidson and S. Hunter (eds) *Community Care in Practice.* London: B. T. Batsford.

Hunter, D. J. and Wistow, G. (1987) The paradox of policy diversity in a unitary state: community care in Britain. *Public Administration,* 65(1): 3–24.

Hunter, D. J., McKeganey, N. P. and MacPherson, I. A. (1988) *Care of the Elderly. Policy and Practice.* Aberdeen: Aberdeen University Press.

Jackson, D. and Haskins, R. (1992) Vouchers in the funding of residential care, in *Market-Type Mechanisms,* Series No. 4. Paris: OECD.

James, A. (1994) *Managing to Care: Public Service and the Market.* London: Longman.

Keen, J. (1994) Should the NHS have an information strategy? *Public Administration* 72(1): 33–53.

Kenny, D. and Edwards, P. (1994) *From Social Security to Community Care. The Impact of the Transfer of Funding on Local Authorities.* Luton: Local Government Management Board.

Knight, B. (1993) *Voluntary Action.* London: Home Office.

Korman, N. and Glennerster, H. (1990) *Hospital Closure.* Buckingham: Open University Press.

Kramer, R. M. (1981) *Voluntary Agencies in the Welfare State.* Berkeley, CA: UCLA Press.

LA (92) 27 National Assistance Act 1948 (Choice of Accommodation) Directions 1992. 23 December 1992.

LAC (92) 3 Supplementary Credit Approval for Information Technology Support in Implementing 'Caring for People'. February 1992.

LAC (93) 4 Community Care Plans (Consultation) Directions 1993. 25 January 1993.

LAC (94) 8 1994/5 Supplementary Credit Approval for Information Technology Support in Implementing 'Caring for People'. 11 February 1994.

LASSL (92) 8 Community Care. 2 October 1992.

LASSL (92) 11 Community Care Special Transitional Grant. 13 November 1992.

LASSL (92) 12 (Amended) Community Care – Special Transitional Grant Conditions and Indicative Allocations. 14 December 1992.

LASSL (93) 19, Department of Health (1993) Community Care – Special Transitional Grant Conditions and Indicative Allocations, 1994/5. London: HMSO.

Laing and Buisson (1995) *Care of Elderly People Market Survey,* 8th edn. London: Laing and Buisson.

Leach, S., Stewart, J. and Walsh, K. (1994) *The Changing Organisation and Management of Local Government.* London: Macmillan.

Leat, D. (1993) *The Development of Community Care by the Independent Sector.* London: Policy Studies Institute.

Leat, D. and Ungerson, C. (1993) *Creating Care at the Boundaries: Issues in the Supply and Management of Domiciliary Care.* Canterbury: Department of Social Policy, University of Kent.

Le Grand, J. and Bartlett, W. (eds) (1993) *Quasi-Markets and Social Policy*. London: Macmillan.

Lewis, J. (1983) *What Price Community Medicine?* Brighton: Harvester Wheatsheaf.

Lewis, J. and Meredith, B. (1988) *Daughters Who Care*. London: Routledge.

Lipsky, M. (1980) *Street Level Bureaucracy. Dilemmas of the Individual in Public Services*. New York: Russell Sage Foundation.

Lipsky, M. and Rathgeb Smith, S. (1989) Nonprofit organizations, government and the welfare state. *Political Science Quarterly*, 104(4): 625–48.

Martin, J. (1984) *Hospitals in Trouble*. Oxford: Blackwell.

Means, R. and Smith, R. (1985) *The Development of Welfare Services for Elderly People*. London: Croom Helm.

Means, R. and Smith, R. (1994) *Community Care Policy and Practice*. London: Macmillan.

National Council for Voluntary Organisations (1993) Contracts rise while grants are cut! *NCVO News*, 47 (September): 1.

Nevitt, D. (1977) Demand and need, in H. Heisler (ed.) *Foundations of Social Administration*. London: Macmillan.

NHS Management Executive and Social Services Inspectorate (1995) *Community Care Monitoring Report, 1994. Findings from Local Authorities' Self-Monitoring and NHS Surveys*. Heywood: NHS Management Executive.

Niskanen, W. A. (1971) *Bureaucracy and Representative Government*. Chicago, IL: Aldine Atherton.

Nixon, J. (1993) Implementation in the hands of senior managers: community care in Britain, in M. Hill (ed.) *New Agendas in the Study of the Policy Process*. Hemel Hempstead: Harvester Wheatsheaf.

Nocon, A. (1994) *Collaboration in Community Care in the 1990s*. Sunderland: Business Education.

NUPE/UNISON (1993) *Bringing it all Home: The NUPE Home Care Survey*. London: NUPE/UNISON.

Pahl, J. (1994) 'Like the job – but hate the organisation': social workers and managers in social services, in R. Page and J. Baldock (eds) *Social Policy Review 6*, pp. 190–210. London: Social Policy Association.

Paton, R. and Cornforth, C. (1991) What's different about managing in voluntary and non-profit organisations? in J. Batsleer, C. Cornforth and R. Paton (eds) *Issues in Voluntary and Non-Profit Management*. Wokingham: Open University and Addison-Wesley.

Phaure, S. (ed.) (1992) *Community Care Plans – A London Review*. London: London Voluntary Service Council.

Pollitt, C. (1990) *Managerialism and the Public Services. The Anglo-American Experience*. Oxford: Blackwell.

Powell, W. W. and Friedkin, R. (1987) Organisational change in non-profit organisations, in W. W. Powell (ed.) *The Non-Profit Sector. A Research Handbook*. New Haven: Yale University Press.

Poxton, R. (1994) *Joint Commissioning. The Story so Far*. London: King's Fund Centre.

Pressman, J. and Wildavsky, A. (1973) *Implementation*. Berkeley: University of California Press.

Propper, C. (1993) Quasi-markets, contracts and quality in health and social care, in J. Le Grand and W. Bartlett (eds) *Quasi-Markets and Social Policy*. London: Macmillan.

Ramon, S. (1994) The implementation of the NHS and Community Care Act: the views of front-line mental health workers. Unpublished typescript.

Ransom, S. and Stewart, J. (1989) Citizenship and government: the challenge for management in the public domain. *Political Studies*, 37(1): 5–24.

Rhodes, R. A. W. (1994) The hollowing out of the state: the changing nature of the public service in Britain. *Political Quarterly*, 65(2): 243–56.

Richards, S. (1994) Making sense of needs assessment. *Research Policy and Planning*, 12(1): 5–9.

Robbins, D. (ed.) (1993) *Community Care. Findings for DH-Funded Research 1988–1992*. London: HMSO.

Robinson, J. and Wistow, G. (1993) *All Change, No Change? Community Care Six Months On. A Second Report of Developments in the Health and Social Care Divide*. London/Leeds: King's Fund Centre/Nuffield Institute.

Rowntree, B. S. (1947) *Old People*. Oxford: Nuffield Foundation and Oxford University Press.

Royal Commission on the Law Relating to Mental Illness and Mental Deficiency (1957) *Report*. London: HMSO.

Sabatier, P. A. (1986) Top-down and bottom-up approaches to implementation research. *Journal of Public Policy*, 6: 21–48.

Sako, M. (1992) *Prices, Quality and Trust. Inter-Firm Relations in Britain and Japan*. Cambridge: Cambridge University Press.

Salomon, L. B. (1987) Partners in public service: the scope and theory of government and non-profit relations, in W. W. Powell (ed.) *The Non-Profit Sector. A Research Handbook*. New Haven, CT: Yale University Press.

Schneider, J. (1993) Care programming in mental health: assimilation and adaptation. *British Journal of Social Work*, 23: 383–403.

Schorr, A. L. (1992) *The Personal Social Services: An Outsider's View*. York: Joseph Rowntree Foundation.

Self, P. (1993) *Government by the Market? The Politics of Public Choice*. London: Macmillan.

Sinclair, I., Parker, R., Leat, D. and Williams, J. (1990) *The Kaleidoscope of Care: A Review of Research on Welfare Provision for Elderly People*. London: HMSO.

Smale, G. and Tuson, G. (with Biehal, N. and Marsh, P.) (1993) *Empowerment, Assessment, Care Management and the Skilled Worker*. London: National Institute of Social Work.

Smale, G., Tuson, G., Ahmad, B., Darvill, G., Domoney, L. and Sainbury, E. (1994) *Negotiating Care in the Community*. London: HMSO.

Smith, G. (1980) *Social Need. Policy, Practice and Research*. London: Routledge.

Smith, S. R. and Lipsky, M. (1993) *Non-profits for Hire. The Welfare State in the Age of Contracting*. Cambridge, MA: Harvard University Press.

Social Services Inspectorate (1993) *Inspection of Assessment and Care Management Arrangements in Social Services Departments. Interim Overview Report*. London: DH.

Stevenson, O. (1994) Social work in the 1990s: empowerment – fact or fiction? in R.

Page and J. Baldock (eds) *Social Policy Review* 6, pp. 170–89. London: Social Policy Association.

Stevenson, O. and Parsloe, P. (1978) *Social Services Teams: The Practitioner's View*. London: HMSO.

Stevenson, O. and Parsloe, P. (1993) *Community Care and Empowerment*. York: Joseph Rowntree Foundation.

Stewart, J. (1993) The limitations of government by contract. *Public Money and Management*, July–September: 7–12.

Stewart, J. and Walsh, K. (1992) Change in the management of public services. *Public Administration*, 70(4): 499–518.

Taylor, M. (1990) *New Times, New Challenges: Voluntary Organisations Facing the 1990s*. London: NCVO.

Taylor, M. and Hoggett, P. (1993) Quasi-markets and the transformation of the independent sector. Conference paper, Quasi-Markets in Public Sector Service Delivery Conference, 22–24 March.

Titmuss, R. M. (1968) Community care: fact or fiction? (Lecture delivered in 1961), in R. M. Titmuss, *Commitment to Welfare*. London: Allen and Unwin.

Townsend, P. (1962) *The Last Refuge*. London: Routledge.

Ungerson, C. (1987) *Policy is Personal. Sex, Gender and Informal Care*. London: Tavistock.

Walker, A. (1982) The meaning and social division of community care, in A. Walker (ed.) *Community Care: The Family, the State, and Social Policy*. Oxford: Blackwell and Martin Robertson.

Walker, A. (1989) Community care, in M. McCarthy (ed.) *The New Politics of Welfare*. London: Macmillan.

Walker, A. (1993) Community care policy: from consensus to conflict, in J. Bornat *et al.* (eds) *Community Care: A Reader*. London: Macmillan and Open University.

Webb, A. and Wistow, G. (1983) Public expenditure and policy implementation: the case of community care. *Public Administration*, 61 (spring): 21–44.

Webb, A. and Wistow, G. (1986) *Planning, Need and Scarcity. Essays on the Personal Social Services*. London: Allen and Unwin.

Webb, A. and Wistow, G. (1987) *Social Work, Social Care and Social Planning. The Personal Social Services since Seebohm*. London: Longman.

Wicks, M. (1985) Enter right: the family patrol group. *New Society*, 24 February.

Wildavsky, A. (1964) *The Politics of the Budgetary Process*. Boston, MA: Little, Brown.

Wilson, G. (1993) Conflicts in case management: the use of staff in community care. *Social Policy and Administration*, 27(2): 109– 23.

Wistow, G. (1983) Joint finance and community care: have the incentives worked? *Public Money*, 3(2): 33–7.

Wistow, G. (1990) *Community Care Planning. A Review of Past Experience and Future Imperatives*, CCI 3. London: DH.

Wistow, G. (1992) Organising for strategic management: the personal social services, in C. Pollitt and S. Harrison (eds) *Handbook of Public Services Management*. Oxford: Blackwell.

Wistow, G. (1994) Coming apart at the seams. *Health Services Journal*, 2 March.

Wistow, G. and Hardy, B. (1994) Community care planning, in N. Malin (ed.) *Implementing Community Care*. Buckingham: Open University Press.

Wistow, G. and Henwood, M. (1990) Planning in a mixed economy: life after Griffiths, in R. Parry (ed.) *Privatisation. Research Highlights in Social Work 18*. London: Jessica Kingsley.

Wistow, G. and Henwood, M. (1991) Caring for people: elegant model or flawed design? in N. Manning (ed.) *Social Policy Review 1990–1*. London: Longman.

Wistow, G. and Henwood, M. (1995) The Task in Hand. *Health Services Journal*, 13 April: 24–5.

Wistow, G., Hardy, B. and Turrell, A. (1990) *Collaboration Under Financial Constraint. Health Authorities' Spending of Joint Finance*. Aldershot: Avebury.

Wistow, G., Knapp, M., Hardy, B. and Allan, C. (1992) From providing to enabling: local authorities and the mixed economy of social care. *Public Administration*, 70(1): 25–45.

Wistow, G., Knapp, M., Hardy, B. and Allan, C. (1994b) *Social Care in a Mixed Economy*. Buckingham: Open University Press.

Wistow, G., Knapp, M., Hardy, B., Forder, J., Manning, R. and Kendall, J. (1994a) *Social Care Markets: Progress and Prospects*. London: DH.

Wistow, G., Leedham, I. and Hardy, B. (1993) *Community Care Plans. A Preliminary Analysis of English Community Care Plans*. London: DH.

Index

IMPLEMENTING COMMUNITY CARE

Nigel Malin (ed.)

This introductory text provides a unique overview of the implementation of community care policy and the process of managing changes in the field. The central thesis is an expansion of the theme of integrating policy and professional practice in order to assess the requirements for providing models of care based upon a user and care management perspective. The book analyses the impact of changes for community nurses, social workers, those employed in residential and home-based care and discusses anticipated new roles and functions. Its examination of changes in policy and planning both at national and local level makes it a valuable sourcebook for health care, social work practitioners and planners, but the volume is designed for use by students and professionals alike. The emphasis throughout is on the design and delivery of services and providing an overview of research findings, particularly in relation to measuring service effectiveness.

Contents
Preface – Section 1: The policy context – Development of community care – Management and finance – Community care planning – Care management – Section 2: Staff and users – The caring professions – The family and informal care – Measuring service quality – The consumer role – Section 3: Models of care – Residential services – Day services – Domiciliary services – Index.

Contributors
Andy Alaszewski, Michael Beazley, John Brown, David Challis, Brian Hardy, Bob Hudson, Aileen McIntosh, Steve McNally, Nigel Malin, Jill Manthorpe, Jim Monarch, John Rose, Len Spriggs, Gerald Wistow, Wai-Ling Wun.

224pp   0 335 15738 6 (Paperback)

SOCIAL CARE IN A MIXED ECONOMY

Gerald Wistow, Martin Knapp, Brian Hardy and Caroline Allen

This book describes the mixed economy of community care in England and analyses the efforts and activities of local authorities to promote and develop it. It is based on national documentary and statistical evidence and on more detailed research with twenty-four local authorities; and includes a case study on the transfer of residential homes to the independent sector.

The roles of social services departments have been progressively redefined to emphasise responsibility for creating and managing a mixed economy. This entails a major cultural shift for departments which may be summarised as involving moves from providing to enabling, and from administration to management. It also implies the need for new skills and structures. *Social Care in a Mixed Economy* traces the historical changes; the local interpretations of central government policy; how authorities actually have been developing mixed economies; the main opportunities or incentives for promoting a mixed economy; and the main obstacles to its development.

Contents

176pp   0 335 19043 X (Paperback)   0 335 19044 8 (Hardback)